SUPPLY CHAIN MANAGEMENT

Processes, Partnerships, Performance

September 29 2004

Peter,

Thanks for being a great friend.

Best regards,

September 29/2009

Thanks for being a

SUPPLY CHAIN MANAGEMENT

Processes, Partnerships, Performance

Douglas M. Lambert, Editor
Fisher College of Business
The Ohio State University

Supply Chain Management Institute
Sarasota, Florida
www.scm-institute.org

For information:

Supply Chain Management Institute
3260 Fruitville Road, Suite C
Sarasota, FL 34237
Phone: (941) 957-1510
Fax: (941) 957-0900
www.scm-institute.org

For Order Information:
sales@scm-institute.org

For Training on the Supply Chain Management Framework:
info@scm-institute.org

Printed in the United States of America.

Lambert, Douglas M.
Supply Chain Management: Processes, Partnerships, Performance
Douglas M. Lambert
       p. cm.
Includes bibliographical references and index.
   ISBN: 0-9759949-0-5

Project Manager: Nancy Bevier
Designer: Stephanie Feria
Printer: The Hartley Press, Inc.
                       4250 St. Augustine Road
                       Jacksonville, FL 32207

To General Raymond E. Mason and his wife, Margaret

Contributing Authors

Douglas M. Lambert is the Raymond E. Mason Chair in Transportation and Logistics and Director of The Global Supply Chain Forum at The Ohio State University. Dr. Lambert has served as a faculty member for over 500 executive development programs in North and South America, Europe, Asia and Australia. He is the author or co-author of seven books and more than 100 articles. In 1986, Dr. Lambert received the CLM Distinguished Service Award for his contributions to logistics management. He holds an honors BA and MBA from the University of Western Ontario and a Ph.D. from The Ohio State University.

Keely L. Croxton is an Assistant Professor of Logistics at The Ohio State University. Her research interests are at the intersection of optimization and supply chain management. She is interested in developing and applying mathematical models in the supply chain and the implementation of supply chain management processes. While at MIT, she was the recipient of a National Science Fellowship and an Eisenhower Fellowship from the Department of Transportation. Dr. Croxton received her Ph.D. from the Operations Research Center at MIT.

Sebastián J. García-Dastugue is the Director of Research at IEEC, Instituto de Estudios para la Excelencia Competitiva in Buenos Aires, Argentina. He is a member of the research team of the The Global Supply Chain Forum at The Ohio State University. His research deals with the use of information technology in the supply chain. He has more than 10 years of experience in industry. Dr. Garcia-Dastugue received his Ph.D. from The Ohio State University, his MBA from IAE - Universidad Austral, and his BA in MIS from Universidad CAECE.

A. Michael Knemeyer is an Assistant Professor of Logistics in the Department of Marketing and Logistics at The Ohio State University. His research focuses on developing and implementing collaborative relationships in the supply chain. His work has been published in major academic journals and has been cited in leading practitioner journals. He received a BSBA in Business Logistics and Marketing from John Carroll University and a Ph.D. in Business Logistics from the University of Maryland.

Dale S. Rogers is Professor of Supply Chain Management and Director of the Center for Logistics Management at the University of Nevada, Reno. He is also, the chairman of the Reverse Logistics Executive Council, a professional organization devoted to the improvement of reverse logistics practices; and the E-Business Supply Chain Council, an organization that provides continued understanding of Internet technologies. He received his Ph.D. from Michigan State University.

Yemisi Bolumole is an Assistant Professor of Logistics at the University of North Florida. Her areas of research are the supply chain implications of third-party logistics and the strategic implications of supply chain management. She received her Ph.D. in Logistics & Supply Chain Management from Cranfield University where her thesis won the best Ph.D. of the year award. She also holds an MA from the University of East London and an MS from Cranfield University.

John T. Gardner is a Professor of Marketing and Logistics at SUNY College of Brockport. He received his BS in Environmental Health and his MBA from East Carolina University, a MBA and a Ph. D. in Marketing from The Ohio State University. Professor Gardner was the recipient of the CLM Dissertation Award in 1990 for a dissertation which included both a set of structured case studies and a quantitative analysis of survey data.

Thomas J. Goldsby is an Assistant Professor of Marketing and Logistics at The Ohio State University. Prior to entering academia, he worked for the Valvoline Company, the Transportation Research Board of the National Academy of Sciences in Washington, D.C. and at the University of Kentucky Transportation Research Center. His research interests focus on customer service and supply chain integration. He received his Ph.D. in Marketing and Logistics from Michigan State University. Dr. Goldsby holds a BS in Business Administration from the University of Evansville and MBA from the University of Kentucky.

Terrance L. Pohlen is an Assistant Professor of Business Logistics, University of North Texas. He has over 20 years of logistics experience in the United States Air Force. His research interests include supply chain metrics and the effect of more accurate cost information on supply chain structure. He received a BS in Marketing from Moorhead State University, a MS in Logistics from the Air Force Institute of Technology and an MA and Ph.D. from The Ohio State University.

Preface

In the fall of 2004, undergraduate students in the first class of a supply chain management course at The Ohio State University were asked what they thought a "supply chain" was. After considerable discussion, the class agreed that a supply chain was a network of companies. Next, they were asked to forget about a network of companies and identify the functions required to manage one company. Without much delay, the students agreed that all functions needed to be involved including: marketing, finance, production, purchasing, logistics, and research and development. Then, they were asked what functions must be involved in managing a supply chain and they quickly reached the conclusion that managing a network of companies requires, at a minimum, involvement of all of the functions that are necessary to manage one company. These bright young people knew that it was not possible to manage a supply chain, a network of companies, with only three functions: purchasing, operations, and logistics. This is the same conclusion that was reached by the executives and researchers involved with The Global Supply Chain Forum a decade earlier.

In 1992, with the encouragement of Gary Ridenhower of 3M, I decided to take the steps to develop a research center that we had been talking about for a number of years. On April 23 and 24, 1992, executives from six companies accepted my invitation to meet and begin a research center which, in 1996 when I moved to The Ohio State University, became The Global Supply Chain Forum. The mission of the Forum is to provide the opportunity for leading practitioners and academics to pursue the critical issues related to achieving excellence in supply chain management. Membership in the Forum consists of representatives of firms recognized as industry leaders. Balance is maintained both as to the nature of the firms and the specific expertise of their representatives. The membership is targeted at fifteen firms. It is expected that members actively participate in Forum activities.

The first research project funded by the Forum was on partnerships. The objective was to determine how to develop and maintain close business relationships with other members of the supply chain. In a progress report, the research team presented a description of characteristics of successful partnerships and the main reasons for failure. The members regarded the progress as positive, but they wanted an assessment tool to set the right expectations of both potential partners. In 1996, the Partnership Model was published followed by a Facilitator's Guide.

In 1994, while the development of the Partnership Model was being finalized, the supply chain management research project began. With the Partnership Model, managers had a tool to determine when a partnership was appropriate and what form the relationship should take. Now, they focused their interest on the development of a framework to assist them in structuring the activities that needed to be coordinated across corporate functions and with other key members of the supply chain.

At its genesis, the Forum members viewed supply chain management positioned within the context of the total business rather than as an initiative within a single function such as logistics or manufacturing. The goal of implementing supply chain management has been to develop competitiveness and to achieve a market advantage through the implementation of cross-functional processes. These processes are the mechanism through which internal and external activities are coordinated.

During the Forum meetings in 1994, the members presented the state of development of supply chain management initiatives in their companies and our definition of supply chain management and the corresponding framework were developed. The group's thinking on the processes that must be implemented to successfully manage the supply chain was strongly influenced by the work that was being done at 3M.

In 1995, it was decided that an executive seminar as well as teaching material needed to be developed and the first seminar was offered at the Marriott Sawgrass Resort in February of 1996. The seminar was structured based on our supply chain management framework which included seven of the eight processes. The eighth process, returns management, was added prior to the second seminar held in April, 1997. With the encouragement of the Forum members, a definition and a framework for supply chain management were published in 1997, based on the contents of the seminars and Forum research to date. In 2000, an MBA course on supply chain management based on the Forum framework was offered for the first time at The Ohio State University.

Since its beginning, the supply chain management framework presented in this book has represented the combined knowledge and experience of the executives who are members of the Forum and the research team. The current state of development of the framework is the result of thousands of hours of reading and writing, uncountable hours of discussions involving executives and researchers during the Forum meetings, and numerous site visits to identify and document best management practices. The supply chain management framework represents more than 10 years of joint effort between industry and academia. Publishing this book is a significant milestone in our on-going research.

Douglas M. Lambert

Acknowledgements

A number of people have contributed to this work. First and foremost, the members of The Global Supply Chain Forum who guided us in the supply chain management research and helped us develop the material in this book. The friendship and guidance provided by the executives who represent the Forum member organizations are a major part of my personal and professional life. Two representatives from the following organizations attend the Forum meetings: 3M, Cargill, The Coca-Cola Company, Colgate-Palmolive Company, Defense Logistics Agency, Hewlett-Packard Company, International Paper, Limited Brands, Lucent Technologies, Masterfoods USA, Moen Incorporated, Shell Global Solutions International B.V., Sysco Corporation, TaylorMade-adidas Golf Company, and Wendy's International.

Colleagues who played a significant role in the development of the supply chain management framework are Keely L. Croxton, Sebastián J. García-Dastugue, A. Michael Knemeyer, Dale S. Rogers, Yemisi Bolumole, John T. Gardner, Thomas J. Goldsby and Terrance L. Pohlen. Martha C. Cooper and Janus Pagh are acknowledged for their help in writing the two initial pieces summarizing the early stages of the research. Yubei Hu, a graduate of the MBA and Master of Accounting programs at the Fisher College of Business, supported us in our work with the Forum part-time while she was a student and also during the first eight months of 2004 while she worked as my office manager, before accepting a position in Supply Chain Services and Operations at 3M.

Dean Joseph A. Alutto of the Fisher College of Business deserves recognition for his support of our vision for supply chain management. Professor Robert Burnkrant, Chair of the Department of Marketing and Logistics, has provided encouragement and support. It is also important to recognize our outstanding colleagues in the Fisher College of Business.

Special thanks are given to General Raymond E. Mason and his wife, Margaret, who are great supporters of the OSU Logistics program and examples of what makes being a Buckeye something special.

Finally, I would like to thank my wife, Lynne, for her love and friendship.

Douglas M. Lambert

Contents

3. The Customer Service Management Process

4. The Demand Management Process

5. The Order Fulfillment Process

6. The Manufacturing Flow Management Process

7. The Supplier Relationship Management Process

8. The Product Development and Commercialization Process

9. The Returns Management Process

1 Supply Chain Management

Douglas M. Lambert

Overview

> *...successful supply chain management requires cross-functional integration of key business processes within the firm and across the network of firms that comprise the supply chain.*

There is a great deal of confusion regarding exactly what supply chain management involves.[1] In fact, most people using the name supply chain management treat it as a synonym for logistics or as logistics that includes customers and suppliers. Others view supply chain management as the new name for purchasing or operations, or the combination of purchasing, operations and logistics. However, successful supply chain management requires cross-functional integration of key business processes within the firm and across the network of firms that comprise the supply chain. The challenge is to determine how to successfully accomplish this integration. In this chapter, supply chain management is defined. Next, sections describing what supply chain management is not and business process management are presented. Then, the framework for supply chain management is described. It is followed by sections on the management components of supply chain management and mapping the supply chain. Finally, suggestions for implementation and conclusions are presented. Case studies conducted at several companies and involving multiple members of their supply chains were used to develop the concepts described.

Introduction

One of the most significant paradigm shifts of modern business management is that individual businesses no longer compete as solely autonomous entities, but rather within supply chains. In this emerging competitive environment, the ultimate success of the single business will depend on management's ability to integrate the company's intricate network of business relationships.[2]

---

[1] This chapter is based on: Martha C. Cooper, Douglas M. Lambert and Janus D. Pagh, "Supply Chain Management: More Than a New Name for Logistics," *The International Journal of Logistics Management*, Vol. 8, No. 1 (1997), pp. 1-14; Douglas M. Lambert, Martha C. Cooper and Janus D. Pagh, "Supply Chain Management: Implementation Issues and Research Opportunities," *The International Journal of Logistics Management*, Vol. 9, No. 2 (1998), pp. 1-19; and, Keely L. Croxton, Sebastián J. García-Dastugue, Douglas M. Lambert, and Dale S. Rogers, "The Supply Chain Management Processes," *The International Journal of Logistics Management*, Vol. 12, No. 2 (2001), pp. 13-36.

[2] Drucker, Peter F., "Management's New Paradigms," *Forbes Magazine*, October 5, 1998, pp. 152-177; and, Martin G. Christopher, "Relationships and Alliances: Embracing the Era of Network Competition," in *Strategic Supply Chain Management*, ed. John Gattorna, Hampshire, England: Gower Press, 1998, pp. 272-284.

Increasingly the management of relationships across the supply chain is being referred to as supply chain management (SCM). Strictly speaking, the supply chain is not a chain of businesses with one-to-one, business-to-business relationships, but a network of businesses and relationships. SCM offers the opportunity to capture the synergy of intra- and inter-company integration and management. In that sense, SCM deals with business process excellence and represents a new way of managing the business and relationships with other members of the supply chain.

Thus far, there has been relatively little guidance from academia, which has in general been following rather than leading business practice.[3] There is a need for building theory and developing normative tools and methods for successful SCM practice. The Global Supply Chain Forum, a group of non-competing firms and a team of academic researchers, has been meeting regularly since 1992 with the objective to improve the theory and practice of SCM. The definition of SCM developed and used by the members of The Global Supply Chain Forum follows:[4]

> Supply chain management is the integration of key business processes from end user through original suppliers that provides products, services, and information that add value for customers and other stakeholders.

This view of SCM is illustrated in Figure 1-1, which depicts a simplified supply chain network structure, the information and product flows, and the SCM processes that integrate functions within the company as well as other firms across the supply chain. Thus, business processes become supply chain processes to manage the links across intra- and inter-company boundaries.

This chapter is organized as follows. First there is a description of what SCM is not. This is followed by a brief overview of business process management. Next, the conceptual framework of SCM is described. Then, the management components of SCM are introduced. Issues regarding how to map business processes across the supply chain, and implement supply chain management are briefly described. Finally, conclusions are outlined.

Supply chain management is the integration of key business processes from end user through original suppliers that provides products, services, and information that add value for customers and other stakeholders.

What SCM Is Not

The term SCM was originally introduced by consultants in the early 1980's[5] and subsequently has become widely used.[6] Since the late 1980's, academics have attempted to give structure to SCM.[7] Bechtel and Jayaram[8] provided an extensive

---

[3] Lambert, Douglas M., Martha C. Cooper, and Janus D. Pagh, "Supply Chain Management: Implementation Issues and Research Opportunities," *The International Journal of Logistics Management*, Vol. 9, No. 2 (1998), pp. 1-19.

[4] The Global Supply Chain Forum, Fisher College of Business, The Ohio State University. See: fisher.osu.edu/scm.

[5] Oliver, R. Keith and Michael D. Webber, "Supply-Chain Management: Logistics Catches Up with Strategy," *Outlook*, (1982), cit. Martin G. Christopher, *Logistics, The Strategic Issue*, London: Chapman and Hall, 1992.

[6] La Londe, Bernard J., "Supply Chain Evolution by the Numbers," *Supply Chain Management Review*, Vol. 2, No. 1 (1998), pp. 7-8.

[7] For example, Graham C. Stevens, "Integration of the Supply Chain," *International Journal of Physical Distribution and Logistics Management*, Vol. 19, No. 8 (1989), pp. 3-8; and, Denis R. Towill, Mohamed M. Naim, and J. Wikner, "Industrial Dynamics Simulation Models in the Design of Supply Chains," *International Journal of Physical Distribution and Logistics Management*, Vol. 22, No. 5 (1992), pp. 3-13.

Figure 1-1
Supply Chain Management:
Integrating and Managing Business Processes Across the Supply Chain

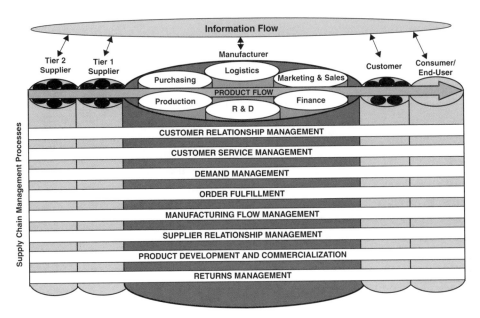

Source: Adapted from Douglas M. Lambert, Martha C. Cooper, and Janus D. Pagh, "Supply Chain Management: Implementation Issues and Research Opportunities," *The International Journal of Logistics Management,* Vol. 9, No. 2 (1998), p. 2.

retrospective review of the literature and research on SCM. They identified generic schools of thought, and the major contributions and fundamental assumptions of SCM that must be challenged in the future.

Until recently most practitioners,[9] consultants[10] and academics[11] viewed SCM as not appreciably different from the contemporary understanding of logistics management, as defined by the Council of Logistics Management (CLM) in 1986.[12] That is, SCM was viewed as logistics outside the firm to include customers and

[8] Bechtel, Christian and Jayanth Jayaram, "Supply Chain Management: A Strategic Perspective," *The International Journal of Logistics Management,* Vol. 8, No. 1 (1997), pp. 15-34.

[9] Davis, Tom, "Effective Supply Chain Management", *Sloan Management Review,* Vol. 34, No. 4, Summer (1993), pp. 35-46; Bruce C. Arntzen, Gerald G. Brown, Thomas P. Harrison and Linda L. Trafton, "Global Supply Chain Management Digital Equipment Corporation," *Interfaces,* Vol. 25, No. 1 (1995), pp. 69-93; and, Robert C. Camp and Dan N. Colbert, "The Xerox Quest for Supply Chain Excellence," *Supply Chain Management Review,* Spring (1997), pp. 82-91.

[10] Scharlacken, John W., "The Seven Pillars of Global Supply Chain Planning," *Supply Chain Management Review,* Vol. 2, No. 1 (1998), pp. 32-40; Gene Tyndall, Christopher Gopal, Wolfgang Partsch and John Kamauff, *Supercharging Supply Chains,* New York: John Wiley & Sons, Inc., 1998; and, William C. Copacino, *Supply Chain Management: The Basics and Beyond,* Boca Raton, FL: St. Lucie Press, 1997.

[11] Fisher, Marshall L., "What is the Right Supply Chain for Your Product?" *Harvard Business Review,* Vol. 75, No. 2, March-April (1997), pp. 105-116; Hau L. Lee and Corey Billington, "Managing Supply Chain Inventory: Pitfalls and Opportunities," *Sloan Management Review,* Vol. 33, No. 3, Spring (1992), pp. 65-73; Robert B. Handfield and Ernest L. Nichols, Jr., *Introduction to Supply Chain Management,* Upper Saddle River, New Jersey, Prentice Hall, 1999; and, Donald J. Bowersox and David J. Closs, *Logistical Management – The Integrated Supply Chain Process,* New York: McGraw-Hill Companies, 1996.

suppliers. Logistics as defined by the CLM always represented a supply chain orientation, "from point of origin to point of consumption." Then why the confusion? It is probably due to the fact that logistics is a function within companies and is also a bigger concept that deals with the management of material and information flows across the supply chain. This is similar to the confusion over marketing as a concept and marketing as a functional area. Thus, the quote from the CEO who said, "Marketing is too important to be left to the marketing department." Everybody in the company should have a customer focus. The marketing concept does not apply just to the marketing department. Everyone in the organization should focus on serving the customer's needs.

Everyone in the organization should focus on serving the customer's needs.

The understanding of SCM has been re-conceptualized from integrating logistics across the supply chain to integrating and managing key business processes across the supply chain. Based on this emerging distinction between SCM and logistics, in 2003, CLM announced a modified definition of logistics. The modified definition explicitly declares CLM's position that logistics management is only a part of SCM. The revised definition follows:

> Logistics is that part of supply chain management that plans, implements, and controls the efficient, effective forward and reverse flow and storage of goods, services, and related information between the point-of-origin and the point-of-consumption in order to meet customers' requirements.[13]

SCM is not just confused with logistics. Those in the operations management area, such as APICS, are renaming what they do as supply chain management[14] as are those working in the procurement area.[15] Some universities have created departments of supply chain management by combining purchasing, operations and logistics faculty, which is a perspective that has appeared in the literature.[16]

Managing the entire supply chain is a very difficult and challenging task, as illustrated in Figure 1-2. Imagine the degree of complexity required managing all suppliers back to the point of origin and all products/services out to the point of consumption. It is probably easy to understand why executives would want to manage their supply chains to the point of consumption because whoever has the relationship with the end-user has the power in the supply chain. Intel created a relationship with the end-user by having computer manufacturers place an "Intel inside" label on their computers. This affects the computer manufacturer's ability to switch microprocessor suppliers. In any case, managing all Tier 1 suppliers' networks to the point of origin is an enormous undertaking.

---

[12] CLM defined logistics management as: The process of planning, implementing, and controlling the efficient, cost-effective flow and storage of raw materials, in-process inventory, finished goods, and related information flow from point-of-origin to point-of-consumption for the purpose of conforming to customer requirements. *What's It All About?*, Oak Brook, IL: Council of Logistics Management, 1986.

[13] The definition is posted at the CLM's homepage: www.CLM1.org.

[14] APICS, *Basics of Supply Chain Management*, CPIM Certification Review Course, Participant Guide, Version 2.1, Alexandira, VA: APICS, The Educational Society for Resource Management, 2001.

[15] Monczka, Robert M., Robert J. Trent and Robert B. Handfield, *Purchasing and Supply Chain Management*, Cincinatic, OH: South-Western College Publishing, 1998.

[16] Wisner, Joel D., G. Keong Leong and Keah-Choon Tan, *Supply Chain Management: Balanced Approach*, Mason, OH: Thomson South-Western, 2004.

Figure 1-2
Supply Chain Network Structure

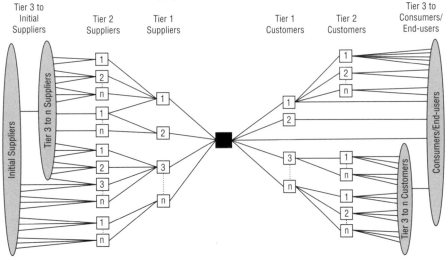

Source: Adapted from Douglas M. Lambert, Martha C. Cooper and Janus D. Pagh, "Supply Chain Management: Implementation Issues and Research Opportunities," *The International Journal of Logistics Management,* Vol. 9, No. 2 1998, p. 3.

Business Process Management

Increasingly, managers want to implement business processes and integrate them with other key members of the supply chain.

Increasingly, managers want to implement business processes and integrate them with other key members of the supply chain.[17] A business process is a structured set of activities with specified business outcomes for customers.[18] Initially, business processes were viewed as a means to integrate corporate functions within the firm. Now, business processes are used to structure the activities between members of a supply chain. Hammer has pointed out that it is in the integration of business processes across firms in the supply chain where the real "gold" can be found.[19]

The concept of organizing the activities of a firm as business processes was introduced in the late 1980s[20] and became popular in the early 1990s, after the publication of books by Hammer and Champy,[21] and Davenport.[22]

[17] This section is based on material included in Douglas M. Lambert, Sebastián García-Dastugue and Keely L. Croxton, "An Evaluation of Process-Oriented Supply Chain Management Frameworks," *Journal of Business Logistics,* forthcoming.

[18] Davenport, Thomas H. and Michael C. Beers, "Managing information about processes," *Journal of Management Information Systems,* Vol. 12, No. 1 (1995), pp. 57-80.

[19] Hammer, Michael, "The Superefficient Company," *Harvard Business Review,* Vol. 79, No. 8 (2001), pp. 82.

[20] Hammer, Michael and Glenn E. Mangurian, "The Changing Value of Communications Technology," *Sloan Management Review,* Vol. 28, No. 2 (1987), pp. 65-71; and, Thomas H. Davenport, Michael Hammer and Tauno J. Metsisto, "How Executives Can Shape Their Company's Information Systems," *Harvard Business Review,* Vol. 67, No. 2 (1989), pp. 130.

[21] Hammer, Michael and James Champy, *Reengineering the Corporation: A Manifesto for Business Revolution,* 1st ed, New York, NY: Harper Business, 1993.

[22] Davenport, Thomas H., *Process Innovation: Reengineering Work through Information Technology,* Boston, MA: Harvard Business School Press, 1993.

The motivation for implementing business processes within and across members of the supply chain might be to make transactions efficient and effective, or to structure inter-firm relationships in the supply chain. Both approaches are customer oriented. The first focuses on meeting the customer's expectations for each transaction, the other on achieving longer term mutual fulfillment of promises.

The transactional view of business process management is rooted in advances in information and communication technology which enabled time compression and availability of information throughout the organization.[23] The focus is not on automating the established business processes, but on redesigning businesses.[24] This transactional approach to redesigning business processes is based on Taylor's principles of scientific management which aim to increase organizational efficiency and effectiveness using engineering principles from manufacturing operations.[25] In this case, business process redesign is based on standardizing transactions and the transfer of information.[26] The goal is to improve outcomes for customers by making transactions more efficient and accurate.

The second view of business process management focuses on managing relationships in the supply chain and is based on an evolving view from the field of marketing. A significant amount of the marketing literature is concerned with market transactions (business transactions with customers) and the fulfillment of orders. Rooted in economic theory, researchers studied the efficiency of transactions with the customers, which raised awareness about the importance of customer retention.[27] Obtaining repeat business from the same customer, that is to conduct multiple transactions, is more cost efficient than obtaining a new customer.[28] This traditional view of marketing as managing transactions with customers is dominated by the "4Ps": product, price, promotion, and place.[29]

The early marketing channels researchers such as Alderson and Bucklin conceptualized why and how channels are created and structured.[30] From a supply chain standpoint, these researchers were on the right track in terms of: 1) identifying who should be a member of the marketing channel, 2) describing the need for channel coordination, and 3) drawing actual marketing channels. However, for the last 35 years most marketing channels researchers ignored two critical issues. First,

The motivation for implementing business processes within and across members of the supply chain might be to make transactions efficient and effective, or to structure inter-firm relationships in the supply chain.

---

[23] Hammer, Michael and Glenn E. Mangurian, "The Changing Value of Communications Technology," *Sloan Management Review*, Vol. 28, No. 2 (1987), pp. 65-71.

[24] Hammer, Michael, "Reengineering Work: Don't Automate, Obliterate," *Harvard Business Review*, Vol. 68, No. 4 (1990), pp. 104.

[25] Taylor, Frederick W., *The Principles of Scientific Management*, New York, NY: Harper & Bros, 1911.

[26] Davenport, Thomas H. and James E. Short, "The New Industrial Engineering: Information Technology and Business Process Redesign," *Sloan Management Review*, Vol. 31, No. 4 (1990), pp. 11.

[27] Weld, Louis D. H., "Marketing Functions and Mercantile Organizations," *The American Economic Review*, Vol. 7, No. 2 (1917), pp. 306-318.

[28] Kotler, Philip, *Marketing Management: Analysis, Planning, Implementation and Control*, 7th ed, Englewood Cliffs, NJ: Prentice-Hall, 1991.

[29] McCarthy, E. Jerome, *Basic Marketing: A Managerial Approach*, Homewood, IL: R.D. Irwin, 1960.

[30] Alderson, Wroe, "Marketing Efficiency and the Principle of Postponement," *Cost and Profit Outlook*, Vol. 3, September (1950); Reavis Cox and Wroe Alderson (eds.) *Theory in Marketing*, Chicago, IL: Richard D. Irwin, Inc., (1950); and, Louis P. Bucklin, *A Theory of Distribution Channel Structure*, IBER Special publication, Berkeley, California (1966).

they did not build on the early contributions by including suppliers to the manufacturer, and thus neglected the importance of a total supply chain perspective. Unlike the marketing channels literature, a major weakness of much of the SCM literature is that the authors appear to assume that everyone knows who is a member of the supply chain. There has been little effort to identify specific supply chain members, key processes that require integration or what management must do to successfully manage the supply chain. Second, they focused on marketing activities and flows across the channel, and overlooked the need to integrate and manage multiple processes within and across companies. In 1992, Webster[31] challenged marketers and marketing researchers to consider relationships with multiple firms. He also called for cross-functional consideration in strategy formulation.

During the 1990s, a paradigm shift occurred with the introduction of the concept of relationship marketing.[32] The goal of relationship marketing "…is to establish, maintain, and enhance… relationships with customers and other partners, at a profit, so that the objectives of the parties involved are met. This is achieved by mutual exchange and fulfillment of promises".[33] Thus, the focus of developing and maintaining relationships in the supply chain is beyond the fulfillment of one or a set of transactions. In the new environment, managers need to focus on helping customers achieve their objectives.

The field of relationship marketing is focused on the customer-side, looking downstream in the supply chain. However, the development and maintenance of relationships with key suppliers should be based on the same pillars, mutuality and fulfillment of promises, in order for suppliers to be profitable. Management needs the support of the firm's key suppliers to fulfill the promises made to customers and meet financial goals. In other words, corporate success is based on relationship management with both suppliers and customers.

The management of inter-organizational relationships with members of the supply chain involves people, organizations, and processes.

The management of inter-organizational relationships with members of the supply chain involves people, organizations, and processes.[34] In fact, the ability to manage inter-organizational relationships "… may define the core competence of some organizations as links between their vendors and customers in the value chain".[35] Several authors have suggested implementing business processes in the context of supply chain management, but there is not yet an "industry standard" on what these processes should be. The value of having standard business processes in place is that managers from organizations in the supply chain can use a common language and can link-up their firms' processes with other members of the supply chain, as appropriate.

---

[31] Webster, Frederick E. Jr., "The Changing Role of Marketing in the Corporation," *Journal of Marketing*, Vol. 56, No. 4 (1992), pp. 1-17; Atul Parvatiyar and Jagdish N. Sheth, Relationship Marketing: Theory, Methods, and Applications, Jagdish N. Sheth and Atul Parvatiyar (eds.), Atlanta: Emory University Center for Relationship Marketing, 1994.

[32] Grönroos, Christian, "Quo Vadis, Marketing? Toward a Relationship Marketing Paradigm," *Journal of Marketing Management*, Vol. 10, No. 5 (1994), pp. 347-360.

[33] Grönroos, Christian, *Service Management and Marketing, Managing the Moments of Truth in the Service Competition*, Lexington, MA: Free Press/Lexington Books, 1990.

[34] Webster, Frederick E. Jr., "The Changing Role of Marketing in the Corporation," *Journal of Marketing*, Vol. 56, No. 4 (1992), pp. 1-17.

[35] Webster, Frederick E. Jr., "The Changing Role of Marketing in the Corporation," *Journal of Marketing*, Vol. 56, No. 4 (1992), pp. 1-17.

In 1994, executives from a group of international companies, later to become The Global Supply Chain Forum (GSCF), began development of a relationship oriented and process-based SCM framework.   In February 1996, the GSCF framework was presented in a three-day executive seminar co-sponsored by the Council of Logistics Management, and was later presented in the literature.[36] The GSCF eight processes are cross-functional and are meant to be implemented inter-organizationally across key members of the supply chain. The eight processes are: customer relationship management, customer service management, demand management, order fulfillment, manufacturing flow management, product development and commercialization, supplier relationship management, and returns management. The motivation for developing the framework was to provide structure to assist academics with their research on supply chain management and practitioners with implementation.

A Conceptual Framework of Supply Chain Management

Figure 1-3 illustrates the inter-related nature of SCM and the need to proceed through several steps to design and successfully manage a supply chain. The SCM framework consists of three closely inter-related elements: the supply chain network structure, the supply chain business processes, and the supply chain management components.

The supply chain network structure is comprised of the member firms and the links between these firms. Business processes are the activities that produce a specific output of value to the customer. The management components are the managerial methods by which the business processes are integrated and managed across the supply chain. Each of the three interrelated elements that constitute the framework is described in the following sections.

Supply Chain Network Structure

All firms participate in supply chains that begin with the source of original materials and end with consumption. How much of these supply chains need to be managed depends on several factors, such as the complexity of the product, the number of available suppliers, and the availability of raw materials. Dimensions to consider include the length of the supply chain and the number of suppliers and customers at each tier. It would be rare for a firm to participate in only one supply chain. The supply chain network will look different depending on a firm's position in the supply chain. For most manufacturers positioned in the middle of the supply chain such as 3M, Colgate-Palmolive and Hewlett-Packard, the supply chain looks less like a pipeline or chain than an uprooted tree where the branches and roots are the extensive network of customers and suppliers (see Figure 1-2).[37] The

The supply chain network will look different depending on a firm's position in the supply chain.

---

[36] Cooper, Martha C., Douglas M. Lambert and Janus D. Pagh, "Supply Chain Management: More than a New Name for Logistics," *The International Journal of Logistics Management*, Vol. 8, No. 1 (1997), pp. 1-14; Douglas M. Lambert, Martha C. Cooper and Janus D. Pagh, "Supply Chain Management: Implementation Issues and Research Opportunities," *The International Journal of Logistics Management*, Vol. 9, No. 2 (1998), pp. 1-19; and, Keely L. Croxton, Sebastián J. García-Dastugue, Douglas M. Lambert and Dale S. Rogers, "The Supply Chain Management Processes," *The International Journal of Logistics Management*, Vol. 12, No. 2 (2001), pp. 13-36.

[37] Cooper, Martha C., Lisa M. Ellram, John T. Gardner and Albert M. Hanks, "Meshing Multiple Alliances," *Journal of Business Logistics*, Vol. 18, No. 1 (1997), pp. 67-89.

Figure 1-3
Supply Chain Management: Elements and Key Decisions

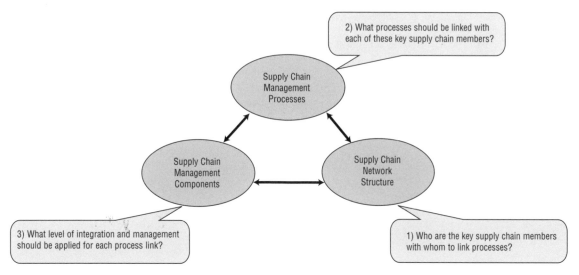

Source: Adapted from Douglas M. Lambert, Martha C. Cooper and Janus D. Pagh, "Supply Chain Management: Implementation Issues and Research Opportunities," *The International Journal of Logistics Management*, Vol. 9, No. 2 1998, p. 4.

question is how many of these branches and roots need to be managed. It should be noted that in each firm, management views its organization as the focal company and the supply chain will look different depending on where the firm is positioned in it. For example, for a retailer such as Wal-Mart, the supply chain looks like a Bayesian decision tree (the root system of the uprooted tree). Figure 1-4 illustrates a supply chain network structure for a retailer. The supply chain network for a Gulf of Mexico shrimper is depicted in Figure 1-5. Logistics providers are not shown as boxes in Figures 1-2, 1-4 and 1-5. Rather they serve as logistics integrators on the linkages.

Management needs to choose the type of relationship appropriate for particular supply chain links.[38] Not all links throughout the supply chain should be closely coordinated and integrated. The most appropriate relationship is the one that best fits the specific set of circumstances.[39] Determining which parts of the supply chain deserve management attention must be weighed against firm capabilities and the importance to the firm.

It is important to have an explicit knowledge of how the supply chain network structure is configured.

It is important to have an explicit knowledge of how the supply chain network structure is configured. The three primary structural aspects of a company's network structure are: 1) the members of the supply chain; 2) the structural dimensions of the network; and, 3) the different types of process links across the supply chain.

[38] Lambert, Douglas M., Margaret A. Emmelhainz and John. T. Gardner, "Developing and Implementing Supply Chain Partnership," *The International Journal of Logistics Management*, Vol. 7, No. 2 (1996), pp. 1-17.

[39] Cooper, Martha C. and John T. Gardner "Good Business Relationships: More Than Just Partnerships or Strategic Alliances," *International Journal of Physical Distribution and Logistics Management*, Vol. 23, No. 6 (1993), pp. 14-20.

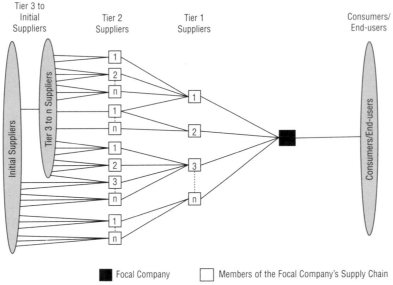

Figure 1-4
Supply Chain Network Structure: Retailer's Perspective

Focal Company · Members of the Focal Company's Supply Chain

Source: Adapted from Douglas M. Lambert, Martha C. Cooper and Janus D. Pagh, "Supply Chain Management: Implementation Issues and Research Opportunities," *The International Journal of Logistics Management*, Vol. 9, No. 2 1998, p. 3.

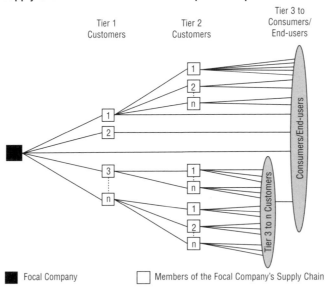

Figure 1-5
Supply Chain Network Structure: Shrimper's Perspective

Focal Company · Members of the Focal Company's Supply Chain

Source: Adapted from Douglas M. Lambert, Martha C. Cooper and Janus D. Pagh, "Supply Chain Management: Implementation Issues and Research Opportunities," *The International Journal of Logistics Management*, Vol. 9, No. 2 1998, p. 3.

Identifying Supply Chain Members. When determining the network structure, it is necessary to identify the member firms of the supply chain. Including all types of members may cause the network to become highly complex, since it may explode in the number of members added from tier to tier.[40] To integrate and manage all process links with all members across the supply chain would, in most cases, be counter-productive, if not impossible. The key is to sort out some basis for determining which members are critical to the success of the company and the supply chain, and thus should be allocated managerial attention and resources.

Marketing channels researchers identified members of the channel based on who takes part in the various marketing flows, including product, title, payment, information, and promotion flows.[41] Each flow included relevant members, such as banks for the payment flow and advertising agencies for the promotion flow. The channels researchers sought to include all members taking part in the marketing flows, regardless of how much impact each member had on the value provided to the end-customer or other stakeholders.

The members of a supply chain include all companies/ organizations with whom the focal company interacts directly or indirectly through its suppliers or customers, from point of origin to point of consumption.

The members of a supply chain include all companies/organizations with whom the focal company interacts directly or indirectly through its suppliers or customers, from point of origin to point of consumption. However, to make a very complex network more manageable, it seems appropriate to distinguish between primary and supporting members. The definitions of primary and supporting members are based on interviews and discussions with the members of The Global Supply Chain Forum, and by applying the definition of a business process by Davenport.[42] Primary members of a supply chain are all those autonomous companies or strategic business units who carry out value-adding activities (operational and/or managerial) in the business processes designed to produce a specific output for a particular customer or market.

In contrast, supporting members are companies that simply provide resources, knowledge, utilities or assets for the primary members of the supply chain. For example, supporting companies include those that lease trucks to the manufacturer, banks that lend money to a retailer, the owner of the building that provides warehouse space, or companies that supply production equipment, print marketing brochures or provide temporary secretarial assistance. These supply chain members support the primary members.

The same company can perform both primary and supporting activities. Likewise, the same company can perform primary activities related to one process and supporting activities related to another process. An example from one of the case studies is an original equipment manufacturer (OEM) that buys some critical and complex production equipment from a supplier. When the OEM develops new products, they work very closely with the equipment supplier to assure there is the right equipment to make the new product. Thus the supplier is a primary member of the OEM's product development and commercialization process. However, once the machinery is in place, the supplier is a supporting and not a primary member for the manufacturing flow management process, since supplying the equipment does not in itself add value to the output of the process even though the equipment adds value.

---

[40] Cooper, Martha C., Lisa M. Ellram, John T. Gardner and Albert M. Hanks, "Meshing Multiple Alliances," *Journal of Business Logistics*, Vol. 18, No. 1 (1997), pp. 67-89.

[41] Stern, Louis W. and Adel El-Ansary, *Marketing Channels*, 5th Edition, Englewood Cliffs, NJ: Prentice Hall, 1995.

[42] Davenport, Thomas H., *Process Innovation - Reengineering Work through Information Technology*, Boston, Massachusetts: Harvard Business School Press, 1993.

The distinction between primary and supporting supply chain members is not obvious in all cases. Nevertheless, this distinction provides a reasonable managerial simplification and yet captures the essential aspects of who should be considered as key members of the supply chain. The approach for differentiating between types of members is to some extent similar to how Porter distinguished between primary and support activities in his "value chain" framework[43].

The definitions of primary and supporting members make it possible to define the point-of-origin and the point-of-consumption of the supply chain. The point-of-origin of the supply chain occurs where no previous primary suppliers exist. All suppliers to the point-of-origin members are solely supporting members. The point-of-consumption is where no further value is added, and the product and/or service is consumed.

The Structural Dimensions of the Network. Three structural dimensions of the network are essential when describing, analyzing, and managing the supply chain. These dimensions are the horizontal structure, the vertical structure, and the horizontal position of the focal company within the end points of the supply chain.

The horizontal structure refers to the number of tiers across the supply chain (see Figure 1-2). The supply chain may be long, with numerous tiers, or short, with few tiers. As an example, the network structure for bulk cement is relatively short. Raw materials are taken from the ground, combined with other materials, moved a short distance, and used to construct buildings. The vertical structure refers to the number of suppliers/customers represented within each tier (see Figure 1-2). A company can have a narrow vertical structure, with few companies at each tier, or a wide vertical structure with many suppliers and/or customers at each tier. The third structural dimension is the company's horizontal position within the supply chain. A company can be positioned at or near the initial source of supply, be at or near to the ultimate customer, or somewhere between these end points of the supply chain.

In the companies studied, different combinations of these structural variables were found. In one example, a narrow and long network structure on the supplier side was combined with a wide and short structure on the customer side. Increasing or reducing the number of suppliers and/or customers effects the structure of the supply chain. For example, as some companies move from multiple to single source suppliers, the supply chain may become narrower. Outsourcing logistics, manufacturing, marketing or product development activities is another example of decision making that may change the supply chain structure. It may increase the length and width of the supply chain, and likewise influence the horizontal position of the focal company in the supply chain network.

Supply chains that burst to many Tier 1 customers/suppliers strain resources in terms of how many process links the focal company can integrate and closely manage beyond Tier 1. In general, our research team has found that in such cases only a few Tier 2 customers or suppliers are actively managing. Some of the companies studied have transferred servicing small customers to distributors, thus, moving the small customers further down the supply chain from the focal company. This principle, known as functional spin-off, is described in the

Supply chains that burst to many Tier 1 customers/suppliers strain resources in terms of how many process links the focal company can integrate and closely manage beyond Tier 1.

[43] Porter, Michael E., *Competitive Advantage - Creating and Sustaining Superior Performance*, New York: The Free Press, 1984, pp. 36.

marketing channels literature,[44] and also can be applied to the focal company's network of suppliers.

In the companies studied, the supply chains looked different from each company's perspective, since management of each company sees its firm as the focal company, and views membership and network structure differently. However, because each firm is a member of the other's supply chain, it is important for management of each firm to understand their interrelated roles and perspectives. The integration and management of business processes across company boundaries will be successful only if it makes sense from each company's perspective.[45]

Supply Chain Management Processes

Successful supply chain management requires a change from managing individual functions to integrating activities into supply chain management processes.

Successful supply chain management requires a change from managing individual functions to integrating activities into supply chain management processes. In many major corporations, such as 3M, management has reached the conclusion that optimizing the product flows cannot be accomplished without implementing a process approach to the business. The supply chain management processes identified by members of The Global Supply Chain Forum are:

- customer relationship management
- customer service management
- demand management
- order fulfillment
- manufacturing flow management
- supplier relationship management
- product development and commercialization
- returns management

These processes are shown in Figure 1-1 and a description of each follows.[46]

Customer Relationship Management. Customer relationship management provides the structure for how the relationships with customers will be developed and maintained. Management identifies key customers and customer groups to be targeted as part of the firm's business mission. The goal is to segment customers based on their value over time and increase customer loyalty by providing customized products and services. Cross-functional customer teams tailor Product and Service Agreements (PSA) to meet the needs of key accounts and for segments of other customers. The PSAs specify levels of performance. The teams work with key customers to improve processes and eliminate demand variability and non-value-added activities. Performance reports are designed to measure the profitability of individual customers as well as the firm's financial impact on the customer.[47]

Customer Service Management. Customer service management is the firm's face to the customer. It provides the key point of contact for administering the PSA.

---

[44] Stern, Louis W. and Adel El-Ansary, *Marketing Channels*, 5th Edition, Englewood Cliffs, NJ: Prentice Hall, 1995.

[45] Cooper, Martha C., Lisa M. Ellram, John T. Gardner and Albert M. Hanks, "Meshing Multiple Alliances," *Journal of Business Logistics*, Vol. 18, No. 1 (1997), pp. 67-89.

[46] Croxton, Keely L., Sebastián J. García-Dastugue, Douglas M. Lambert, and Dale S. Rogers, "The Supply Chain Management Processes," *The International Journal of Logistics Management*, Vol. 12, No. 2 (2001), pp. 13-36.

[47] Lambert, Douglas M. and Terrance L. Pohlen, "Supply Chain Metrics," *The International Journal of Logistics Management*, Vol. 12, No. 1 (2001), pp. 1-19.

Customer service provides the customer with real-time information on promised shipping dates and product availability through interfaces with the firm's functions such as manufacturing and logistics. The customer service management process may also include assisting the customer with product applications.

Demand Management. Demand management is the SCM process that balances the customers' requirements with the capabilities of the supply chain. With the right process in place, management can match supply with demand proactively and execute the plan with minimal disruptions. The process is not limited to forecasting. It includes synchronizing supply and demand, increasing flexibility, and reducing variability. A good demand management system uses point-of-sale and "key" customer data to reduce uncertainty and provide efficient flows throughout the supply chain. Marketing requirements and production plans should be coordinated on an enterprise-wide basis. Thus, multiple sourcing and routing options are considered at the time of order receipt which allows market requirements and production plans to be coordinated on an organization-wide basis. In advanced applications, customer demand and production rates are synchronized to manage inventories globally.

Order Fulfillment. The order fulfillment process involves more than just filling orders. It includes all activities necessary to define customer requirements, design a network and enable a firm to meet customer requests while minimizing the total delivered cost as well as filling customer orders. This is not just the logistics function, but instead needs to be implemented cross-functionally and with the coordination of key suppliers and customers. The objective is to develop a seamless process from the supplier to the organization and to its various customer segments.

Manufacturing Flow Management. Manufacturing flow management is the SCM process that includes all activities necessary to move products through the plants and to obtain, implement and manage manufacturing flexibility in the supply chain. Manufacturing flexibility reflects the ability to make a wide variety of products in a timely manner at the lowest possible cost. To achieve the desired level of manufacturing flexibility, planning and execution must extend beyond the four walls of the manufacturer in the supply chain.

Supplier Relationship Management. Supplier relationship management is the process that defines how a company interacts with its suppliers. As the name suggests, this is a mirror image of customer relationship management. Just as a company needs to develop relationships with its customers, it also needs to foster relationships with its suppliers. As in the case of customer relationship management, a company will forge close relationships with a small subset of its suppliers, and manage arm-length relationships with others. A PSA is negotiated with each key supplier that defines the terms of the relationship. For segments of less critical suppliers, the PSA is not negotiable. Supplier relationship management is about defining and managing these PSAs. Long-term relationships are developed with a small core group of suppliers. The desired outcome is a win-win relationship where both parties benefit.

As in the case of customer relationship management, a company will forge close relationships with a small subset of its suppliers, and manage arm-length relationships with others.

Product Development and Commercialization. Product development and commercialization is the SCM process that provides the structure for developing and bringing products to market jointly with customers and suppliers. The product development and commercialization process team must coordinate with the customer relationship management process team to identify customers' articulated and unarticulated needs; select materials and suppliers in conjunction with the supplier relationship management process; and, develop production technology in manufacturing flow to manufacture and integrate into the best supply chain flow for the product/market combination.

Returns Management. Returns management is the SCM process by which activities associated with returns, reverse logistics, gatekeeping, and avoidance are managed within the firm and across key members of the supply chain. The correct implementation of this process enables management not only to manage the reverse product flow efficiently, but to identify opportunities to reduce unwanted returns and to control reusable assets such as containers. Effective returns management is an important part of SCM and provides an opportunity to achieve a sustainable competitive advantage.

Types of Business Process Links

As previously noted, integrating and managing all business process links throughout the entire supply chain is likely not appropriate. Since the drivers for integration are situational and differ from process link to process link, the levels of integration should vary from link to link, and over time. Some links are more critical than others.[48] As a consequence, the task of allocating scarce resources among the different business process links across the supply chain becomes crucial. The GSCF research indicates that four fundamentally different types of business process links can be identified between members of a supply chain. These are managed process links, monitored process links, not-managed process links, and non-member process links.

...the task of allocating scarce resources among the different business process links across the supply chain becomes crucial.

Managed Process Links. Managed process links are links that the focal company finds important to integrate and manage. In the supply chain drawn in Figure 1-6, the managed process links are indicated by the thickest solid lines. The focal company will integrate and manage process links with Tier 1 customers and suppliers. As indicated by the remaining thick solid lines in Figure 1-6, the focal company is actively involved in the management of a number of other process links beyond Tier 1.

Monitored Process Links. Monitored process links are not as critical to the focal company; however, it is important to the focal company that these process links are integrated and managed appropriately between the other member companies. Thus, the focal company, as frequently as necessary, simply monitors or audits how the process link is integrated and managed. The thick dashed lines in Figure 1-6 indicate the monitored process links.

Not-managed Process Links. Not-managed process links are links that the focal company is not actively involved in managing, nor are they critical enough to use resources for monitoring. In other words, the focal company fully trusts the other members to manage the process links appropriately, or because of limited resources leaves it up to them. The thin solid lines in Figure 1-6 indicate the not-managed process links. For example, a manufacturer has a number of potential suppliers for cardboard shipping cartons. Usually the manufacturer will not choose to integrate and manage the links beyond the cardboard carton supplier all the way back to the

---

[48] Håkansson, Håkan and Ivan Snehota, *Developing Relationships in Business Networks*, London: Routledge, 1995.

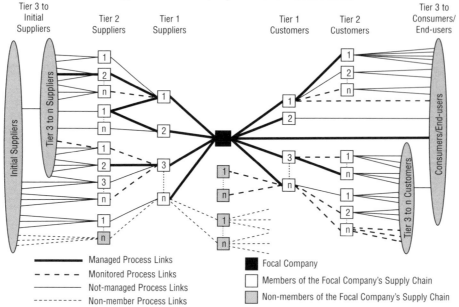

Figure 1-6
Types of Inter-company Business Process Links

Tier 3 to Initial Suppliers · Tier 2 Suppliers · Tier 1 Suppliers · Tier 1 Customers · Tier 2 Customers · Tier 3 to Consumers/End-users

Initial Suppliers · Tier 3 to n Suppliers · Consumers/End-users · Tier 3 to n Customers

——————— Managed Process Links
– – – – – Monitored Process Links
——————— Not-managed Process Links
----------- Non-member Process Links

■ Focal Company
☐ Members of the Focal Company's Supply Chain
▨ Non-members of the Focal Company's Supply Chain

Source: Adapted from Douglas M. Lambert, Martha C. Cooper and Janus D. Pagh, "Supply Chain Management: Implementation Issues and Research Opportunities," *The International Journal of Logistics Management*, Vol. 9, No. 2 (1998), p. 7.

growing of the trees. The manufacturer wants certainty of supply, but it may not be necessary to integrate and manage the links beyond the cardboard carton supplier.

Non-member Process Links. The case studies indicated that managers are aware that their supply chains are influenced by decisions made in other connected supply chains. For example, a supplier to the focal company is also a supplier to the chief competitor, which may have implications for the supplier's allocation of manpower to the focal company's product development process, availability of products in times of shortage, and/or protection of confidentiality of information. Non-member process links are process links between members of the focal company's supply chain and non-members of the supply chain. Non-member links are not considered as links of the focal company's supply chain structure, but they can and often will affect the performance of the focal company and its supply chain. The thin dashed lines in Figure 1-6 illustrate examples of non-member process links.

Based on the described process links, our research reveals variation in how closely companies integrate and manage links further away from the first tier. In some companies, management works through or around other members/links in order to achieve specific supply chain objectives, such as product availability, improved quality, or reduced overall supply chain costs. For example, a tomato ketchup manufacturer in New Zealand conducts research on tomatoes in order to develop plants that provide larger tomatoes with fewer seeds. Their contracted growers are provided with young plants in order to ensure the quality of the output. Since the growers tend to be small, the manufacturer negotiates contracts with suppliers of equipment and agricultural chemicals such as fertilizer and pesticides.

…our research reveals variation in how closely companies integrate and manage links further away from the first tier.

The farmers are encouraged to purchase materials and machinery using the manufacturer's contract rates. This results in higher quality raw materials and lower prices without sacrificing the margins and financial strength of the growers.

There are several examples of companies who, in times of shortage, discovered that it was important to manage beyond Tier 1 suppliers for critical times. One example involves a material used in the manufacture of semi-conductors. It turned out that the six Tier 1 suppliers all purchased from the same Tier 2 supplier. When shortages occurred, it became apparent that the critical relationship was with the Tier 2 supplier. It is important to identify the critical links in the supply chain and these may not be the immediately adjacent firms.

The Requirement for Standard Business Processes

Thousands of activities are performed and coordinated within a company, and every company is by nature in some way involved in supply chain relationships with other companies.[49] When two companies build a relationship, certain of their internal activities will be linked and managed between the two companies.[50] Since both companies have linked some internal activities with other members of their supply chain, a link between two companies is thus a link in what might be conceived as a supply chain network. For example, the internal activities of a manufacturer can affect the internal activities of a distributor, which in turn have an effect on the internal activities of a retailer. Ultimately, the internal activities of the retailer are linked with and can affect the activities of the end-user.

Empirical research has led to the conclusion that "the structure of activities within and between companies is a critical cornerstone of creating unique and superior supply chain performance".[51] In our research, executives believed that competitiveness and profitability could increase if internal key activities and business processes are linked and managed across multiple companies. Thus, "corporate success requires a change from managing individual functions to integrating activities into supply chain management processes."[52]

..."corporate success requires a change from managing individual functions to integrating activities into supply chain management processes."

Our research team has found that in some companies, executives emphasize a functional structure (see Figure 1-7, Tier 1 Supplier) and others a process structure (see Figure 1-7, Manufacturer, Tier 2 Supplier and both tiers of customers). Those companies with processes had different numbers of processes consisting of different activities and links between activities. Different names were used for similar processes, and similar names for different processes. This lack of inter-company consistency is a cause for significant friction and inefficiencies in supply chains. It is important that managers in different firms speak the same language (use

[49] Bowersox, Donald J., "Integrated Supply Chain Management; A Strategic Perspective," *Annual Conference Proceedings*, Chicago, Illinois: Council of Logistics Management (1997), pp. 181-189; George E. Stigler, "The Division of Labor Is Limited by the Extent of the Market," *Journal of Political Economy*, Vol. 59, No. 3 (1951), pp. 185-193; and, R. H. Coase, "The Nature of the Firm," *Economica*, Vol. 4 (1937), pp. 386-405.

[50] Håkansson, Håkan and Ivan Snehota, *Developing Relationships in Business Networks*, London: Routledge, 1995.

[51] Håkansson, Håkan and Ivan Snehota, *Developing Relationships in Business Networks*, London: Routledge, 1995.

[52] Lambert, Douglas M., James R. Stock, and Lisa M. Ellram, *Fundamentals of Logistics Management*, Boston: Irwin/McGraw-Hill, 1998.

Figure 1-7
Supply Chain Management: The Disconnects

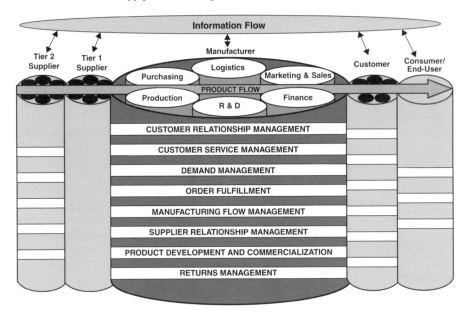

Source: Adapted from Douglas M. Lambert, Martha C. Cooper, and Janus D. Pagh, "Supply Chain Management: Implementation Issues and Research Opportunities," *The International Journal of Logistics Management*, Vol. 9, No. 2 (1998), p. 10.

the same terminology). There is generally an understanding of what corporate functions like marketing, manufacturing and accounting/finance represent. If management in each firm identifies its own set of processes, how can these processes be linked across firms?

In some of the case study companies, business processes extended to suppliers and were managed to some extent between the two firms involved. This may imply that when a leadership role is taken, firms in the supply chain will use the same business processes. The obvious advantage when this is possible is that each member of the band is playing the same tune.

The number of business processes that should be integrated and managed between companies will likely vary. However, in each specific case, it is important that executives thoroughly analyze and discuss which key business processes to integrate and manage. The major components for integrating and managing a supply chain network are addressed next.

If management in each firm identifies its own set of processes, how can these processes be linked across firms?

The Management Components of Supply Chain Management

The management components of SCM are the third element of the SCM framework (see Figure 1-3). The level of integration and management of a business process link is a function of the number and level, ranging from low to high, of components added to the link.[53] Consequently, adding more management components or increasing the level of each component can increase the level of integration of the business process link.

---

[53] Lambert, Douglas M., Margaret A. Emmelhainz and John T. Gardner, "So You Think You Want a Partner?" *Marketing Management*, Vol. 5, No. 2 (1996), pp. 25-41.

The literature on business process reengineering,[54] buyer-supplier relationships,[55] and SCM[56] suggests numerous possible components that must receive managerial attention when managing supply chain relationships. Based on the management components identified in our previous work, review of the literature, and interviews with 80 managers, nine management components are identified for successful SCM: planning and control, work structure, organization structure, product flow structure, information flow structure, management methods, power and leadership structure, risk and reward structure, and culture and attitude. These are briefly described below.

- Planning and control of operations are keys to moving an organization or supply chain in a desired direction. The extent of joint planning is expected to bear heavily on the success of the supply chain and different components may be emphasized at different times but planning transcends the phases.[57] The control aspects can be operationalized as the best performance metrics for measuring supply chain success.

- The work structure indicates how the firm performs its tasks and activities. The level of integration of processes across the supply chain is a measure of organizational structure. All but one of the literature sources examined cited work structure as an important component.

- Organizational structure can refer to the individual firm and the supply chain; the use of cross-functional teams would suggest more of a process approach. When these teams cross organizational boundaries, such as in-plant supplier personnel, the supply chain should be more integrated.

- Product flow structure refers to the network structure for sourcing, manufacturing, and distribution across the supply chain. Since inventory is necessary in the system, some supply chain members may keep a disproportionate amount of inventory. As it is less expensive to have unfinished or semi-finished goods in inventory than finished goods, upstream members may bear more of this burden.

- Virtually every author indicates that the information flow structure is key. The kind of information passed among channel members and the frequency of information updating has a strong influence on the efficiency of the supply chain. This may well be the first component integrated across part or all of the supply chain.

- Management methods include the corporate philosophy and management techniques. It is very difficult to integrate a top-down organization structure

The kind of information passed among channel members and the frequency of information updating has a strong influence on the efficiency of the supply chain.

[54] Hammer, Michael and James Champy, *Reengineering the Corporation: A Manifesto for Business Revolution*, New York: Harper Business, 1993; Stephen Towers, *Business Process Re-engineering: A Practical Handbook for Executives*, Stanley Thorns, 1994.; and, Fred Hewitt, "Supply Chain Redesign," *The International Journal of Logistics Management*, Vol. 5, No. 2 (1994), pp. 1-9.

[55] Ellram, Lisa M. and Martha C. Cooper, "Supply Chain Management, Partnership, and the Shipper – Third Party Relationship," *The International Journal of Logistics Management*, Vol. 1, No. 2 (1990), pp. 1-10; and, Graham C. Stevens, "Integration of the Supply Chain," *International Journal of Physical Distribution and Logistics Management*, Vol. 19, No. 8 (1989), pp. 3-8.

[56] See literature review by Martha C. Cooper, Douglas M. Lambert and Janus D. Pagh, "Supply Chain Management: More Than a New Name for Logistics," *The International Journal of Logistics Management*, Vol. 8, No. 1 (1997), pp. 1-14; and, Rasmus F. Olsen and Lisa M. Ellram, "A Portfolio Approach to Supplier Relationships," *Industrial Marketing Management*, Vol. 26 (1997), pp. 101-113.

[57] Cooper, Martha C., Lisa M. Ellram, John T. Gardner and Albert M. Hanks, "Meshing Multiple Alliances," *Journal of Business Logistics*, Vol. 18, No. 1 (1997), pp. 67-89.

with a bottom-up structure. The level of management involvement in day-to-day operations can differ across supply chain members.

- The power and leadership structure across the supply chain will affect its form. One strong leader will drive the direction of the chain. In most supply chains studied to date, there are one or two strong leaders among the firms. The exercise of power, or lack of, can affect the level of commitment of other members. Forced participation will encourage exit behavior, given the opportunity.[58]
- The anticipation of sharing of risks and rewards across the supply chain affects long-term commitment of its members.
- The importance of corporate culture and its compatibility across members of the supply chain cannot be underestimated. Meshing cultures and individuals' attitudes is time consuming but is necessary at some level for the channel to perform as a chain. Aspects of culture include how employees are valued and incorporated into the management of the firm.

Figure 1-8 illustrates how the management components can be divided into two groups. The first group is the physical and technical group, which includes the most visible, tangible, measurable, and easy-to-change components. Our research and the literature on change management[59] shows that if this group of management components is the only focus of managerial attention, the results will be disappointing at best.

The second group is comprised of the managerial and behavioral components. These components are less tangible and visible and are often difficult to assess and alter. The managerial and behavioral components define the organizational behavior and influence how the physical and technical management components can be implemented. If the managerial and behavioral components are not aligned to drive and reinforce an organizational behavior supportive of the supply chain objectives and operations, the supply chain will likely be less competitive and profitable. If one or more components in the physical and technical group are changed, management components in the managerial and behavioral group likewise may have to be readjusted. The groundwork for successful SCM is established by understanding each of these SCM components and their interdependence. Hewitt stated that true intra- and inter-company business process management, or redesign, is only likely to be successful if it is recognized as a multi-component change process, simultaneously and explicitly addressing all SCM components.[60]

If the managerial and behavioral components are not aligned to drive and reinforce an organizational behavior supportive of the supply chain objectives and operations, the supply chain will likely be less competitive and profitable.

---

[58] Macneil, Ian R., *The New Social Contract, and Inquiry into Modern Contractual Relations*, New Haven, CT; Yale University Press, 1980; and, Oliver E. Williamson, *Markets and Hierarchies; Analysis and Antitrust Implications*, New York, Free Press, 1975.

[59] Jaffe, Dennis T. and Cynthia D. Scott, "Reengineering in Practice: Where Are the People? Where Is the Learning," *Journal of Applied Behavioral Science*, Vol. 34, No. 3 (1998), pp. 250-267; Dorine C. Andrews and Susan K. Stalick, *Business Reengineering: The Survival Guide*, 1st ed., Englewood Cliffs, NJ: Yourdon Press, 1994; Michael Hammer, "Reengineering Work: Don't Automate, Obliterate," *Harvard Business Review*, Vol. 68, No. 4 (1990), pp. 104-112; Michael Hammer and James Champy, *Reengineering the Corporation: A Manifesto for Business Revolution*, New York: Harper Business, 1993; and, Stephen Towers, *Business Process Re-engineering: A Practical Handbook for Executives*, Stanley Thorns, 1994.

[60] Hewitt, Fred, "Supply Chain Redesign," *The International Journal of Logistics Management*, Vol. 5, No. 2 (1994), pp. 1-9.

Figure 1-8
The Management Components of Supply Chain Management

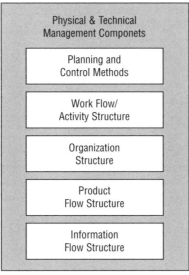

Physical & Technical
Management Componets

Planning and
Control Methods

Work Flow/
Activity Structure

Organization
Structure

Product
Flow Structure

Information
Flow Structure

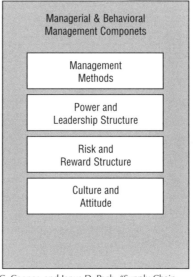

Managerial & Behavioral
Management Componets

Management
Methods

Power and
Leadership Structure

Risk and
Reward Structure

Culture and
Attitude

Source: Adapted from Douglas M. Lambert, Martha C. Cooper, and Janus D. Pagh, "Supply Chain Management: Implementation Issues and Research Opportunities," *The International Journal of Logistics Management,* Vol. 9, No. 2 (1998), p. 12.

All nine management components were found in the business process links studied, including examples of successful SCM applications. However, the number, levels of components and combinations of representations varied. A finding is that the physical and technical components were well understood and managed the farthest up and down the supply chain. For example, in one case, the focal company had integrated its demand management process across four links by applying the following components: planning and control methods, work flow/activity structure, communication and information flow facility structure and product flow facility structure. The managerial and behavioral management components were less well understood and more difficulties were encountered in their implementation.

Mapping the Supply Chain

The first step in managing the supply chain is to map the supply chain network structure as shown in Figure 1-6 and determine which links will be: (1) managed process links; (2) monitored process links; (3) not-managed process links; and (4) non-member process links. Because a supply chain map can become very complex in terms of the number of companies included in each tier, it will be necessary to determine which firms are key and need to be represented on the map. A firm may be considered key for a number of reasons including: (1) the volume of sales or purchases; (2) the criticality of the component purchased; (3) the ability to innovate; and (4) access to markets.

The next step is to determine which processes should be linked with each firm on the supply chain map. The key processes for integrating and managing the supply chain are customer relationship management and supplier relationship

The key processes for integrating and managing the supply chain are customer relationship management and supplier relationship management.

management. Each of the other six processes will be coordinated through these process teams. However, not every process will be linked with every member of the supply chain. For example, including all suppliers and customers in the product development and commercialization process would result in "too many cooks in the kitchen".

The final step is to determine the level of integration and management that should be applied for each link. This is where the partnership model that will be described in Chapter 10 plays an important role since it can be used to help structure business relationships.

Implementing Supply Chain Management

Implementing SCM requires making the transition from a focus on functions to a focus on supply chain management processes. Figure 1-9 illustrates examples of how each function within the organization provides input to the eight processes.

In the customer relationship management process, sales and marketing provides the account management expertise, engineering provides the specifications which define the requirements, logistics provides knowledge of logistics capabilities, manufacturing provides production capabilities, purchasing provides the sourcing capabilities, and finance provides customer profitability reports. The customer service requirements must be used as input to manufacturing, sourcing, and logistics strategies. Customers and suppliers are shown in Figure 1-9 to make the point that each of these processes, to be properly implemented, requires the involvement of customers and suppliers. When logistics third-party providers are used, representatives from these firms should serve on the process teams to provide their logistics expertise.

Implementing SCM requires making the transition from a focus on functions to a focus on supply chain management processes.

If the proper coordination mechanisms are not in place across the various functions, the process will be neither effective nor efficient. By taking a process focus, all functions that touch the product or provide information must work together. For example, purchasing depends on sales/marketing data fed through a production schedule to assess specific order levels and timing of requirements. These orders drive production requirements which in turn are transmitted upstream to suppliers.

The use of outsourcing has accelerated the need to coordinate supply chain processes since the organization becomes more dependent on outside contractor suppliers. Consequently, coordination mechanisms must be in place within the organization. It is important that representatives from third-party providers serve on the process teams.

Typically, firms within the supply chain will have their own functional silos that must be overcome and a process approach must be accepted in order to successfully implement SCM. However, the functional structure will not be replaced by processes because functional expertise is necessary and the activities required to operate the business are performed within the functions. The requirements for successful implementation of SCM include:
- Executive support, leadership and commitment to change.
- An understanding of the degree of change that is necessary.
- Agreement on the SCM vision and the key processes.
- The necessary commitment of resources and empowerment to achieve the stated goals.

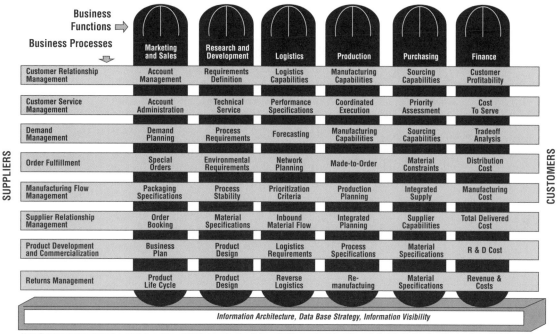

Figure 1-9
Functional Involvement in the Supply Chain Management Processes

Business Processes	Marketing and Sales	Research and Development	Logistics	Production	Purchasing	Finance
Customer Relationship Management	Account Management	Requirements Definition	Logistics Capabilities	Manufacturing Capabilities	Sourcing Capabilities	Customer Profitability
Customer Service Management	Account Administration	Technical Service	Performance Specifications	Coordinated Execution	Priority Assessment	Cost To Serve
Demand Management	Demand Planning	Process Requirements	Forecasting	Manufacturing Capabilities	Sourcing Capabilities	Tradeoff Analysis
Order Fulfillment	Special Orders	Environmental Requirements	Network Planning	Made-to-Order	Material Constraints	Distribution Cost
Manufacturing Flow Management	Packaging Specifications	Process Stability	Prioritization Criteria	Production Planning	Integrated Supply	Manufacturing Cost
Supplier Relationship Management	Order Booking	Material Specifications	Inbound Material Flow	Integrated Planning	Supplier Capabilities	Total Delivered Cost
Product Development and Commercialization	Business Plan	Product Design	Logistics Requirements	Process Specifications	Material Specifications	R & D Cost
Returns Management	Product Life Cycle	Product Design	Reverse Logistics	Re-manufacturing	Material Specifications	Revenue & Costs

SUPPLIERS — Business Functions — CUSTOMERS

Information Architecture, Data Base Strategy, Information Visibility

Note: Process sponsorship and ownership must be established to drive the attainment of the supply chain vision and eliminate the functional barriers that artificially separate the process flows.

Source: Adapted from Douglas M. Lambert, Larry C. Guinipero and Gary J. Ridenhower, "Supply Chain Management: A Key to Achieving Business Excellence in the 21st Century," unpublished manuscript.

Conclusions

Executives are becoming aware of the emerging paradigm that the successful integration and management of key supply chain management processes across members of the supply chain will determine the ultimate success of the single enterprise.

Executives are becoming aware of the emerging paradigm that the successful integration and management of key supply chain management processes across members of the supply chain will determine the ultimate success of the single enterprise. Managing the supply chain cannot be left to chance. For this reason, executives are striving to interpret and determine how to manage the company's supply chain network, and achieve the potential of SCM.

Research with member firms of The Global Supply Chain Forum at The Ohio State University indicates that managing the supply chain involves three closely inter-related elements: 1) the supply chain network structure; 2) the supply chain business processes; and, 3) the management components. The structure of activities/processes within and between companies is vital for creating superior competitiveness and profitability. Successful SCM requires integrating business processes with key members of the supply chain. Waste of valuable resources results when supply chains are not integrated, appropriately streamlined and managed. A prerequisite for successful SCM is that management accepts the eight processes and manages them using cross-functional teams.

Marketing researchers were in the forefront of studying critical aspects of what we now call supply chain management, particularly with respect to identifying the members of a channel of distribution. The focus was from the manufacturer to the customer for the most part. The approach to SCM presented in this book ensures inclusion of suppliers and customers. There are several implications for practitioners and researchers. There is a need to integrate activities across the firm and across firms in the supply chain. While marketing strategy formulation has always considered internal and external constraints, SCM makes the explicit evaluation of these factors even more critical. Additionally, traditional roles of marketing and sales are changing. Team efforts are becoming more common for developing and marketing new products, as well as managing current ones. The role of the firm's sales force is changing to one of measuring and selling the value that the firm is providing for the customer.

The implementation of SCM involves identifying: the supply chain members, with whom it is critical to link; the processes that need to be linked with each of these key members; and, the type/level of integration that applies to each process link. The objective of SCM is to create the most value not simply for the company but the whole supply chain network including the end-customer. Consequently, supply chain process integration and reengineering initiatives should be aimed at boosting total process efficiency and effectiveness across members of the supply chain.

The remaining 11 chapters of this book are organized as follows. Chapters 2 through 9 contain detailed descriptions of the eight supply chain management processes: customer relationship management, customer service management, demand management, order fulfillment, manufacturing flow management, supplier relationship management, product development and commercialization, and returns management. Chapter 10 presents a systematic process for developing, implementing and continuously improving relationships with key members of the supply chain. Chapter 11 deals with supply chain management performance measurement. Finally, Chapter 12, Implementing Supply Chain Management, provides a comparison of The Global Supply Chain Forum and Supply Chain Council supply chain management frameworks including how each might be used. In addition, guidelines are provided regarding how to assess where an organization stands in terms of implementation and recommendations are provided on how to best implement The Global Supply Chain Forum framework.

The implementation of SCM involves identifying: the supply chain members, with whom it is critical to link; the processes that need to be linked with each of these key members; and, the type/level of integration that applies to each process link.

The Customer Relationship Management Process

Douglas M. Lambert

Overview

The customer relationship management process provides the structure for how relationships with customers will be developed and maintained. The goal is to segment customers based on their value over time and increase customer loyalty by providing customized products and services. In this chapter, detailed descriptions of the strategic and operational sub-processes that comprise customer relationship management are provided. Also, there are descriptions of the interfaces that are necessary with the other seven supply chain management processes and each of the corporate functions. Guidelines for successful implementation are described.

Introduction

In a business-to-business environment, customer relationship management is the supply chain management process that provides the structure for how relationships with customers are developed and maintained.

Typically, large sums of money are spent by corporations to attract new customers; yet these same companies are often complacent when it comes to nurturing existing customers to build and strengthen relationships with them.[1] However, for most companies, existing customers represent the best opportunities for profitable growth. There are direct and strong relationships between profit growth; customer loyalty; customer satisfaction; and, the value of goods delivered to customers.[2] "Relationship marketing concerns attracting, developing, and retaining customer relationships".[3] In a business-to-business environment, customer relationship management is the supply chain management process that provides the structure for how relationships with customers are developed and maintained. Management identifies key customers and customer groups to be targeted as part of the firm's business mission. The decision regarding who represents key customers requires evaluation of the profitability and potential profitability of individual customers. Often it is assumed that the marketing

---

[1] Berry, Leonard L. and A. Parasuraman, "Marketing to Existing Customers" in *Marketing Services: Competing Through Quality*, New York, NY: The Free Press, 1991, p.132.

[2] Heskett, James L., W. Earl Sasser, Fr. and Leonard A. Schlesinger, *The Service Profit Chain*, New York, NY: The Free Press, 1997, p.11.

[3] Berry, Leonard L. and A. Parasuraman, "Marketing to Existing Customers" in *Marketing Services: Competing Through Quality,* New York, NY: The Free Press, 1991, p.133.

function is responsible for creating, maintaining and strengthening relationships with business-to-business customers because it does this with consumers. However, for two large organizations to be able to coordinate their complex operations, all corporate functions must be involved and actively participate in the relationship in order to align corporate resources with the profit potential of each relationship. The customer teams tailor product and service agreements (PSAs) to meet the needs of key accounts and segments of other customers.[4] PSAs come in many forms, both formal and informal, and may be referred to by different names from company to company. However, for best results they should be formalized as written documents. Teams work with key accounts to improve processes, and eliminate demand variability and non-value-added activities. Performance reports are designed to measure the profitability of individual customers as well as the firm's financial impact on those customers.

The customer teams tailor product and service agreements (PSAs) to meet the needs of key accounts and segments of other customers.

Customer relationship management has become a critical business process as a result of: competitive pressures; the need to achieve cost efficiency in order to be a low-cost supplier; a recognition of the fact that customers are not equal in terms of their profitability; and, knowledge that customer retention can significantly affect profitability. Customer relationship management is one of the eight processes and it must interface with each of the other seven (see Figure 2-1). A description of the strategic and operational processes that comprise customer

Figure 2-1
Supply Chain Management:
Integrating and Managing Business Processes Across the Supply Chain

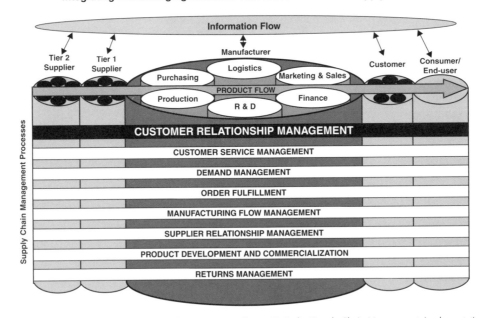

Source: Adapted from Douglas M. Lambert, Martha C. Cooper, and Janus D. Pagh, "Supply Chain Management: Implementation Issues and Research Opportunities," *The International Journal of Logistics Management*, Vol. 9, No. 2 (1998), p. 2.

[4] Seybold, Patrica B., "Get Inside the Lives of Your Customers", *Harvard Business Review*, Vol. 78, No. 5 (2001), pp. 81-89.

relationship management is provided along with the sub-processes and their activities. Also, there are descriptions of the interfaces with functions, the other supply chain management processes and other firms. Finally, conclusions are presented.

Customer Relationship Management as a Supply Chain Management Process

Customer relationship management and supplier relationship management provide the critical linkages throughout the supply chain.

Customer relationship management and supplier relationship management provide the critical linkages throughout the supply chain (see Figure 2-2). For each supplier in the supply chain, the ultimate measure of success for the customer relationship management process is the change in profitability of an individual customer or segment of customers. For each customer, the most comprehensive measure of success for the supplier relationship management process is the impact that a supplier or supplier segment has on the firm's profitability. The goal is to increase the joint profitability by developing the relationship. The biggest potential roadblock is failure to reach agreement on how to split the gains that are made through joint process improvement efforts. The overall performance of the supply chain is determined by the combined improvement in profitability of all of its members from one year to the next.

The customer relationship management process has both strategic and operational elements. For this reason, the process has been divided into two parts, the strategic process in which the firm establishes and strategically manages the process, and the operational process which is the actualization of the

Figure 2-2
Customer Relationship Management (CRM) and Supplier Relationship Management (SRM): The Critical Supply Chain Management Linkages

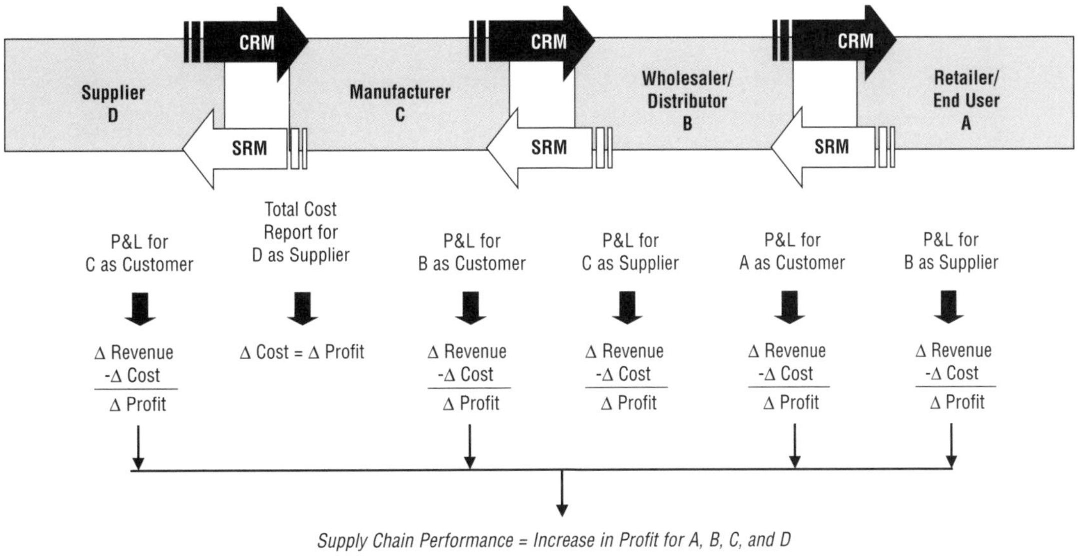

Supply Chain Performance = Increase in Profit for A, B, C, and D

Source: Adapted from Douglas M. Lambert and Terrance L. Pohlen, "Supply Chain Metrics," *The International Journal of Logistics Management,* Vol. 12, No. 1 (2001), p. 14.

process once it has been established (see Figure 2-3). Implementation of the strategic process within the firm is a necessary step in integrating the firm with other members of the supply chain, and it is at the operational level that the day-to-day activities take place. The strategic process is led by a management team that is comprised of executives from several functions: marketing (including sales), finance, production, purchasing, logistics and, research and development. The team is responsible for developing the procedures at the strategic level and seeing that they are implemented. At the operational level, there will be a customer team for each key account and for each segment of non-key customers. It is important that teams calling on competitors do not have overlapping members since it will be very hard for these individuals to not be influenced by what has been discussed as part of developing a PSA for a competitor of the customer. Business ethics dictate that it is important to reach agreement on what data to share and there is a fine line between using process knowledge gained versus using competitive marketing knowledge gained from a customer. The account teams will have day-to-day responsibility for managing the process at the operational level. Firm employees outside of the team might execute parts of the process, but the team still maintains managerial control.

The strategic process is led by a management team that is comprised of executives from several functions: marketing (including sales), finance, production, purchasing, logistics and, research and development.

Figure 2-3
Customer Relationship Management

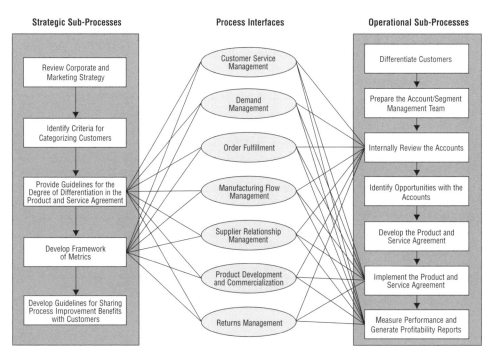

Source: Adapted from Keely L. Croxton, Sebastián J. García-Dastugue, Douglas M. Lambert and Dale S. Rogers, "The Supply Chain Management Processes," *The International Journal of Logistics Management,* Vol. 12, No. 2 (2001), p. 15.

The Strategic Customer Relationship Management Process

At the strategic level, the customer relationship management process provides the structure for how relationships with customers will be developed and managed. An objective is to align functional expertise from the supplier and the customer to support implementation of the other seven supply chain management processes. The strategic customer relationship management process is comprised of five sub-processes (see Figure 2-4) and includes a key account management component.

While there is a great deal of software that is being marketed as customer relationship management, these technology tools should not be confused with the relationship-focused supply chain management process.

While there is a great deal of software that is being marketed as customer relationship management, these technology tools should not be confused with the relationship-focused supply chain management process. Customer relationship management software has the potential to enable management to gather customer data quickly, identify the most valuable customers over time, and provide the customized products and services that should increase customer loyalty.[5] When it works, the costs to serve customers can be reduced making it easier to acquire more, similar customers. However, according to Gartner Group, 55% of all customer relationship management (software solutions) projects do not produce results.[6] In a Bain Survey of 451 senior executives, 25% reported that these software

Figure 2-4
The Strategic Customer Relationship Management Process

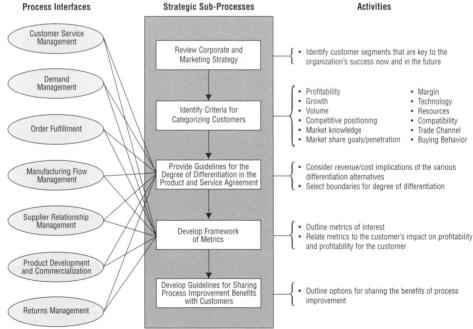

---

[5] Rigby, Darrell K., Frederick F. Reichheld and Phil Scheffer, "Avoid the Four Perils of CRM,", *Harvard Business Review,* Vol. 80, No. 2 (2002), pp. 101-109.

[6] Rigby, Darrell K., Frederick F. Reichheld and Phil Scheffer, "Avoid the Four Perils of CRM,", *Harvard Business Review,* Vol. 80, No. 2 (2002), pp. 101-109.

tools had failed to deliver profitable growth and in many cases had damaged long-standing customer relationships. One firm spent over $30 million only to scrap the entire project.[7]

There are four major reasons for failure: (1) implementing software solutions before creating a customer strategy; (2) rolling out software before changing the organization; (3) assuming that more technology is better; and, (4) trying to build relationships with the wrong customers.[8]

To be successful, management must place its primary focus on the customer relationship management process and the people and the procedures that make the technology effective. Relying on the technology by itself will most often lead to failure.[9]

Review Corporate and Marketing Strategies

The customer relationship management process team reviews the corporate strategy and the marketing strategy in order to identify customer segments that are critical to the organization's success now and in the future. Strategies are directional statements that provide guidance in terms of: (1) the markets to serve and customer segments to target; (2) the positioning theme that differentiates the business from its competitors; (3) the channels used to reach the market; and, (4) the appropriate scale and scope of activities to be performed.[10]

The customer relationship management process team reviews the corporate strategy and the marketing strategy in order to identify customer segments that are critical to the organization's success now and in the future.

Identify Criteria for Categorizing Customers

In the second sub-process, the team identifies the criteria that can be used to categorize customers. This includes providing guidelines for determining which customers qualify for tailored PSAs and which customers will be grouped into segments and offered a standard PSA that is developed to provide value to the segment. Customer categories must have clear differences in their PSAs or they are not distinct segments. Potential criteria include: profitability, growth potential, volume, competitive positioning issues, access to market knowledge, market share goals, margin levels, level of technology, resources and capabilities, compatibility of strategies, channel of distribution and buying behavior (what drives their buying decision). As part of this sub-process, the team develops the firm's strategy for dealing with segments of customers who do not qualify for individually tailored PSAs.

Provide Guidelines for the Degree of Differentiation in the Product and Service Agreement

In the third sub-process, the team develops guidelines for the degree of differentiation in the PSA. This involves developing the differentiation alternatives and considering the revenue and cost implications of each. The output is the degree of

---

[7] Rigby, Darrell K., Frederick F. Reichheld and Phil Scheffer, "Avoid the Four Perils of CRM,", *Harvard Business Review,* Vol. 80, No. 2 (2002), pp.101-109.

[8] Rigby, Darrell K., Frederick F. Reichheld and Phil Scheffer, "Avoid the Four Perils of CRM,", *Harvard Business Review,* Vol. 80, No. 2 (2002), pp. 101-109.

[9] Turchan, Mark P. and Paula Mateus, "The Value of Relationships," *Journal of Business Strategy,* Vol 22, No. 6 (2001), pp. 29-32.

[10] Day, George, S., *Market Driven Strategy: Processes for Creating Value,* New York, NY: The Free Press, 1990, p.6.

customization that can be offered to customers based on the potential of the customer(s). The goal is to offer PSAs that enhance the profitability of the firm and its customers. For some customers, PSAs will be enhanced and in other cases the offerings included in the PSAs will be trimmed. Basically, it is a matter of matching the company's resources to the customers' short-term and long-term value to the firm. Profitability reports by customer are a key input when making these decisions. In order to find and understand the opportunities to customize the PSAs, in this sub-process the team will interface with all of the other processes.

At 3M, PSAs contain: the contacts including name, title, telephone, e-mail for both 3M and the customer representatives; details related to transportation including deliveries, order minimums, driver instructions, will calls and appointments; bills of lading (combine or do not combine purchase orders); pallets to be used; purchase order confirmations; order status including names of contact individuals, Internet order status website with user name and password; details related to pricing inquires; availability of market development funds; marketing promotional allowances; acceptability of backorders and how they will be handled; and contract items. For key customers, the PSAs are customized and for segments of other customers standard values are provided for each parameter.

Develop Framework of Metrics

Developing the framework of metrics involves outlining the metrics of interest and relating them to the customer's impact on the firm's profitability as well as the firm's impact on the customer's profitability.

Developing the framework of metrics involves outlining the metrics of interest and relating them to the customer's impact on the firm's profitability as well as the firm's impact on the customer's profitability. The customer relationship management process has the responsibility for assuring that the metrics used to measure all of the other processes are not in conflict. Management needs to insure that all internal and external measures are driving consistent and appropriate behavior.[11]

Figure 2-5 shows how the customer relationship management process can affect the firm's financial performance as measured by economic value added (EVA). It illustrates how customer relationship management can impact sales, cost of goods sold, total expenses, inventory investment, other current assets, and the investment in fixed assets. For example, customer relationship management can lead to higher sales volume as a result of strengthening relationships with profitable customers, selling higher margin products, increasing the firm's share of the customer's expenditures for the products/services sold, and/or improving the mix, that is, aligning services and the costs to serve.

Cost of goods sold can be reduced as a result of the better planning that comes from collaboration with customers. Cost savings occur due to fewer last minute production changes and, less expediting of inbound materials and shipments to customers. For wholesalers, significant cost savings can occur as a result of fewer order changes.

Customer relationship management leads to better targeting of marketing expenditures. A number of expenses can be reduced as a result of better tailoring of the firm's marketing and logistics programs to customer needs while giving full

---

[11] Lambert, Douglas M., Martha C. Cooper, and Janus D. Pagh, "Supply Chain Management: Implementation Issues and Research Opportunities," *The International Journal of Logistics Management,* Vol. 9, No. 2 (1998), pp. 1-19.

Figure 2-5
How Customer Relationship Management Affects Economic Value Added (EVA)

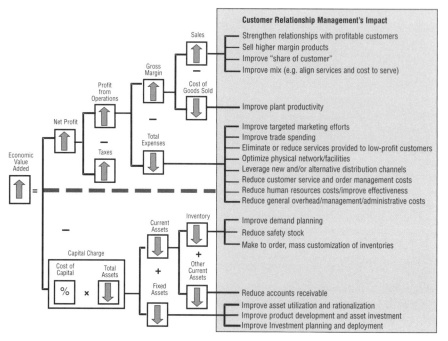

Source: Adapted from Douglas M. Lambert and Terrance L. Pohlen, "Supply Chain Metrics," *The International Journal of Logistics Management,* Vol. 12, No. 1 (2001), p. 10.

consideration to the profitability of each customer. Trade spending also can be improved. Services to low profit customers can be eliminated or reduced and reallocated to more profitable customers to drive revenue growth. Better knowledge of customer requirements and the reduction of services to low-profit customers can lead to a reconfiguration of the physical network of facilities resulting in cost savings. Less profitable customers may be served using wholesalers/distributors which may represent a new channel of distribution. Reductions are also possible in the costs of customer service and order management, human resources, and in general overhead and administrative. In addition to reducing expenditures, there is the opportunity through customer relationship management to better allocate resources to customers which can be measured in terms of increased revenue.

Better knowledge of customer requirements and the reduction of services to low-profit customers can lead to a reconfiguration of the physical network of facilities resulting in cost savings.

Properly implemented, customer relationship management can reduce current assets such as inventories and accounts receivable as well as fixed assets. Inventories will be reduced as a result of improved demand planning, lower safety stocks, and the shift to a make-to-order manufacturing environment. Accounts receivable will be reduced as a result of fewer disputed invoices that typically are caused by incomplete orders, missed deliveries, incorrect pricing, and/or products shipped in error. Finally, successful customer relationship management can lead to lower fixed assets as a result of improved utilization/rationalization of plant and warehousing facilities, and improved investment planning and deployment.

Once the team has an understanding of how customer relationship management impact the firm's financial performance as measured by EVA, metrics must be developed for each of the individual activities performed and these metrics must be tied back to the firm's financial performance. However, management should focus on those activities that increase the profitability of the total supply chain not just the profitability of a single firm. It is the goal of supply chain management to encourage actions that benefit the whole supply chain while at the same time equitably sharing in the risks and the rewards. If the management team of a firm makes a decision that positively affects that firm's EVA at the expense of the EVA of customers or suppliers, every effort should be made to share the benefits in a manner that improves the financial performance of each firm involved and thus gives each one an incentive to improve overall supply chain performance.

It is the goal of supply chain management to encourage actions that benefit the whole supply chain while at the same time equitably sharing in the risks and the rewards.

The development of customer profitability reports enables the process team to track performance over time. If calculated as shown in Table 2-1, these reports reflect all of the cost and revenue implications of the relationship. Variable manufacturing costs are deducted from net sales to calculate a manufacturing contribution. Next, variable marketing and logistics costs, such as sales commissions, transportation, warehouse handling, special packaging, order processing and a charge for account receivable, are deducted to calculate a contribution margin. Assignable nonvariable costs, such as salaries, customer related advertising expenditures, slotting allowances and inventory carrying costs, are subtracted to obtain a segment controllable margin. The net margin is obtained after deducting a charge for dedicated assets. These statements contain opportunity costs for investment in receivables and inventory and a charge for dedicated assets.

Table 2-1
Customer Profitability Analysis:
A Contribution Approach with Charge for Assets Employed

	Customer A	Customer B	Customer C	Customer D
Net Sales				
Cost of Goods Sold (Variable Manufacturing Cost)	———	———	———	———
Manufacturing Contribution				
Variable Marketing and Logistics Costs:				
Sales Commissions				
Transportation				
Warehousing (Handling in and out)				
Special Packaging				
Order Processing				
Charge for Investment in Accounts Receivable	———	———	———	———
Contribution Margin				
Assignable Nonvariable Costs:				
Salaries				
Segment Related Advertising				
Slotting Allowances				
Inventory Carrying Costs				
Controllable Margin				
Charge for Dedicated Assets Used				
Net Margin	———	———	———	———

Consequently, they are much closer to cash flow statements than a traditional profit and loss statement. They contain revenues minus the costs (avoidable costs) that disappear if the revenue disappears.

At Sysco, a $23.4 billion food distributor, profitability reports by customer were implemented in 1999. These reports enabled management to make strategic decisions about the allocation of resources to accounts. The results are illustrated in Figure 2-6. The five year cumulative annual growth rate for the period 1999 to 2003 was 11.3% for sales and 19.1% for net earnings. As shown in Figure 2-6, net earnings growth improved sharply after the profitability reports were implemented.

In addition to measuring current performance, these profitability reports can be used to track performance of customers over time and to generate pro-forma statements that evaluate potential process improvement projects. Decision analysis can be performed to consider what if scenarios such as best case, worst case and most likely customers.

Develop Guidelines for Sharing Process Improvement Benefits with Customers

In the final sub-process, the team develops the guidelines for sharing process improvement benefits with customers. The goal is to make process improvements win-win solutions for both the firm and the customer. If all of the parties involved do not gain from process improvement efforts, it will be difficult to obtain their full commitment. The customer relationship management team must quantify the benefits of process improvements in financial terms.

The goal is to make process improvements win-win solutions for both the firm and the customer.

For example, in a project that involved Cargill and a key customer, representatives from the two firms needed to address the following issue as they worked to develop a method for sharing the benefits:

• An agreement in principle on a fair location of benefits. For example,

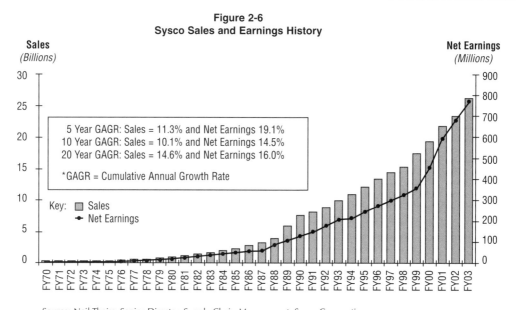

Figure 2-6
Sysco Sales and Earnings History

5 Year GAGR: Sales = 11.3% and Net Earnings 19.1%
10 Year GAGR: Sales = 10.1% and Net Earnings 14.5%
20 Year GAGR: Sales = 14.6% and Net Earnings 16.0%

*GAGR = Cumulative Annual Growth Rate

Key: ▢ Sales
— Net Earnings

Source: Neil Theiss, Senior Director, Supply Chain Management, Sysco Corporation

should it be 50% and 50% or 60% and 40%?
- Timeframe for benefit sharing. Should it be the life of the agreement, five years, or re-assessed annually?
- Decision on what benefits/costs to include.
- A fair approach to handling capital expenditure costs.
- Accurate baseline to use as a starting point for measuring savings.
- Common process to measure value captured and the cost to get.
- Benefit review and approval procedures.
- Mechanics to accrue for and transfer value (where, how, how often, etc.).
- Methodology review.

It was decided that a 50/50 split was in keeping with the overall spirit of the partnership, would motivate both parties to maximize the opportunities, and would acknowledge that neither party could have achieved the savings without the other party.

Both companies' process improvement teams agreed that benefits should be derived from supply chain initiatives, be explicitly recognized in supply chain project outcomes (e.g. reduced freight, reduced inventory carrying costs, reduced administrative transaction costs, etc.), and be in excess of a predetermined "baseline" for each area. The costs to be considered should be directly related to recommended supply chain initiatives (capital costs, transaction costs, system related costs, etc.), represent only incremental, full time staff adds, and be documented costs, greater than an agreed upon minimum dollar amount.

In the view of Cargill's management, it was important to identify the range of the expectations that each team brought to the project. It was also necessary to agree on the specific objectives that were realistic and that were shared with regard to process efficiency, growth/profit stability, costs savings, improved customer service, organizational alignment, clear metrics, and any other areas that were viewed as important by the parties.

The key learnings for the management team were summarized as follows:

Determine gain sharing at the outset so it does not undermine the joint objectives.

- Determine gain sharing at the outset so it does not undermine the joint objectives. Collaborative projects pursue opportunities that cannot be achieved independently, so the value will only be captured if jointly implemented.
- Working between business units is challenging - adding an external trading partner is even harder – trust, culture, process and system differences have an impact.
- Skeptics abound: success requires focused leadership and management support.
- Partnerships work – they take longer and are harder, but they work. Once trust is established, there are many opportunities to learn from each other.
- All involved enhance their knowledge and capabilities, which will be applied outside of the partnership, which should be acknowledged and encouraged.
- Enhanced collaboration and cooperation between customers and Cargill has led to unique results.
- Next step is to consider opportunities to jointly approach retailer or the next trading partner in the supply chain.

In summary, the objective of customer relationship management at the strategic level is to identify customer segments, provide criteria for categorizing customers, provide customer teams with guidelines for customizing the product and service offering, develop a framework for metrics, and provide guidelines for the sharing of process improvement benefits with the customers.

The Operational Customer Relationship Management Process

At the operational level, the customer relationship management process deals with writing and implementing the PSAs. It is comprised of seven sub-processes: differentiate customers, prepare the account/segment management team, internally review the accounts, identify opportunities with the accounts, develop the product and service agreement, implement the product and service agreement, and measure performance and generate profitability reports (see Figure 2-7).

All customers do not contribute equally to the firm's success and the goal is to identify those customers who desire and deserve special treatment so that the firm's offerings can be tailored to meet their needs while achieving the firm's profit goals for the customer.

Differentiate Customers

All customers do not contribute equally to the firm's success and the goal is to identify those customers who desire and deserve special treatment so that the firm's offerings can be tailored to meet their needs while achieving the firm's profit goals for the customer. In the first sub-process, customers are differentiated based on the criteria that were established in the strategic process. A key measure is the current

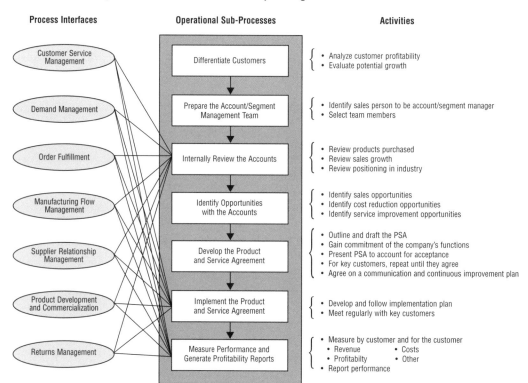

Figure 2-7
The Operational Customer Relationship Management Process

and potential profitability of each customer measured as shown in Table 2-1. Other criteria for differentiating customers might include: competitive positioning, market knowledge, market share goals/penetration, margin, technological capabilities, resources, compatibility, and class of trade.

Table 2-2 shows how one major corporation has categorized customers based on profitability. The most profitable customers were classified as Platinum followed by Gold, Silver, Bronze and Lead (unprofitable). Platinum customers only represented 8.4% of the accounts but they produced 65% of the pretax earnings. At the other extreme, unprofitable customers represented 34.3% of the accounts and actually reduced overall pretax earnings by 6%. This information is used to prioritize customers for the customer relationship management process. Table 2-3 shows how the profitability and thus classification can change from year to year. Not only did some Platinum customers turn to Gold, Silver, Bronze and Lead in 2003, but unprofitable customers became profitable with some even becoming Platinum. The goal is to understand what is driving the numbers and reassign resources on that basis.

Prepare the Account/Segment Management Team

In this sub-process, the account or segment management teams are formed, including the salesperson who will be the account or segment manager. The teams are cross-functional with representation from each of the functional areas such as marketing, research and development, manufacturing, logistics, information

Table 2-2
Customer Classification Based on Pretax Profit Contribution

Classification	Percentage of Accounts	Percentage of Pretax Earnings
Platinum	8.4%	65%
Gold	17.1%	25%
Silver	18.2%	11%
Bronze	22.0%	5%
Lead (Unprofitable)	34.3%	-6%
Total	100%	100%

Table 2-3
Customer Classification for 2002 and 2003

	2002 Classification Percentage of Customers Mix	2003 Classification					
		Platinum	Gold	Silver	Bronze	Lead (Unprofitable)	Total
Platinum	7.71%	5.89%	1.35%	0.21%	0.09%	0.15%	7.71%
Gold	16.49%	1.74%	10.44%	2.82%	0.79%	0.70%	16.49%
Silver	17.90%	0.26%	3.61%	8.79%	3.47%	1.77%	17.90%
Bronze	22.05%	0.15%	0.93%	4.37%	11.59%	5.02%	22.05%
Lead (Unprofitable)	35.85%	0.32%	0.80%	2.04%	6.06%	26.04%	35.85%
Total	100%	8.36%	17.13%	18.23%	21.99%	34.29%	100%

systems, finance and in some cases purchasing. Some of the team members may be more important to a specific customer relationship. For example, if the business drivers for both firms are to collaborate on the development of new products, personnel from research and development in both firms will play a key role on the teams. In the case of key accounts, each team is dedicated to a specific account and meets regularly with the customer's team. In most instances, the team members, with the exception of the account representatives, will have full-time positions in one of the functions. For very large customers, such as Wal-Mart, suppliers such as Colgate-Palmolive, have dedicated team members who work full-time on the customer relationship management team and are located near the customer's corporate headquarters. In the case of customer segments, a team manages a group of customers, and develops and manages a standard PSA for the segment.

In the case of key accounts, each team is dedicated to a specific account and meets regularly with the customer's team.

Internally Review the Accounts

Each account team reviews their account or segment of accounts to determine the products purchased, sales growth and their position in the industry. The value that the firm brings to the customer is based on the customer relationship management team's ability to understand and meet the customer's priorities. The customers' top priorities are so important that they will pay a premium for them or, when they are not being provided, they will switch some or all of their business to another supplier.[12] The link between understanding customers' priorities and the firm's profitability is established by the following sequence of activities:
- Understand priorities (the objective of the next sub-process).
- Design products and services that address these priorities.
- Sell the value proposition to the customers and within the firm.
- Measure the impact in terms of the profitability of each customer and customer segment.

Identify Opportunities with the Accounts

In order to understand the customer, the team must ask the right people the right questions. With a business-to-business customer, there are many individuals throughout the customer's organization who must be identified in order to gain knowledge about the customer's needs, behavior, decision-making process, price sensitivities and preferences.[13] A major part of this effort is to identify customer priorities that are being ignored and find a way to profitably provide for them. Once the team has an understanding of the customer(s), they work with each account or segment of accounts to develop improvement opportunities in sales, costs and service. These opportunities might arise from any part of the business, so the account teams need to interface with each of the other supply chain management processes.

In a supply chain management context, it is important to also understand what brings value to customers beyond Tier 1. For example, "a component supplier must understand the economic motivations of the manufacturer who buys the

---

[12] Slywotzky, Adrian J. and David J. Morrison, *The Profit Zone*, New York, NY: Times Books, 1997.
[13] Slywotzky, Adrian J. and David J. Morrison, *The Profit Zone*, New York, NY: Times Books, 1997.

components, the distributor who takes the manufacturer's products to sell, and the end-use consumer".[14]

Develop the Product and Service Agreement

In the fifth sub-process, each team develops the PSA for their account or segment of accounts. Each team first outlines and drafts the PSA, and then gains commitment from the internal functions. For key accounts, they present the PSA for acceptance, and work with the customer until agreement has been reached. It is important that the PSA for key accounts include a communication and continuous improvement plan. For other accounts, the PSA is presented to the customer. The PSA is an agreement that matches the requirements of the customer with the capabilities of the firm and the firm's profit goals for the customer. This sub-process aligns the business goals of the customer and the firm so that the expectations of each side are realistic and understood by both organizations.

Implement the Product and Service Agreement

In the sixth sub-process, the team implements the PSA, which includes holding regular planning sessions with key customers. The customer relationship management teams provide input to each of the other supply chain management processes that are affected by the customizations that have been made in the PSAs. Customer relationship management teams must work with the other process teams to make sure that the PSA is being implemented as planned, and schedule regular meetings with customers to review progress and performance. Implementation of the PSA might require an investment in new information systems, the re-engineering of a transactional activity, or a new employee such as a dedicated person for planning.

Measure Performance and Generate Profitability Reports

In the last operational sub-process, the team captures and reports the process performance measures. Metrics from each of the other processes also are captured in order to generate the customer profitability reports. These profitability reports provide information for measuring and selling the value of the relationship to each customer and internally to upper management. The value provided should be measured in terms of costs, impact on sales, and associated investment, otherwise the efforts incurred will go unrewarded.[15]

The other process teams communicate customer-related performance to the customer relationship management teams who tie these metrics back to the profitability of the firm as well as to the profitability of the customer. For example, Heinz in the United Kingdom has the capability of generating profitability reports showing the profitability of customers such as Tesco and Sainsbury to Heinz. In addition, they generate reports for each of these customers showing how much profit Heinz has contributed to their firms. The ability to generate profitability reports of this type is a powerful tool that enables fact-base negotiation between the process teams of each firm.

Each team first outlines and drafts the PSA, and then gains commitment from the internal functions. For key accounts, they present the PSA for acceptance, and work with the customer until agreement has been reached.

---

[14] Slywotzky, Adrian J. and David J. Morrison, *The Profit Zone*, New York, NY: Times Books, 1997.

[15] Lambert, Douglas M. and Renan Burduroglu, "Measuring and Selling the Value of Logistics," *The International Journal of Logistics Management*, Vol. 11, No. 1 (2000), pp. 1-17.

Conclusions

Customer relationship management provides the structure for how relationships with customers are developed and maintained, including the establishment of PSAs between the firm and its customers. It is a key supply chain management process which along with the supplier relationship management process form the critical linkages that connect firms in the supply chain. Supply chain management is about relationship management and so much of the success depends on individual relationships. A top-to-top relationship is necessary to achieve buy-in and the resources to support the relationship but there must be multiple one-to-one relationships "where the rubber meets the road." The requirements for successful customer relationship management include trust, open books, senior executives who walk the talk, key connections and quick wins.

The ultimate measure of success for each relationship is the impact that it is having on the financial performance of the firms involved. Consequently, it is necessary for each firm to have the capability to measure the performance of both customer relationship management and supplier relationship management in terms of their impact on incremental revenues and costs as well as incremental investment. The supply chain is managed relationship-by-relationship, link-by-link. With the proper information regarding the costs and benefits associated with process improvement and a willingness to share the gains, over time the supply chain should migrate to the most efficient and effective structure.

The ultimate measure of success for each relationship is the impact that it is having on the financial performance of the firms involved.

The Customer Service Management Process

Yemisi A. Bolumole, A. Michael Knemeyer and Douglas M. Lambert

Overview

Customer service management is the supply chain management process that represents the firm's face to the customer.[1] The process is the key point of contact for administering product and service agreements (PSAs) developed by customer teams as part of the customer relationship management process. The goal is to provide a single source of customer information, such as product availability, shipping dates and order status. Customer service management requires a real-time system to respond to customer inquires and facilitate order placement. In this chapter, we describe the customer service management process in detail to demonstrate how it can be implemented and managed. To do this, we detail the activities of each strategic and operational sub-process; evaluate the interfaces with the business functions and the other seven supply chain management processes; and describe examples of successful implementation.

Introduction

In a competitive business environment, it is necessary that firms actively manage their customer service management process in order to provide a focused point of contact for all customer inquiries.

Driven by an increasing expectation for timely and accurate information before, during and after transactions, customers expect an ease of doing business that entails adoption of a process approach towards customer service. Management is moving away from the traditional isolated approach towards a more coordinated and integrated design and control of the supply chain in order to provide goods and services to customers at low costs and high service levels.[2] The motivation for management to provide high levels of service comes from the need to grow sales through the ultimate satisfaction of demanding customers who are involved in their own complex businesses. In the words of a former Director of Customer Service at 3M, "The fact that 3M is a multi-national, multi-division, and multi-product company is not our customers' problem".[2] In a competitive business environment, it is necessary that firms actively manage their customer service management process in order to provide a focused point of contact for all customer inquiries.

---

[1] This chapter is based on Yemisi A. Bolumole, A. Michael Knemeyer and Douglas M. Lambert, "The Customer Service Management Process," *The International Journal of Logistics Management*, Vol. 14, No. 2 (2003), pp. 15-31.

[2] Fabozzi, Dennis S., "Customer Service Management," Supply Chain Management Seminar, Marriott Sawgrass, February 14, 1996.

The well-managed customer service management process includes efficiently utilizing on-line information systems with current and consistent information to serve the customer. When effectively managed, this process can allow a company to be more proactive to service requests, and more responsive to service problems. A key component of customer service management is planning how the commitments made in PSAs, developed by the customer relationship management process teams, are going to be delivered and managed. Another important component is working with the order fulfillment process in actively addressing customer inquires and orders. The goals of customer service management are to develop the necessary infrastructure and coordination for implementing the PSAs and to provide a key point of contact to the customer.[3]

From a logistics perspective, customer service has been shown to significantly impact the performance of a firm. Superior customer service can positively influence purchasing decisions,[4] serve as a method of building a sustainable competitive advantage,[5] increase the likelihood of repurchase[6] and be used to secure and maintain customers for the firm.[7] While many managers view customer service only within the bounds of the logistics function, it is the integration with other internal functions and other members of the supply chain that defines customer service management as a supply chain process. Improvements in the customer service management process should be beneficial not only within the firm, but should extend to other members of the supply chain.

In this chapter, we describe the sub-processes and activities for implementing an efficient and effective customer service management process. Customer service management is one of the eight processes and it requires interfaces with the other seven (see Figure 3-1). Next, customer service as a supply chain management process is described with particular emphasis on the distinction between customer service management as a supply chain process and customer service from a logistics perspective. We also delineate the distinction between the customer service management process and the customer relationship management process, and describe the interface between the two processes. We then detail the strategic and operational processes that comprise customer service management, and describe the sub-processes and their activities, and the interfaces with business functions, the other supply chain management processes and other firms. Finally, we present an example of the operational customer service management process at Shell UK and conclusions.

While many managers view customer service only within the bounds of the logistics function, it is the integration with other internal functions and other members of the supply chain that defines customer service management as a supply chain process.

---

[3] Croxton, Keely L., Sebastian J. Garcia-Dastugue, Douglas M. Lambert, and Dale S. Rogers, "The Supply Chain Management Processes," *The International Journal of Logistics Management*, Vol. 12, No. 2 (2001), pp. 13-36.

[4] Levy, Michael, "Toward an Optimal Customer Service Package," *Journal of Business Logistics*, Vol. 2, No. 2 (1981), pp. 87-101.

[5] Stock, James R. and Douglas M. Lambert, "Becoming a 'World Class' Company with Logistics Service Quality," *The International Journal of Logistics Management*, Vol. 3, No. 1 (1992), pp. 73-81.

[6] Innis, Daniel E. and Bernard J. La Londe, "Modeling the Effects of Customer Service Performance on Purchase Intentions in the Channel," *Journal of Marketing Theory and Practice*, Vol. 2, No. 2 (1994), pp. 45-59.

[7] Lambert, Douglas M., "Developing a Customer-focused Logistics Strategy," *International Journal of Physical Distribution and Materials Management*, Vol. 22, No. 6 (1992), pp. 12-19; and, Philip B. Schary and Boris W. Becker, "The Impact of Stock-Out on Market Share: Temporal Effects," *Journal of Business Logistics*, Vol. 1, No. 1 (1979), pp. 31-43.

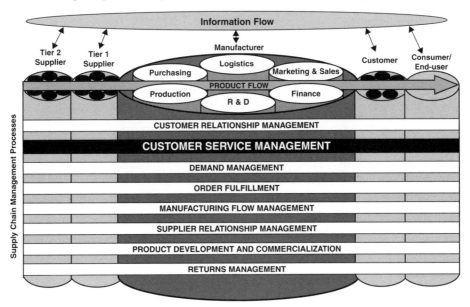

Figure 3-1
Supply Chain Management:
Integrating and Managing Business Processes Across the Supply Chain

Source: Adapted from Douglas M. Lambert, Martha C. Cooper, and Janus D. Pagh, "Supply Chain Management: Implementation Issues and Research Opportunities," *The International Journal of Logistics Management,* Vol. 9, No. 2 (1998), p. 2.

Customer Service Management as a Supply Chain Management Process

The customer service management process has both strategic and operational elements, as shown in Figure 3-2. In the strategic process, a management team establishes the structure for managing the process, and in the operational process it is implemented. Strategic sub-processes typically involve a longer time horizon, are closely linked to the corporate strategy and establish the framework for process implementation. Implementation of the strategic customer service management process within the firm is a necessary first step in integrating the firm's process with other members of the supply chain. Operational sub-processes focus on the implementation of the customer service management process on a day-to-day basis. Figure 3-2 also shows the interfaces between each sub-process and the other seven supply chain management processes. These interfaces might take the form of a transfer of data or might involve a sharing of information or ideas with another process team.

The customer service management process should not be confused with logistics customer service, which represents a measure of the logistics system performance in creating time and place utility, measuring its ability to satisfy existing customers and attract new ones.[8] From this perspective, customer service provides the key interface between the marketing and logistics functions. A clear distinction must be made between the internal logistics perspective of customer

A clear distinction must be made between the internal logistics perspective of customer service and that of customer service management as a supply chain management process.

---

[8] Lambert, Douglas M., James J. Stock and Lisa M. Ellram, *Fundamentals of Logistics Management,* Irwin/McGraw-Hill, 1998.

Figure 3-2
Customer Service Management

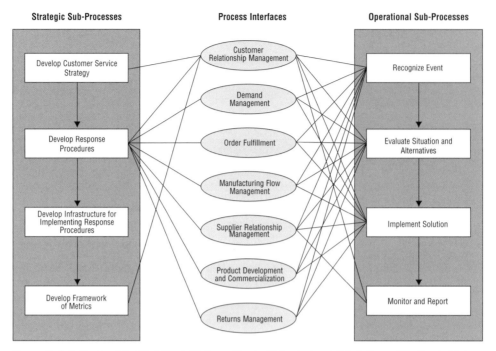

Source: Keely L. Croxton, Sebastián J. García-Dastugue, Douglas M. Lambert, and Dale S. Rogers, "The Supply Chain Management Processes," *The International Journal of Logistics Management*, Vol. 12, No. 2 (2001), p. 17.

service and that of customer service management as a supply chain management process. The customer service management process provides the firm's face to customers. It includes the management and administration of PSAs, and provides a single point of contact and source of customer information. Customer service management involves developing proactive response procedures for addressing specific customer service events, facilitated by the establishment of system infrastructure for implementing effective service solutions. It is more extensive and proactive than logistics customer service which emphasizes specific pre-, post- and transactional service events. The customer service management process also involves a higher-level focus on supply chain relationships.

Customer service management deals with administering the customer's PSA. PSAs are documents that match specific customer or customer segment needs with a firm's products and services. They represent a firm's commitment to a customer based on a realistic understanding of customer expectations and the firm's own capabilities and profitability requirements. The customer relationship management process teams develop PSAs of varying complexity and formality depending on a needs-based definition of specific variables including the number and extent of products within the firm's portfolio; shipping locations; frequency of orders; contractual limitations; purchasing and delivery specifications; and price/service guarantees. The inclusion of some or all of these variables, within the PSA means that the agreement can range from a low level of customization, which would be typical for most segments of customers, to a high level of customization for a few key accounts (see Figure 3-3). As an example, 3M varies the components of their PSAs based on customer importance, customer requirements, and their own capabilities. As the level of customization increases, the PSAs will include additional value-added services.

In order to identify opportunities to more efficiently and effectively administer PSAs, it is necessary to work with the sales, marketing and manufacturing functions as well as customers and suppliers. Increasingly technology is being leveraged to provide on-line/real-time product, pricing and order status information in support of customer orders and inquiries. For example, Moen Inc. introduced CustomerNet, an interactive website designed to provide customers with world-class service through round-the-clock access to real-time order and shipping information. This customer service management tool continues to evolve as Moen Inc. customizes the website functionality for specific customers or customer segments. In all cases, process teams need to understand and consider the implications of their solutions to meet customer requirements, as defined by the PSA, on the other members of the supply chain.

While the customer relationship management process teams develop the PSAs, customer service management teams service and support the PSAs. TaylorMade-adidas Golf Company Inc. demonstrates this distinction through their use of a customer relationship management process team to establish the PSA that delineates a basic set of parameters for managing the relationship with a particular golf equipment retailer. This agreement involves a mutual understanding of each other's goals and requirements for the relationship. TaylorMade-adidas Golf Company Inc. then tasks their customer service management process team to

Figure 3-3
Potential Components of a Product and Service Agreement

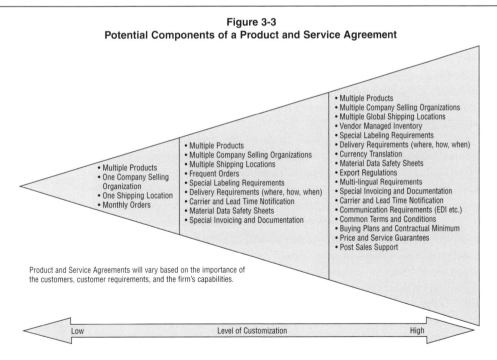

- Multiple Products
- One Company Selling Organization
- One Shipping Location
- Monthly Orders

- Multiple Products
- Multiple Company Selling Organizations
- Multiple Shipping Locations
- Frequent Orders
- Special Labeling Requirements
- Delivery Requirements (where, how, when)
- Carrier and Lead Time Notification
- Material Data Safety Sheets
- Special Invoicing and Documentation

- Multiple Products
- Multiple Company Selling Organizations
- Multiple Global Shipping Locations
- Vendor Managed Inventory
- Special Labeling Requirements
- Delivery Requirements (where, how, when)
- Currency Translation
- Material Data Safety Sheets
- Export Regulations
- Multi-lingual Requirements
- Special Invoicing and Documentation
- Carrier and Lead Time Notification
- Communication Requirements (EDI etc.)
- Common Terms and Conditions
- Buying Plans and Contractual Minimum
- Price and Service Guarantees
- Post Sales Support

Product and Service Agreements will vary based on the importance of the customers, customer requirements, and the firm's capabilities.

Low ← Level of Customization → High

Source: Adapted from Dennis S. Fabozzi, "Customer Service Management," Supply Chain Management Seminar, Marriott Sawgrass, February 14, 1996.

service and support these agreements. Based on the customers' PSA, the customer service management process team serves as the internal advocate for the retailer by developing account-focused process improvements and value-added services.

Customer service managers are dedicated full-time to a particular customer or segment of customers. They are necessary because, with the exception of very large customer accounts such as Wal-Mart Stores for which suppliers might have a dedicated team, the only person other than the salesperson who is dedicated full-time to a particular customer or segment of customers is the customer service manager. The salesperson is the company's in-the-field representative who should be focused on finding solutions to customer problems, not dealing with customer service issues. The customer service manager is the internal advocate for the customer or segment of customers. The success of an organization's customer service management process is only as effective as its knowledge of its customers and of its own internal capabilities. The PSAs articulate commitments based on customer requirements and expectations as well as the firm's capabilities and profit goals for the customer or customer segment.

...the only person other than the salesperson who is dedicated full-time to a particular customer or segment of customers is the customer service manager.

Effective customer service management is dependent on the supply chain's overall service ethic with a philosophy that envisions the service environment as a critical component of the business. Management is tasked with prioritizing the firm's investment strategies so these align with a diverse set of customer needs. Achieving this is a holistic, enterprise-wide responsibility, not just the job of sales and customer service. It involves understanding changing customer needs and focusing resources on the highest priority customer or customer segments, and reengineering transactional activities to develop service levels which are aligned to customer expectations as defined within the PSA. The customer service management process team must communicate changing requirements and capabilities with the customer relationship management process team in order to ensure this fit.

A process team comprised of managers from functions including marketing, finance, production, purchasing and logistics, leads the strategic process. This team might also include members from outside the firm such as representatives from key customers, key suppliers or third-party logistics providers. This team is not full-time, that is, members come together from different functions and firms to carry out process activities which cut across traditional functional responsibilities and expertise. The strategic process team is responsible for defining the customer service strategy and designing the infrastructure and framework to be used for its implementation. The team is also responsible for developing the procedures at the strategic level and overseeing their implementation. The operational process can be managed by a team for large critical customers or by assigning an individual customer service manager the day-to-day responsibility for the process. This team or customer service manager is responsible for implementing the activities, on a day-to-day basis as established, and within the framework set, by the strategic process team. Firm employees outside of the team might be involved in implementation of the process, but the customer service management process team or customer service manager maintains managerial responsibility.

The role of the customer service manager within the customer service management process is different from that of a traditional customer service representative, an order entry clerk who may also provide information on order status and resolve invoicing problems.

The role of the customer service manager within the customer service management process is different from that of a traditional customer service representative, an order entry clerk who might also provide information on order status and resolve invoicing problems. The customer service managers interface and work with other supply chain management process teams and customer service representatives to provide effective solutions to customer inquiries and complaints. At 3M, compensation for the customer service manager position corresponds to the pay scale for field sales representatives. This differentiates the position from traditional day-to-day order-taking responsibilities. This practice of matching extends back down the pay scale connecting various levels of sales representatives with customer service representatives as they progress towards the managerial level.

The customer service manager will serve as the company liason to the customer, initiate proactive communication, facilitate the resolution of customer issues and questions, identify and communicate up-sale opportunities to the sales force, obtain feedback on company and product performance, and issue reports to functional and/or process managers as needed to administer the PSA.[9] The customer service manager's primary responsibility is to ensure that the firm is fulfilling the promises made within its PSAs, following up to implement the PSA as members of the customer relationship management process team return to their functional responsibilities. The decision by Moen Inc. to have an on-site customer service manager at Home Depot also supports this perspective of the customer service manager becoming an advocate for the customer.

The Strategic Customer Service Management Process

Strategic customer service management includes four sub-processes that deal with the necessary framework and infrastructural basis for implementing PSAs. At this level, the process team is responsible for planning how each of the potential products and services to be included in the PSA are going to be delivered and managed. Figure 3-4 shows the strategic customer service management sub-processes, the activities that comprise each one, and the interfaces with the other seven supply chain management processes. Based on our discussions with a number of corporate executives, the expected trend is for companies to move from a reactive operational approach to customer service management towards a more strategic approach that establishes proactive ways to deal with service issues. The strategic process team is responsible for achieving this through the establishment of an effective customer service management process.

Develop Customer Service Management Strategy

The customer service management process is focused on developing an overall customer service strategy that meets the commitments made in the PSAs.

The customer service management process is focused on developing an overall customer service strategy that meets the commitments made in the PSAs. A company's identified target markets will influence the development of the customer service management strategy. For example, TaylorMade-adidas Golf Company Inc. targets 0-10 handicap golfers, who typically have deeper technical questions about their golfing products. To address the particular needs of this target market, the company provides in-depth technical information on its products through its corporate website. The website provides answers for typical inquires from this group of consumers and is a valuable resource for the company's retailers.

---

[9] "Customer Advocates: Putting a Face on CRM," *IOMA's Report on Customer Relationship Management,* Vol. 2, No. 5 (2002), pp. 3-4.

Figure 3-4
The Strategic Customer Service Management Process

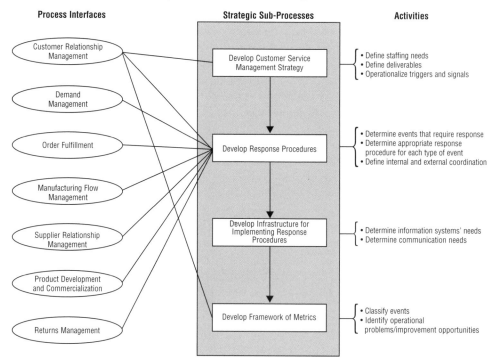

The information that is available on the website assists retailers with their customer service activities in support of TaylorMade-adidas products.

In this sub-process, the customer service management team identifies the deliverables of the customer service management process, operationalizes the triggers and signals for initiating action, and defines the staffing needs. The deliverables of the process are standardized responses to standardized events that occur while administering the PSA. The output is a list of relevant events with corresponding triggers, signals and deliverables. When implementing the first strategic sub-process, the customer service management team interfaces with the customer relationship management team. The driving force is the recognition that you cannot be everything to everyone. PSAs will vary based on the importance of customers, customer requirements, and the firm's capabilities. Therefore, many organizations develop a tiered customer service strategy as a direct result of the level of PSA customization.

At Shell UK, the customer service management strategy is defined within individual operating units, based on their pre-defined customer segments. The decentralization across these units means that there are no expectations that all customer service management modules should be acceptable within all operating units. Shell UK has developed a Customer Relationship Implementation Solution Pack (CRISP) as a way to respond to problems within its commercial department. CRISP provides a "live resolution" of getting whatever the customer wants across several silos. Shell UK's development of a customer service management strategy

PSAs will vary based on the importance of customers, customer requirements, and the firm's capabilities.

also involves defining accreditation levels and CRISP helps define customer service staffing needs, infrastructure and deliverables. An example of its implementation is the development of the information technology infrastructure for Shell's Central American operations. This helps to improve workflow performance through a system that sets up and captures service triggers throughout the entire system. In the past, call centers used an ERP system that did not capture customer information. Today, CRISP helps to catalog customer complaints and ensuing responses, thus building a database of these "triggers" and signals which helps provide consistency in the responses and actions of customer service managers and customer service representatives across all call centers.

Prior to the development of response procedures in the next sub-process, organizations define a customer service structure that identifies what staffing, administrative, and technological resources are needed and available, matching resource availability with the organization's strategic alignment. This sub-process interfaces with the customer relationship management process to differentiate customers into segments based on behavior, profitability, and loyalty.

Develop Response Procedures

In the second sub-process, the team determines the types of events that require responses and develops response procedures for each of these events. This includes developing the internal and external coordination required to respond, and distinguishing between customer and internal responses. The sub-process requires organizations to have clearly segmented their customers. Specific to these identified customer segments, events are determined and the appropriate response procedures are established for the organization. For example, Shell UK has developed response procedures for potential events that might occur while administering their PSAs. Shell UK equips each customer service manager with a set of service-process maps with functional interfaces identified for potential events. As an example, Figure 3-5 shows the response procedures developed to manage a customer request to cancel an order. The arrows on the map represent the customer event. Each square details the set of standardized response procedures for the particular event; circles establish a required intermediate step; diamonds are decision points; and rounded rectangles represent deliverables. At Shell UK, each operating unit - depending on individual circumstances - can modify these guides but financial and managerial controls are fixed and inflexible. For each decision point, an explanation is provided listing the internal and external groups involved with the administration of response procedures for the event.

Moen's customer service management process team determines the events that require a response by assessing the severity of the issue to their customers.

Moen Inc. also develops detailed response procedures at a strategic level. For example, if a supplier's manufacturing operation goes down for an extended period of time, the customer service manager contacts the customers whose orders are affected and communicates the problem, expected consequences to the customers in the most factual way possible, and provides them with a solution. Typical response procedures are scripted and integrated into customer service manager training activities. Moen's customer service management process team determines the events that require a response by assessing the severity of the issue to their customers. When determining an appropriate response procedure, Moen has found internal and external communication to be critical. They often assemble a

Figure 3-5
Shell UK - Standardized Response Procedure for Order Cancellation

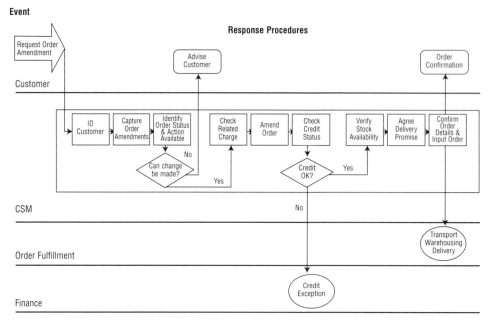

Source: Shell International Petroleum Company

response team that coordinates the message to the customer, with the goal of maintaining the integrity of the product as well as the company's reputation. The response team may include representatives from marketing, logistics, business planning, sales and other affected functional areas.

Communication is important for implementing this sub-process. How does the customer service management team determine events that require a response? At Moen Inc., any activity that fails to deliver on its commitments as defined within the PSA requires a response. When standardized responses are lacking, customer inquiries can be used as a launch-pad for developing a database of formal responses and procedures. At Taylor Made-adidas Golf Company Inc., no key performance indicators (KPIs) have been established but account managers have been successful in identifying the level of service that is expected by tracking and classifying customer complaints, questions, and inquiries through an internal mechanism. For example, the customer service management team tracks and measures warranty information, volume, and contact time and uses these data as an input to developing standard procedures related to warranty, fill rate, and damage issues. The data collected over time are published annually in a Customer Service Index Report. As a feedback mechanism, these data are provided to other process teams to improve the customer service management process. As a result of this procedure, the frequency of customer service inquiries has been reduced.

At Shell UK, there also is an interface with the team that is charged with standardizing data that are used and transferred across the organization, as originally defined by CRISP. Within the CRISP process map (see Figure 3-5) other

When standardized responses are lacking, customer inquiries can be used as a launch-pad for developing a database of formal responses and procedures.

internal functional interfaces and external supply chain interfaces, necessary for resolving customer inquiries, are also identified. The customer service management process team also interfaces with the manufacturing flow management process team in providing adequate visibility to support the firms' customer service efforts.

Develop Infrastructure for Implementing Response Procedures

Once the customer service management process team decides on appropriate response procedures to the relevant events, the team identifies the infrastructure for implementing them. The sources of the information needed to handle each event and determining the appropriate communication protocols for internal and external coordination must be identified. The team must also determine the information technology and communication needs for managing the PSAs efficiently and effectively. If there are technical constraints restricting the establishment of this infrastructure, the components of the PSA that are affected have to be re-evaluated and eventually modified to make them feasible.

Customer service tracking software can be used to identify when there is non-compliance, provide documentation of this occurrence as well as establish the immediate action required. Responsibility for this action is then assigned to individual customer service managers and tracked until an effective solution is provided. For example, FAW-Volkswagen Automotive Company Ltd. - a large-scale, joint-venture car manufacturing collaboration between First Automobile Works of China and German automakers Volkswagen and Audi - has utilized SAP to integrate all customer service functions on a single platform, from the contact center through sales, service, and marketing. The system allows customer service managers to get the latest product information and address customer issues at any time, anywhere. FAW-Volkswagen sells through regional dealers and the use of SAP has enabled them to get the direct customer feedback it needed to ensure superior customer service. Moen Inc. also uses SAP to formalize a "work list" that enables recurring process information to reach all internal and external parties who need to act on the information. They utilize a process specialist who can assist in laying out the appropriate administrative and technological infrastructure for implementing response procedures, mapping the process, and defining the appropriate work steps to respond to events.

Develop Framework of Metrics

The customer service management metrics should provide managers with the information necessary to identify problems and improvement opportunities in the administration of the PSA.

Finally, the team develops the framework of metrics to be used to measure and monitor the performance of the process, and sets goals for performance improvement. A uniform approach should be used throughout the firm to develop these metrics.[10] The customer service management metrics should provide managers with the information necessary to identify problems and improvement opportunities in the administration of the PSA. These measurements are used not only for managing the process, but also for improving its efficiency. The team interfaces with the customer relationship management team to assure that the metrics developed are consistent with the firm's objectives.

---

[10] Lambert, Douglas M. and Terrance L. Pohlen, "Supply Chain Metrics," *The International Journal of Logistics Management*, Vol. 12, No. 1 (2001), pp. 1-19.

Metrics selected should reflect the customer's perspective and expectations. These metrics should also reflect the impact of customer service management on the organization's efficiency, its return on assets and ultimately, on its financial performance as measured by Economic Value Added (EVA).[11] Figure 3-6 provides a framework for examining how customer service management can impact sales, total expenses, inventory investment, other current assets and fixed assets. For example, improved customer service management can result in higher sales by retaining and strengthening relationships with key customers. The information about the customer obtained through this process can assist the firm by identifying opportunities to sell higher margin products or increase the overall "share of customer" through superior service delivery. Similarly, improved customer service management may increase overall sales by avoiding lost sales associated with inadequate performance. Close monitoring of the PSAs should result in fewer last minute production changes. Several expenses can be reduced through the improved planning and communication between a firm and its customers including: reducing returns, order processing and transaction costs; minimizing or eliminating claims; improved management of warranty, replacement, and repair programs; and, reducing the number of expedited shipments.

Figure 3-6
How Customer Service Management Affects Economic Value Added (EVA®)

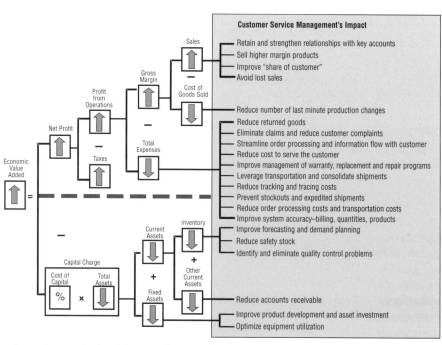

Source: Framework adapted from Douglas M. Lambert and Terrance L. Pohlen, "Supply Chain Metrics," *The International Journal of Logistics Management,* Vol. 12, No. 1 (2001), p. 10.

[11] Stewart, G. Bennet III, *The Quest for Value: A Guide for Senior Managers,* 2nd Edition, New York, NY: Harper Collins, 1999; and, Joel M. Stern, "One Way to Build Value in Your Firm, a la Executive Compensation," *Financial Executive,* Vol. 3, No. 6 (1990), pp. 51-54.

The customer knowledge gained through improvements in customer service management can lead to better forecasting and demand planning, lower levels of safety stock, and an improved ability to identify and eliminate quality control problems. Accounts receivables can be improved since fewer invoices will be disputed as a result of incomplete orders and missed delivery dates. Finally, improved customer involvement facilitated by the customer service management process can lead to improved product development efforts, better asset investment planning and equipment utilization. Although other activities and processes in the supply chain affect these holistic metrics, the team responsible for customer service management needs to estimate how this process affects the firm's financial performance. The determination of potential financial implications will help to justify future investments in the process and to determine rewards for superior performance.

Once the team has an understanding of the impact that customer service management can have on financial performance as measured by EVA, metrics need to be developed for the activities performed and these metrics must be tied back to financial measures.

Once the team has an understanding of the impact that customer service management can have on financial performance as measured by EVA, metrics need to be developed for the activities performed and these metrics must be tied back to financial measures. Relevant metrics for the customer service management process are those that target areas within the organization that touch the customer. These metrics enable the measurement of the value of each process. Typical process measures include accessibility of customer service representatives, input accuracy, and the ability of the customer service management process team to effectively respond to customer inquiries.

At Shell UK, metrics are defined with input from finance at executive, managerial, and operational levels. Each operating unit decides which metrics are appropriate. The responsibility for the choice of metrics lies with individual operating units. Metrics must be constantly reviewed and reassessed by the customer service management process team. To ensure this knowledge transfer, the CRISP team works closely with operating units within Shell UK during the initial stages of implementation. This also ensures control and sustainability of procedures.

It is important that firms implement processes that positively affect the profitability of the supply chain as a whole, not just that of an individual firm within it. There are advantages to using aligned metrics throughout the supply chain as these enable each organization to encourage the right behaviors from the other members. A primary goal of supply chain management should be to encourage behavior that benefits the entire supply chain while sharing the risks and rewards among its members. If management of one firm makes a decision that positively affects their firm's EVA but negatively affects the EVA of a key supplier or customer, the two firms should work out an agreement where the benefits are shared so that both firms' management teams have the incentive to implement the improvements.

The Operational Customer Service Management Process

At the operational level, customer service management process teams are responsible for the execution of the process as it was designed by the strategic process team.

At the operational level, customer service management process teams are responsible for the execution of the process as it was designed by the strategic process team. Figure 3-7 shows the four operational sub-processes, the activities within each of these, and the interfaces of each sub-process with the other supply chain management processes.

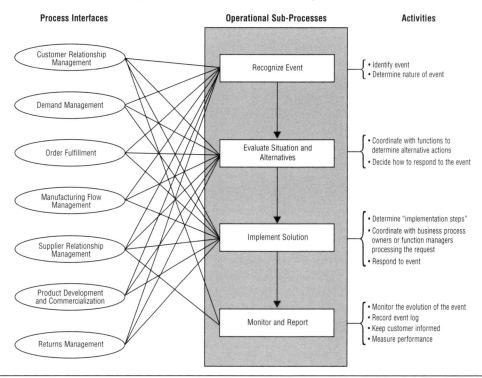

Figure 3-7
The Operational Customer Service Management Process

Process Interfaces	Operational Sub-Processes	Activities

Process Interfaces:
- Customer Relationship Management
- Demand Management
- Order Fulfillment
- Manufacturing Flow Management
- Supplier Relationship Management
- Product Development and Commercialization
- Returns Management

Operational Sub-Processes:
- Recognize Event
- Evaluate Situation and Alternatives
- Implement Solution
- Monitor and Report

Activities:
- Recognize Event:
  - Identify event
  - Determine nature of event
- Evaluate Situation and Alternatives:
  - Coordinate with functions to determine alternative actions
  - Decide how to respond to the event
- Implement Solution:
  - Determine "implementation steps"
  - Coordinate with business process owners or function managers processing the request
  - Respond to event
- Monitor and Report:
  - Monitor the evolution of the event
  - Record event log
  - Keep customer informed
  - Measure performance

Recognize Event

The first step of this operational sub-process is to recognize the event or at least be informed of it. The aim is to distinguish between inbound and outbound, or proactive or reactive responses. Being proactive makes this a challenging part of administering the PSAs. Examples of customer service events include queries regarding warranty issues, stockouts, quality complaints, technical questions, order request and inquiries. The team needs to have a thorough understanding of the firm's operations, and try to foresee the effects of a given event on the customer and on the internal operations of the firm. Events that require action might originate in any one of the other processes so coordination is essential. It is necessary to classify events and responses accordingly, based on internally set triggers. As an example, Moen Inc. treats large or significant orders with unique requirements in packaging, quantity or shipping execution over and above the normal stock replenishment orders as an event. When such an order enters the system, a cross-functional team is alerted. The team works with sales and marketing to identify what is coming down the pipeline and communicate internally the customer requirements. Internal communication is critical for identifying potential obstacles to fulfilling the customers' unique requirements.

Once the event is recognized, the customer service management process team evaluates alternatives for managing the event with the least disruption to the customer and internal operations.

Evaluate Situation and Alternatives

Once the event is recognized, the customer service management process team evaluates alternatives for managing the event with the least disruption to the customer and internal operations. They follow a pre-determined set of alternative actions working jointly with the specialists in each of the functions affected by the event or that can contribute to implementing the solution. This requires interfacing with other processes that might be affected by the alternative responses. For Moen Inc., the customer service manager gathers information to effectively evaluate potential alternatives for handling the order. Another key consideration when evaluating the situation and alternatives is to fully understand both the customer's operational limitations as well as Moen's. For example, a Moen customer service manager alerted a corporate buyer of the potential negative consequences of the buyer's decision to scale back some existing orders which would have caused a significant shipping delay because of the requirement that Moen ship in full truckload quantities. A shipping delay might have adversely affected the level of stock availability at the store level.

Implement Solution

The implementation of the selected solution is coordination intensive, as other business process owners or functional managers often need to participate in the implementation. At TaylorMade-adidas Golf Company Inc., a response might actually be to refer the consumer back to a member of the company's retailer network. While the customer service manager might have the ability to respond to the event, the nature of the golf industry supply chain dictates the need to refer the customer back to the retailer. The fear of disintermediation within the retailer network requires that TaylorMade-adidas be cognizant of the implications of their solutions on other members of their supply chain. The detail involved in this sub-process can change depending on the supply chain position of the firm. The customer service management process can be more intricate for business-to-business transactions and more generic for business-to-consumer transactions.

Monitor and Report

Finally, the customer service management process includes monitoring and reporting the process performance. This includes identifying possible process improvements to avoid future events or improve the responses to them. The sub-process also involves recording the event in a database that can be used for future reference, and monitoring the evolution of the event in order to know to what extent the response has been implemented. Part of the sub-process is informing the customer about how the issue is being resolved. Performance of the process is measured and conveyed to the customer relationship management and supplier relationship management teams. The most effective feedback occurs in a continuous stream, providing guidance and clear direction yielding process improvements.

A periodic review can be performed using specific metrics defined in the strategic process. Each opportunity for process improvement should bring about a change to the process. TaylorMade-adidas Golf Company Inc. improved its monitoring and reporting capabilities through the implementation of i2 systems which provides real-time customer service information that more closely monitors the evolution of events. The system increases the ability of TaylorMade-adidas to access timely customer service information.

Performance of the process is measured and conveyed to the customer relationship management and supplier relationship management teams.

The Operational Customer Service Management Process at Shell UK

As an example of the operational customer service management process, Figure 3-8 shows the service process map to manage a customer order amendment at Shell UK. The arrows on the map represent the customer event; each rectangle details the set of response procedures for the particular event; and rounded rectangles represent deliverables.

Recognize Event

At Shell UK, recognizing customer service events involves receiving calls and requests from customers who wish to make changes to their order. The sub-process used for delivering this service applies to all products. The service owner (i.e., the functional business area owning the service regardless of who performs the task) is the department responsible for service delivery. Using customer reference information, customer service managers verify the customer's identity to ensure they have the authority to carry out the inquiry and determine ship to location information. Capturing the order amendments involves establishing and categorizing the details of changes required by the customer.

Evaluate Situation and Alternatives

Shell UK utilizes a customer service impact scale to classify the potential severity of events. High impact events are assigned an 'S' (stoppage) where the

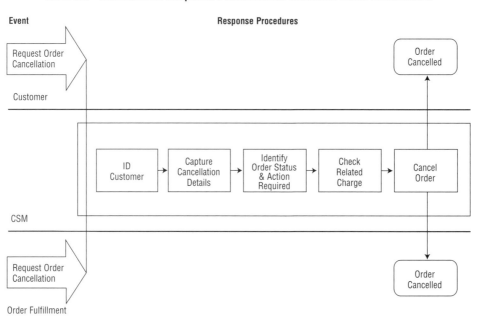

Figure 3-8
Shell UK – Standardized Response Procedure for Customer Order Amendment

Source: Shell International Petroleum Company

service promised is not delivered and the effect upon, and potential damage to, the customer relationship is determined as severe. Events with mid-level severity are assigned a 'D' (disruptions) where the service promised is disrupted or significantly hampered. The impact upon the customer relationship is potentially undermining. Events with the least severe impact where the service promised does or could result in a minor inconvenience to the customer are assigned an 'A' (annoyance). Using this customer service impact scale, the process of amending customer orders is awarded an 'S', to demonstrate the potential severity of this situation on customer relationship, indicating that not fulfilling the service promise would have a high and severe impact on the customer relationship. The next level of evaluation is to determine whether the sub-process changes (in terms of actions, people, IT, product, etc.) depending on the customer classification. In this example, it varies by product and is differentiated according to the service level agreements and service segments defined in the PSA. Decisions on the most appropriate service provider, available media, and standard/specific application types to be used remain the responsibility of the operating unit involved.

Implement Solution

Following the procedure laid out in Figure 3-8, customer service managers implement a resolution of the customer request. Major steps taken include identifying where the order is in the delivery process; understanding and advising the customer of any associated changes; amending the order with new details, ascertaining stock and transportation availability. This sub-process requires a working knowledge of the execution of the normal order taking, amendment, and cancellation procedures, the use and application of credit checking systems, procedures for credit exceptions, and a working knowledge of the system that manages delivery date and time information. When implementing an order amendment process, customer service managers refer to the PSAs. These rules must be applied to each situation and monitored for compliance.

Monitor and Report

Cost measures are used to determine and compare the cost to serve individual customer categories.

Cost measures are used to determine and compare the cost to serve individual customer categories. These cost measures represent a mechanism and tool used to provide costing data. Key performance indicators used within Shell UK to measure performance and monitor the evolution of the customer order amendment sub-process include:
- Total number of amendments.
- Percentage of calls abandoned.
- Speed of acknowledgment by channel.
- Percentage of calls with live resolution.
- Percentage of calls resolved within x time.
- Percentage of calls receiving a date and time commitment.
- Total number of rework activities.
- Number of amended orders as a percentage of total orders (re-work & customer education).

The objective is that customer service managers resolve the customer's order amendment without further contact with or from the customer.

Conclusions

A well thought-out implementation and seamless execution of the customer service management process can have substantial benefits on the firm's EVA through, for example, increased revenue, lower expenses, reduced inventory levels, improved asset utilization and improved product availability. The customer service management process operationalizes PSAs to minimize and proactively avoid service failures. It increases operational flexibility and facilitates the implementation of an effective system and infrastructure so that management can either quickly react to or proactively respond to unplanned issues. Working as a supply chain, management can find ways to improve both the internal and external coordination that needs to take place as part of the customer service management process.

Working as a supply chain, management can find ways to improve both the internal and external coordination that needs to take place as part of the customer service management process.

The Demand Management Process

Keely L. Croxton, Douglas M. Lambert, Sebastián J. García-Dastugue and Dale S. Rogers

Overview

Demand management is the supply chain management process that balances the customers' requirements with the capabilities of the supply chain.[1] With the right process in place, management can match supply with demand proactively and execute the plan with minimal disruptions. The process is not limited to forecasting. It includes synchronizing supply and demand, increasing flexibility, and reducing variability. In this chapter, we describe the demand management process in detail to show how it can be implemented within a company and managed across firms in the supply chain. We examine the activities of each sub-process; evaluate the interfaces with corporate functions, processes and firms; and provide examples of successful implementation.

Introduction

The demand management process is concerned with balancing the customers' requirements with the capabilities of the supply chain. This includes forecasting demand and synchronizing it with production, procurement, and distribution capabilities. A good demand management process can enable a company to be more proactive to anticipated demand, and more reactive to unanticipated demand. An important component of demand management is finding ways to reduce demand variability and improve operational flexibility. Reducing demand variability aids in consistent planning and reduces costs. Increasing flexibility helps the firm respond quickly to internal and external events. Most customer-driven variability is unavoidable, but one of the goals of demand management is to eliminate management practices that increase variability, and to introduce policies that foster smooth demand patterns. Another key part of demand management is developing and executing contingency plans when there are interruptions to the operational plans. The goal of demand management is to

A good demand management process can enable a company to be more proactive to anticipated demand, and more reactive to unanticipated demand.

[1] This chapter is based on Keely L. Croxton, Douglas M. Lambert, Sebastián J. García-Dastugue and Dale S. Rogers "The Demand Management Process," *The International Journal of Logistics Management*, Vol. 13, No. 2 (2002), pp. 51-66.

meet customer demand in the most effective and efficient way.

The demand management process can have a significant impact on the profitability of a firm, its customers and suppliers. Improving the process can have far-reaching implications. Having the right product on the shelves will increase sales and customer loyalty.[2] Improved forecasting can reduce raw materials and finished goods inventories. Smoother operational execution will reduce logistics costs and improve asset utilization. These improvements will be realized not only within the firm, but will extend to other members of the supply chain.

Demand management is one of the eight processes and it requires interfaces with the other seven (see Figure 4-1). We describe the strategic and operational processes that comprise demand management, including the sub-processes and their activities. In addition, we identify the interfaces with the corporate functions, the other supply chain management processes and other firms. Finally, we present conclusions.

Demand Management as a Supply Chain Management Process

The demand management process has both strategic and operational elements, as shown in Figure 4-2. In the strategic process, the team establishes the structure for managing the process. The operational process is the actualization of demand management. Implementation of the strategic process is a necessary first

---

Figure 4-1
Supply Chain Management:
Integrating and Managing Business Processes Across the Supply Chain

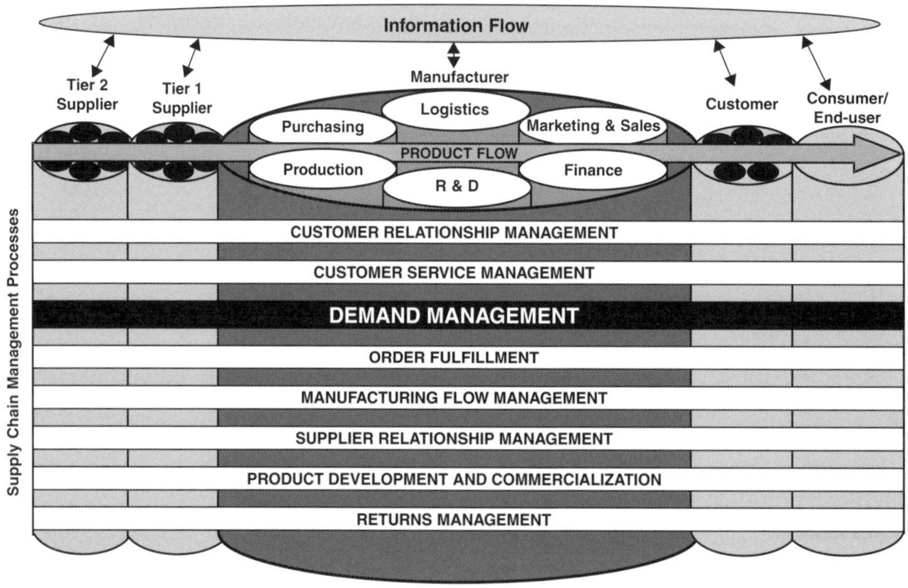

Source: Adapted from Douglas M. Lambert, Martha C. Cooper, and Janus D. Pagh, "Supply Chain Management: Implementation Issues and Research Opportunities," *The International Journal of Logistics Management,* Vol. 9, No. 2 (1998), p. 2.

---

[2] Zinn, Walter and Peter C. Liu, "Customer Response to Retail Stockouts" *Journal of Business Logistics,* Vol. 22, No. 1 (2001), pp. 50-53; Mike Duff, "Loyalty Wanes when Stock is Low," *DSN Retailing Today,* Vol. 40, Issue 20 (2001), pp. 37-38.

Figure 4-2
Demand Management

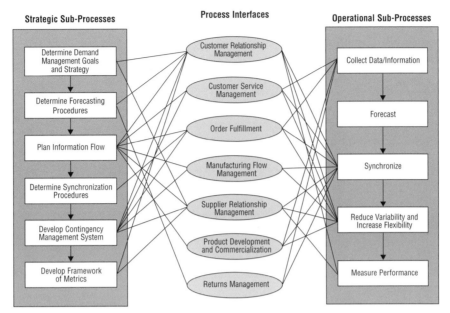

Source: Adapted from Keely L. Croxton, Sebastián J. García-Dastugue, Douglas M. Lambert, and Dale S. Rogers, "The Supply Chain Management Processes," *The International Journal of Logistics Management*, Vol. 12, No. 2 (2001), p. 19.

step in integrating the firm with other members of the supply chain, and it is at the operational level that the day-to-day activities are executed. Figure 4-2 also shows the interfaces between each sub-process and the other seven processes. These interfaces might take the form of a transfer of data that other processes require, or might involve sharing information or ideas with another process team.

A process team comprised of managers from several functions including marketing, finance, production, purchasing and logistics, leads both the strategic and operational processes. The team might also include members from outside the firm. For example, the team might include customers as well as representatives from a key supplier or a third-party provider. The team is responsible for developing the procedures at the strategic level and seeing that they are implemented. This team also has day-to-day responsibility for managing the process at the operational level. Firm employees outside of the team might execute parts of the process, but the team maintains managerial responsibility.

The Strategic Demand Management Process

Demand management is about forecasting and synchronizing. The strategic process is comprised of six sub-processes that are aimed at designing an efficient operational system for matching supply and demand. Figure 4-3 shows the sub-processes, the activities that comprise each one, and the interfaces with the other seven supply chain management processes.

There is an abundance of technology on the market to help managers with components of the demand management process. The team needs to determine

Figure 4-3
The Strategic Demand Management Process

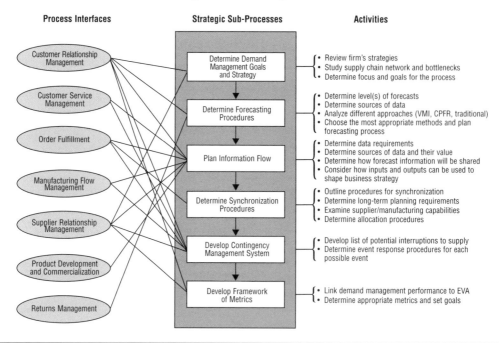

how the firm will use technology within the demand management process, and how information systems will need to be integrated with other members of the supply chain to facilitate the process. It is important that the technology solution is consistent with the expected benefits. Some firms will require more investment in information technology than others.[3] It is critical that managers concentrate on the people and the procedures that make the technology effective and not rely simply on the technology.

It is critical that managers concentrate on the people and the procedures that make the technology effective and not rely simply on the technology.

Determine Demand Management Goals and Strategy

The demand management process is focused on predicting customer demand and determining how that demand can be synchronized with the capabilities of the supply chain. The process team must have a broad understanding of the firm's strategy, the customers and their needs, the manufacturing capabilities, and the supply chain network. In order to accomplish this, information is required from individuals in functions as well as the customer relationship management and supplier relationship management processes.

With this understanding, the process team can have a high-level discussion about the goals and the focus of the process, which may vary across different firms and industries. For instance, business in the telecommunications industry has become so unpredictable that Lucent Technologies, a global network provider, has decided to place priority on increasing flexibility in response to the demand, and

---

[3] Smith, Todd, Jay Mabe and Jeff Beech, "Components of Demand Planning: Putting Together the Details for Success" *Strategic Supply Chain Alignment*, John Gattorna, Editor; Aldershot, England: Gower Publishing Limited, 1998, pp. 123-137.

put less focus on trying to accurately forecast it. In industries, where demand is more stable, reducing forecast error might be more cost effective than increasing flexibility. The discussion that the process team has in this sub-process will set the tone for how demand management is structured.

Determine Forecasting Procedures

In the second sub-process, the process team develops a critical piece of demand management; that is, forecasting. The team needs to select the appropriate forecasting approaches. This includes determining the levels and time frames of the forecasts needed throughout the firm, identifying the sources of data, and then defining forecasting procedures for each forecast required.

Different parts of the firm might need different levels of the forecast.[4] For instance, manufacturing planning might require an SKU-level forecast. Transportation planning, on the other hand, might need a forecast aggregated at the product-family level but disaggregated by region. Marien[5] suggested five levels of forecasting, all based on the time frame of the forecast. However, the decision should not be based solely on the time frame required. Other factors play a role, such as the units being forecasted and the use of the forecasts. Ross Products, a division of Abbott Laboratories and a market leader in pediatric and adult nutritionals, found that the forecasting needs of the entire firm could be met with three forecasts, one for operations, one for marketing and one for finance.[6]

A firm might also use different forecasting procedures for new products or limited-time offers than they do for their standard products. For instance, the management team at a global beverage company recognized the difficulty in developing long-term forecasts for new products. Consequently, when introducing a new product, the forecasting team now works with key suppliers and the sales organization to develop a pipeline-fill forecast; that is, a gross sales figure for the duration of the supply chain lead-time. Based on cross-functional input and risk assessment, they determine an initial production quantity. This quantity is produced before the introduction of the product so that the beverage company can meet demand through the initial stage of the introduction. Once management observes the level of demand in the first few weeks, they can begin to generate a reasonably accurate forecast for the future.

If managers of each function develop their own forecasts independently, the firm will lose control over the forecasting process.

It is important that these strategic decisions regarding the number of forecasts used are made collectively by a team of managers and that the resulting forecasts are coordinated. Although there might be several forecasts used in the firm, they should be consistent and represent one truth. If managers of each function develop their own forecasts independently, the firm will lose control over the forecasting process.

Next, the team determines the sources of the data required to generate each forecast. These might include historical data, sales projections, promotion plans,

---

[4] Helms, Marilyn M., Lawrence P. Ettkin and Sharon Chapman, "Supply Chain Forecasting - Collaborative Forecasting Supports Supply Chain Management," *Business Process Management Journal,* Vol. 6, No. 5 (2000), p. 392.

[5] Marien, Edward J., "Demand Planning and Sales Forecasting: A Supply Chain Essential," *Supply Chain Management Review,* Vol. 2, No 4, (1999), pp. 76-86.

[6] Robeano, Steven, "Demand Forecasting: Reality vs. Theory," unpublished speech at the National Management Science Roundtable, Nashville, 1991.

corporate objectives, market share data, trade inventory, and market research. In order to determine how to use these data, the team should understand the value of the information from each source; for instance, determining how good each source is at predicting demand.

It is at this point that the team might also consider Collaborative Planning, Forecasting and Replenishment (CPFR) or Vendor Managed Inventory (VMI).[7] If these systems are being implemented, the customer is a direct source of data. If this is the case, the team needs to interface with the customer relationship management process team to determine what systems will be used to efficiently transfer data between the firms.

Once the team has an understanding of what type of forecast is needed, and what data are available, they can select a forecasting method and define a process to follow for each required forecast. There are many methods from which to choose, from quantitative, such as time series methods, to more people-driven, such as focus groups and the Delphi approach.[8] The appropriate method will depend on the environment in which the forecasting is taking place. In fact, different methods might be used for different products. In one of the companies interviewed, management segments products according to demand variability and demand volume in order to make decisions about the appropriate forecasting approaches. Each product is plotted using a two-by-two matrix as shown in Figure 4-4. The quadrant of the matrix in which a product is categorized will determine the appropriate forecasting approach. Quantitative methods based on historical data are used for products with low demand variability. Products with high variability and high volume require more human input, perhaps from the sales force or the customers themselves. If a product has low volume and high variability, make-to-order production is used, which avoids the need for an SKU-level forecast and allows management to concentrate on an aggregated forecast for raw-materials or components.

Products with high variability and high volume require more human input, perhaps from the sales force or the customers themselves.

After the appropriate forecasting approach is determined, the team selects the specific forecasting method. When making this decision, it is important for the team to understand the nature of the demand. For instance, if the demand is seasonal, they will want to select a method that incorporates seasonality. Should the team decide to use a quantitative approach like time series or regression, they might consider using forecasting software. There are numerous stand-alone software packages on the market that can handle the forecasting component of demand management and do not require significant financial investments.[9] It is important that the capabilities of the software package align with the forecasting needs of the firm. Considerations when selecting a software package include the span of statistical methods that the system uses, the ability to adjust the forecast,

---

[7] Sherman, Richard J., "Collaborative Planning, Forecasting & Replenishment (CPFR): Realizing the Promise of Efficient Consumer Response through Collaborative Technology," *Journal of Marketing Theory & Practice*, Vol. 6, No. 4 (1998), pp. 6-9; and, Matt Waller, Eric M. Johnson and Tom Davis, "Vendor-Managed Inventory in the Retail Supply Chain," *Journal of Business Logistics*, Vol. 20, No. 1 (1999), pp. 183-203.

[8] Makridakis, Spyros, Steven C. Wheelwright and Rob J. Hyndman, *Forecasting: Methods and Applications*, New York: John Wiley & Sons, Inc., 1998.

[9] Elikai, Fara, Ravija Badaranathi and Vince Howe, "A Review of 52 Forecasting Software Packages," *Journal of Business Forecasting Methods & Systems*, Vol. 21, Issue 2 (2002), pp. 19-27.

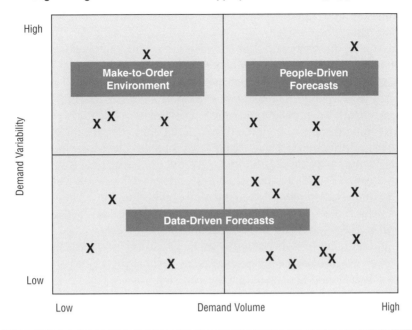

Once the team decides on the method of forecasting and the sources of data, they plan the information flow; that is, they determine the sources of data, how this input data will be transferred, and what output needs to be communicated to whom.

the ability to use the software in a collaborative mode (either internally or externally), and the sophistication of the output reports that are offered.[10]

The team also needs to determine how often the forecasting procedures will be reevaluated. For instance, if the nature of the demand changes or the forecast errors begin to worsen, the team will need to convene and make necessary changes to the procedures being used.

Plan Information Flow

Once the team decides on the method of forecasting and the sources of data, they plan the information flow; that is, they determine the sources of data, how this input data will be transferred, and what output needs to be communicated to whom. Input to the forecasting process will likely come from several functions, the customer relationship management process, and in a CPFR environment, the customers themselves. The forecasts are communicated internally to the other process teams that are affected by them.

In addition, the firm needs to determine what data will be shared with other members of the supply chain. For instance, in a CPFR environment, SKU-level forecasts are jointly developed with next-tier customers. Management might decide to share these forecasts in an aggregated form with suppliers, perhaps including key second tier suppliers. For example, Wendy's International, a quick service restaurant chain, shares its forecasts with both the lettuce processors and the lettuce growers.

[10] Safavi, Alex, "Choosing the Right Forecasting Software and System," *Journal of Business Forecasting Methods & Systems*, Vol. 19, Issue 3 (2000), pp. 6-10.

The team also needs to consider if information systems need to be developed or enhanced in order to efficiently transfer appropriate information. Within a single firm, Enterprise Resource Planning (ERP) systems can provide consistent data that can be used throughout the company. In many cases, however, the demand management process needs information to flow between firms in the supply chain. For instance, information systems can be put into place to provide inventory visibility in the supply chain or manage the information flow of a VMI or CPFR implementation. Considerable effort is often required to integrate systems between firms. In some cases, web-based applications, which do not require integration of information systems between supply chain members, provide an effective means for sharing information with suppliers and customers. Companies like Moen Inc., the world's largest manufacturer of plumbing products, have developed applications to share forecasts, production schedules and inventory levels with their supplier base through the Internet. A web-enabled application can be a first point of contact for status reports.

As an extension to the information flow, the team should consider ways in which both the inputs and outputs of demand management can be used to define the future business strategy. Langabeer[11] differentiates the tactical use of demand information from its strategic uses. He argues that the same information that is used in the demand management process can be used to shape the marketing strategy and the direction the firm takes. For instance, analyzing demand and forecast data allows management to plan the life cycle of products, including the determination of when to introduce new products and phase out existing ones. Data on where the bottlenecks in the supply chain are can be used in conjunction with product profitability reports to guide management on its investment strategies. The process team should look for ways to share insight that is gained as part of executing the demand management process with other key decision makers in the firm.

As an extension to the information flow, the team should consider ways in which both the inputs and outputs of demand management can be used to define the future business strategy.

The activities and learnings of the demand management process can also influence the supply chain strategy. Supply chain strategy should be determined, at least in part, by the supply and demand uncertainty that exists in the firm's supply chain.[12] As shown in Figure 4-5, managers need to align their firm's supply chain strategy with the uncertainties inherent in the system. Since firms often have products with different levels of uncertainty, managers should follow different supply chain strategies for different products. As the demand management team gains an understanding of system uncertainties and works to reduce them, the information they glean can be used to guide and perhaps evolve the supply chain strategies so that they maintain proper alignment.

Determine Synchronization Procedures

Next, the team determines the synchronization procedures required to match the demand forecast to the supply chain's manufacturing, supply and logistics capabilities. Frequently, this is referred to as sales and operations planning (S&OP). As shown in Figure 4-6, the synchronization requires coordination with marketing,

---

[11] Langabeer, Jim R. II, "Aligning Demand Management with Business Strategy," *Supply Chain Management Review,* Vol. 4, No. 2 (2000), pp. 66-72.

[12] Lee, Hau L., "Aligning Supply Chain Strategies with Product Uncertainties," *California Management Review,* Vol. 44, No. 3 (2002), pp. 105-119.

Figure 4-5
Aligning Supply Chain Strategies with Uncertainty

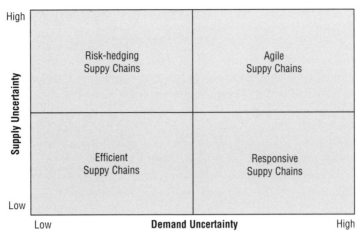

Source: Adapted from Hau L. Lee, "Aligning Supply Chain Strategies with Product Uncertainties," *California Management Review*, Vol. 44, No. 3 (2002), pp. 105-119. Copyright © 2002, by The Regents of the University of California. Reprinted by permission of The Regents.

Figure 4-6
Synchronizing the Supply Chain

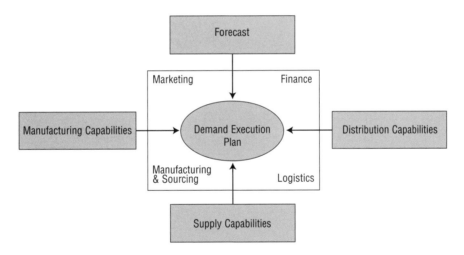

manufacturing and sourcing, logistics and finance. When executed at the operational level, this synchronization process includes examining the forecasted customer demand and determining the requirements back through the supply chain. It requires not only understanding the level of demand, but also the velocity at which product is required at each touch point in the supply chain. The output of this synchronization will be a single execution plan that will balance the needs and costs of manufacturing, logistics, sales, and the suppliers to meet anticipated demand. This execution plan will provide the basis for the detailed manufacturing and sourcing plan that is developed within the manufacturing flow management process through manufacturing requirement planning (MRP), and the detailed distribution plan that is developed within order fulfillment through distribution requirement planning (DRP).

At the strategic level, the team is responsible for developing the synchronization procedures that will be used at the operational level, including who will be included in the synchronization process and the structure for how they will meet. Some firms have a two-stage synchronization process whereby a cross-functional team of managers will meet, for instance monthly, to develop an initial demand execution plan. If there are any unresolved issues from this meeting, they will be directed to a meeting of upper-level managers who resolve them and sign-off on a final demand execution plan.

Once a firm has an effective internal synchronization process, management should consider integrating key suppliers and customers directly into it. For instance, a beverage company includes internal suppliers in their monthly S&OP meeting. These suppliers are under the company's corporate umbrella, but they are different strategic business units and they have their own income statements and balance sheets.

Part of determining the synchronization procedures is defining policies about stockpiling and allocating; that is, where to stock inventory when supply is greater than demand, and how to reposition inventory when demand is greater than supply. These guidelines will be rather generic. Within the order fulfillment process, the customer-specific rules will be developed.

The team needs to gain a complete understanding of the capacity and flexibility available at key points along the supply chain. They also need to determine the long-term planning requirements, particularly in the case of demand with high seasonality or long-term changes, such as sustained growth. In the case of limited capacity and a product with seasonal demand, it might be necessary to ramp-up production several months prior to the high demand periods. At this point in the process, the team might also recognize future capacity issues and make recommendations to proactively address them before they cause problems.

The team needs to gain a complete understanding of the capacity and flexibility available at key points along the supply chain.

It is important to realize that different product-lines might require different synchronization procedures. This is part of aligning supply chain strategy with product characteristics. For instance, a product with high demand uncertainty, and therefore expected high forcast errors, should have a synchronization process in place that does not rely too heavily on the forecast, and instead designs supply chain flexibility into the system. To Moen Inc., this has meant developing different procedures for core, custom and new products. For new products, the focus is on attaining the most flexibility possible, as the demand of new products is the most uncertain. For Moen's core product-lines, management is interested in driving the costs out since products are mature and competitive price pressure is high. For custom products that are low-volume, the goal is asset optimization, which suggests an assemble-to-order system. When Moen used the same procedures for all products, they had problems because the goals of all three classifications could not be attained with one set of procedures. They moved to a differentiated system where the methods vary over the three classifications. In fact, even the organizational structure is differentiated; that is, different people are responsible for planning in each area.

Systems such as those provided by i2, Manugistics, and SAP[13] can be implemented to facilitate the synchronization process and help develop the demand execution plan. These systems are designed to examine the real-time constraints on the sources of supply and match them with the forecasted demand. Combining the functionality of information flow and synchronization, some of these systems can offer inventory deployment tools that provide real-time decision support for managing inventory in the supply chain. Although these systems are useful, they should be used in conjunction with human decision-making in a team setting. There are too many factors involved in the synchronization process to leave it entirely to an automated system.

Develop Contingency Management System

Another important component of the strategic demand management process is developing contingency plans to respond to significant internal or external events that disrupt the balance of supply and demand.[14] For example, how should the firm react if a manufacturing facility is unexpectedly shut down, or a port strike interrupts the flow of raw materials? Determining reaction procedures prior to the possible events will allow management to respond quickly in the case that one of these events occurs. In addition, the process team should consider what will be done if there is an interruption to any portion of data flow through the supply chain due to system errors.

This contingency management system should be developed in accordance with the expectations of the customers outlined in the customer relationship management process, and with input from order fulfillment, manufacturing flow management and supplier relationship management. Once developed, the contingency plans need to be communicated to the affected process teams.

Develop Framework of Metrics

The team should start by understanding how demand management can influence key performance metrics that directly affect the firm's financial performance, as measured by economic value added (EVA).

Finally, the team develops the framework of metrics to be used to measure and monitor the performance of the process, and sets the goals for performance improvement. A uniform approach should be used throughout the firm to develop these metrics.[15] The team should start by understanding how demand management can influence key performance metrics that directly affect the firm's financial performance, as measured by economic value added (EVA).[16] Figure 4-7 provides a framework for examining these relationships. It shows how demand management can impact sales, cost of goods sold, total expenses, inventory investment, other current assets, and fixed assets. For example, better demand management can result in higher sales by increasing customer loyalty and repeat

---

[13] See: www.i2.com; www.manugistics.com; www.sap.com.

[14] Dobie, Kathryn, L. Milton Glisson and James Grant, "Terrorism and the Global Supply Chain: Where Are Your Weak Links?" *Journal of Transportation Management,* Vol. 12, No. 1 (2000), pp. 57-66.

[15] Lambert, Douglas M. and Terrance L. Pohlen, "Supply Chain Metrics," *The International Journal of Logistics Management,* Vol. 12, No. 1 (2001), pp. 1-19.

[16] Stewart, G. Bennett III, *The Quest for Value: A Guide for Senior Managers,* 2nd Edition, New York, NY: Harper Collins, 1999; and, Joel M. Stern, "One Way to Build Value in Your Firm, a la Executive Compensation," *Financial Executive,* November-December 1990, pp. 51-54.

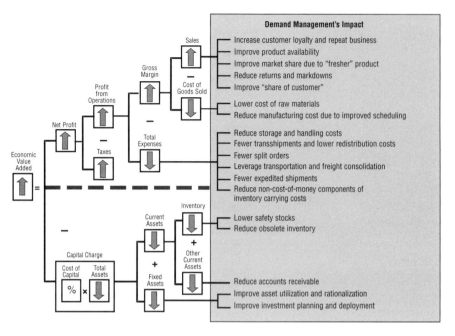

Figure 4-7
How Demand Management Affects Economic Value Added (EVA®)

Source: Adapted from Douglas M. Lambert and Terrance L. Pohlen, "Supply Chain Metrics," *The International Journal of Logistics Management*, Vol. 12, No. 1 (2001), p. 10.

business due to better forecasting and the associated customer service improvements. Also, improved product availability can lead to higher levels of retail sales and/or lower inventory carrying costs which can lead to a larger portion of the customer's purchases in this category. Product freshness results in better assortment and consumer appeal. A reduction in returns and markdowns can lead to the company becoming a more preferred supplier.

Cost of goods sold can be reduced as a result of lower cost of raw materials due to fewer expedited shipments and fewer last minute production changes by the supplier. Manufacturing costs can decrease as a result of improved scheduling.

A number of expenses can be reduced through better planning and scheduling that comes from less demand variability, including: storage and handling, transportation, order processing and the non-cost of money components of inventory carrying cost.

Better demand management can lead to lower safety stocks and less obsolete inventory which delivers higher inventory turns and lower inventory investment. Accounts receivable can be improved since fewer invoices will be disputed as a result of incomplete orders and missed delivery dates. Finally, better demand management can lead to lower fixed assets as a result of improved asset utilization and facility rationalization, and better investment planning and deployment.

Although these holistic metrics are affected by other activities and processes in the supply chain, the team responsible for demand management needs to estimate how this process impacts the firm's financial performance. Doing so will help to justify future investments in the process and to determine rewards for good performance.

Once the team has an understanding of the impact that demand management can have on financial performance as measured by EVA, metrics need to be developed for the activities performed and these metrics must be tied back to financial measures. Typical process measures for demand management include forecast error and capacity utilization. If steps are taken to actively reduce variability or increase flexibility, it is appropriate to include metrics that monitor the results of these activities, as well as to measure how improvements in these non-financial measures affect financial performance. The role of the customers in reducing demand variability and the role of suppliers in increasing flexibility need to be measured and their contributions rewarded. The team needs to confirm these measures with the customer relationship management team to assure consistency across the firm.

Management should implement processes that positively affect the profitability of the supply chain as a whole, not just that of their firm. It is the goal of supply chain management to drive behavior that benefits the entire supply chain while sharing risks and rewards among its members. If management of one firm in the supply chain makes a decision that positively affects their firm's EVA but negatively affects the EVA of a key supplier or customer, the two firms should work out an agreement where the benefits are shared so that the bottom lines of both firms improve.

If steps are taken to actively reduce variability or increase flexibility, it is appropriate to include metrics that monitor the results of these activities, as well as to measure how improvements in these non-financial measures affect financial performance.

The Operational Demand Management Process

At the operational level, the process team must execute the forecasting and synchronization as it was designed at the strategic level. Figure 4-8 shows the five operational sub-processes, the activities within each of these, and the interfaces between processes.

Collect Data/Information

At the strategic level, the data requirements for developing the forecast were determined, and the information systems were put in place to facilitate this data collection. In order to collect the relevant data that were specified in the strategic process, the team must interface with the marketing function as well as the order fulfillment, customer service management, product development and commercialization, and returns management processes. When designing the forecasting system at the strategic level, important input comes from the customer relationship management team, but at the operational level, it is the order fulfillment and customer service management processes that provide the most relevant information on anticipated demand. The product development and commercialization process team provides information regarding the rollout of new products. Data from the returns management process are used for generating the forecast because it provides input to understanding the actual demand. If a forecaster only uses sales figures as a measure of past demand, and does not consider what was returned, the forecast will be based on inflated numbers.

Forecast

With all the required data in hand, the team develops the forecasts. It is

Figure 4-8
The Operational Demand Management Process

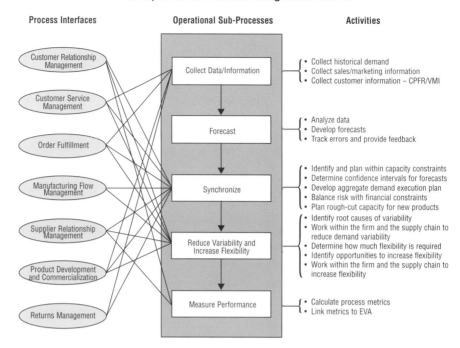

Process Interfaces	Operational Sub-Processes	Activities

- Customer Relationship Management
- Customer Service Management
- Order Fulfillment
- Manufacturing Flow Management
- Supplier Relationship Management
- Product Development and Commercialization
- Returns Management

Collect Data/Information
- Collect historical demand
- Collect sales/marketing information
- Collect customer information – CPFR/VMI

Forecast
- Analyze data
- Develop forecasts
- Track errors and provide feedback

Synchronize
- Identify and plan within capacity constraints
- Determine confidence intervals for forecasts
- Develop aggregate demand execution plan
- Balance risk with financial constraints
- Plan rough-cut capacity for new products

Reduce Variability and Increase Flexibility
- Identify root causes of variability
- Work within the firm and the supply chain to reduce demand variability
- Determine how much flexibility is required
- Identify opportunities to increase flexibility
- Work within the firm and the supply chain to increase flexibility

Measure Performance
- Calculate process metrics
- Link metrics to EVA

important that they track and analyze the forecast error and incorporate this feedback to fine-tune the forecasting methods. This is an important component of the learning process associated with good forecasting. For example, at a global beverage company, managers examine forecast errors and perform a root-cause analysis when errors are unusually large. This analysis involves tracing the source of the unexpected demand (or shortage of demand) to see if it is a particular customer, brand, region, or product. Once the source is known, it is necessary to determine what the cause was and how long the change in demand will last. This provides a starting point for improving future forecasts.

Synchronize

The forecast provides one input for matching demand with supply. This synchronization process follows the procedures determined at the strategic level. This is where the team turns the forecast into a demand execution plan (see Figure 4-6); that is, a plan for how the firm will meet the demand. In addition to the forecast, the team must consider capacities throughout the supply chain, financial limitations, and current inventory positioning (including saleable product that is being repositioned as a result of returns).

Understanding the capacity limitations requires the team to look both upstream and downstream. Ideally, the team should know both the capacity and the current inventory levels for key members of the supply chain. Comparing this information to the forecast will tell the team what constraints are in the system. Once the constraints are identified, the team can work with the other process

Once the constraints are identified, the team can work with the other process teams to determine how to resolve the bottlenecks, or to allocate the available resources and prioritize demand.

teams to determine how to resolve the bottlenecks, or to allocate the available resources and prioritize demand.

Although most forecasting methods are focused on determining the point forecast, calculating confidence intervals can provide management with valuable information on which to base their decisions. Using past forecast error values, the team can calculate confidence intervals for the forecasts. For instance, a manufacturing firm might forecast the demand to be 100 units and the 95% confidence interval to be 80 to 120 units. This means they are 95% sure the actual demand will fall in this range. In addition to the point forecast, this range could be shared with suppliers to provide information that they can use for planning, or even to negotiate available capacity. Management can also use this information to determine how much demand they want to meet. To offer high customer service, they should produce 120, but if the cost of inventory or risk of obsolescence is high, they might choose to produce only 80. In order to make this determination, the team needs to understand the firm's cost structure and strategic objectives.

In addition to supply and manufacturing constraints, the forecast might introduce a financial constraint. In turning the forecast into a demand plan, the team might need to practice risk management. This is the practice of balancing risk with financial rewards. When it is not financially feasible to meet all the demand, management must decide how to most effectively allocate resources. The contingency management plans developed at the strategic level might also need to be considered if an internal or external event causes a disruption to supply or large forecast errors.

The team also develops a rough-cut capacity plan for any new products soon to be launched. At Moen, Inc., management not only determines existing capacities, but talks to key suppliers to understand how quickly they could respond if demand exceeds the forecast for a new product.

The output of the synchronization sub-process is a demand execution plan that includes aggregate production plans and inventory-positioning plans, which need to be communicated internally and to key members of the supply chain. Developing and communicating these plans requires interfaces with the customer relationship management, customer service management, order fulfillment, manufacturing flow management, supplier relationship management, and product development and commercialization processes.

Reduce Variability and Increase Flexibility

There are two things managers can do to minimize the negative impact of variability. One is to reduce the variability itself, and the other is to increase the flexibility to react to it.

Many people see variability as the enemy of planning. It is easy to plan for the average, but it is the deviations from the norm that cause problems. Managers spend substantial time and money dealing with the consequences of demand and supply variability. There are two things managers can do to minimize the negative impact of variability. One is to reduce the variability itself, and the other is to increase the flexibility to react to it. A key component of demand management is an ongoing effort aimed at doing both these things. Increasing flexibility helps the firm respond quickly to internal and external events and reducing demand and supply variability aids in consistent planning and reduces costs.

Management should first try to reduce variability and then manage the

---

[17] Slack, N.D.C., *The Manufacturing Advantage*, London: Mercury, 1991.

unavoidable variability by building-in flexibility.[17] Flexibility usually comes with a price tag so it should not be used as a Band-Aid to fix problems that can otherwise be avoided. There are many sources of variability in the supply chain. One of the most problematic is demand variability. Many managers see demand as an uncontrollable input. Bolton states that demand management "actively seeks to ensure that the customer demand 'profile' that is the input into the demand-planning process is as smooth as possible".[18] This is the difference between demand planning and demand management. Within the demand management process, the team should look for sources of variability and implement solutions to reduce it.

Table 4-1 provides examples of sources of demand variability and potential solutions. For example, the team might work with the customer relationship management team and help customers better plan promotions, or implement scheduled ordering policies.[19] The team might also find that internal practices are driving demand variability, such as end-of-quarter loads. If the demand for new products is highly variable, they could work with the product development teams to implement controlled roll-outs where the products are introduced first in test markets where demand patterns can be evaluated. In some scenarios, it could be the competition that is driving demand variability. For instance, demand could be affected by a competitor engaged in end-of-quarter loading or offering a promotion. In these cases, the variability is unavoidable, but can often be planned for when developing the forecast. Likewise, the team should also look for ways to reduce supply variability and work with the supplier relationship management team and the procurement function to implement changes. It is easier to manage supply chains that fall towards the bottom and left portions of Figure 4-5, so the demand management process team should look for ways to reduce uncertainties in both dimensions.[20] Then they should assure that the company's executives adjust the supply chain strategies accordingly.

Table 4-1
Sources of Variability and Possible Solutions

Causes of Lumpy Demand	Possible Supply Chain Solutions
Consumer promotions	Plan promotions collaboratively with customers.
Sales metrics	Design consistent metrics that avoid actions such as end-of-quarter loads.
Credit terms	Revise credit terms with customer input to ensure that the terms of sale are not negatively affecting purchase patterns.
Pricing/Incentives	Work with sales/marketing to only offer incentives that truly increase long-term sales.
Minimum order quantities	Assure that all costs are included when calculating the appropriate minimum order size.
Long distribution channels	Incorporate demand volatility into network design decisions.

[18] Bolton, Jamie, "Effective Demand Management: Are You Limiting the Performance of Your Own Supply Chain?" *Strategic Supply Chain Alignment*, John Gattorna, Editor; Aldershot, England: Gower Publishing Limited, 1998, p. 139.

[19] Cachon, Gerard, "Managing Supply Chain Demand Variability with Scheduled Ordering Policies," *Management Science*, Vol. 45, No. 6, pp. 843-856.

[20] Lee, Hau L., "Aligning Supply Chain Strategies with Product Uncertainties," *California Management Review*, Vol. 44, No. 3 (2002), pp. 105-119.

[21] Towill, Denis R. and Peter McCullen, "The Impact of Agile Manufacturing on Supply Chain Dynamics," *The International Journal of Logistics Management*, Vol. 10, No. 1 (1999), p. 86.

"The supply chain which best succeeds in reducing uncertainty and variability is likely to be the most successful in improving its competitive position."[21]

Gaining flexibility allows a company to better manage the system variability that cannot be eliminated – both anticipated and unanticipated variability. When a beverage company introduced one of its new products, demand was more than double the amount forecasted. Because management had developed a flexible system, they were able to manage through this without affecting customer service. Increasing flexibility can influence the reliability, quality, cost and speed of the process and its products.[22] The team should first determine how much flexibility is needed. Because building flexibility into a system is often expensive, it is important that the level of flexibility developed is consistent with the needs of the supply chain. To make this determination, the process team needs to fully understand customers' needs, demand patterns, and the capabilities of the entire supply chain.

Because building flexibility into a system is often expensive, it is important that the level of flexibility developed is consistent with the needs of the supply chain.

Once the team understands how much flexibility is needed, they should look for ways to attain it. This involves working with the other process teams within the firm, as well as with suppliers and customers to determine where there are opportunities to add flexibility into the supply chain. For example, the team might work with the manufacturing flow management team to find ways to introduce postponement into the manufacturing process, implement agile manufacturing practices, or find ways to multi-source.[23] They might work with the customer relationship management team to stratify customers so that the firm can be most responsive to a small set of key customers, or work with the product development teams to standardize materials. The team might work with the order fulfillment team to make changes to the network, such as reducing lead-times or increasing capacity at buffers. Solutions might also exist from within the demand management process, such as implementing VMI.

In order to find ways to increase flexibility and reduce variability, the process team works with the sales, marketing and manufacturing organizations, customers and suppliers. To increase flexibility, they identify bottlenecks and pinch points, and develop cost-effective solutions. To reduce variability, the team highlights root causes and develops solutions that are consistent with the business strategy. Identifying these opportunities involves process interfaces with manufacturing flow management, supplier relationship management, customer relationship management and customer service management, as well as the corporate functions. In all cases, the team needs to consider the implications of the solutions on the other members of the supply chain.

Measure Performance

Finally, the process team is responsible for measuring the performance of the process with the metrics developed at the strategic level. These metrics are used internally to improve the process and are provided to the customer relationship management team and supplier relationship management team who will convey

---

[22] Correa, Henrique Luiz, *Linking Flexibility, Uncertainty and Variability in Manufacturing Systems,* Aldershot, England: Avebury Publishing, 1994.

[23] van Hoek, Remko I., "The Rediscovery of Postponment: A Literature Review and Directions for Research," *Journal of Operations Management,* Vol. 19, No. 2 (2001), pp. 161-184; and, Y. Y. Yusef and A. Gunasekaran, "Agile Manufacturing: A Taxonomy of Strategic and Technological Imperatives," *International Journal of Production Research,* Vol. 40, No. 6 (2002), pp. 1357-1385.

[24] Lambert, Douglas M. and Terrance L. Pohlen, "Supply Chain Metrics," *The International Journal of Logistics Management,* Vol. 12, No. 1 (2001), pp. 1-19.

the firm's performance to the key members of the supply chain and generate the customer profitability and supplier profitability or cost reports.[24]

Conclusions

Demand management is an important component of successful supply chain management. A well thought-out implementation and seamless execution of the process can have substantial benefits on the firm's EVA through, for example, reduced inventory levels, improved asset utilization and improved product availability. It is not enough to forecast well and have a good operations planning system. Demand management should include finding ways to reduce demand variability and increase operational flexibility, and implementing a good contingency management system so that the firm can quickly react to unplanned issues.

Although it is possible to implement many portions of the demand management process without going outside the four walls of the firm, the real opportunities come when management reaches out to the other members of the supply chain and integrates this process with the processes of suppliers and customers. It is through these integration efforts that the benefits of supply chain management will be achieved.

Although it is possible to implement many portions of the demand management process without going outside the four walls of the firm, the real opportunities come when management reaches out to the other members of the supply chain and integrates this process with the processes of suppliers and customers.

CHAPTER

5

The Order Fulfillment Process

Keely L. Croxton

Overview

Order fulfillment is a key process in managing the supply chain.[1] It is the customers' orders that put the supply chain in motion, and filling them efficiently and effectively is the first step in providing customer service. However, the order fulfillment process involves more than just filling orders. It is about designing a network and a process that permits a firm to meet customer requests while minimizing the total delivered cost. In this chapter, the order fulfillment process is described in detail to show how it can be implemented cross-functionally within a company, and managed across firms in the supply chain. The activities of each sub-process are examined; the interfaces with functional silos, processes and firms are evaluated; and, examples of successful implementations are provided.

Introduction

Order fulfillment involves generating, filling, delivering and servicing customer orders. In some cases, it is only through this process that the customer interacts with the firm, and therefore, the order fulfillment process can determine the customer's experience.[2] To accomplish these tasks, management must design a network and a fulfillment process that permits a firm to meet customer requests while minimizing the total delivered cost. This requires integration of logistics, marketing, finance, purchasing, research and development, and production within the firm, and coordination with key suppliers and customers. At the operational level, the order fulfillment process focuses on transactions, while at the strategic level, management can focus on making critical improvements to the process that influence the financial performance of the firm, its customers and its suppliers. For instance, order fulfillment directly affects product availability which influences total sales volume. An optimized network minimizes total delivered costs, including sourcing costs. A streamlined process reduces the order-to-cash cycle which frees up capital, and reduces the delivery lead-time which allows for reduced inventory levels. Thus, order fulfillment can affect the financial performance of the focal-firm, as well as other members of the supply chain.

> *At the operational level, the order fulfillment process focuses on transactions, while at the strategic level, management can focus on making critical improvements to the process that influence the financial performance of the firm, its customers and its suppliers.*

[1] This chapter is based on Keely L. Croxton, "The Order Fulfillment Process," *The International Journal of Logistics Management*, Vol. 14, No. 1 (2002), pp. 19-32.

[2] Shapiro, Benson P., V. Kasturi Rangan, and John J. Sviokla, "Staple Yourself to an Order," *Harvard Business Review*, Vol. 40, No. 4 (1992), pp.113-122.

In this chapter, the framework for implementing the order fulfillment process is developed. The process is described as it would be implemented at a firm in the middle of the supply chain, for instance a manufacturer or distributor. For a retailer, the process is similar in some respects, but it would need to be adapted before being implemented. Order fulfillment is one of the eight supply chain management processes and it requires interfaces with the other seven (see Figure 5-1). The strategic and operational processes that comprise order fulfillment are described, including the sub-processes and their activities. In addition, the interfaces with the corporate functions, the other supply chain management processes and other firms are identified. Finally, conclusions are presented.

Order Fulfillment as a Supply Chain Management Process

The order fulfillment process has both strategic and operational elements, as shown in Figure 5-2. Therefore, the process has been divided into two parts, the strategic process in which management establishes the structure for managing the process, and the operational process that is the execution of the process once it has been established. Implementation of the strategic process within the firm is a necessary first step in integrating the firm with other members of the supply chain, and it is at the operational level that the day-to-day activities take place. Figure 5-2 also shows the interfaces between each sub-process and the other seven supply chain processes. These interfaces might take the form of a transfer of some data that the other process requires, or might involve sharing information or ideas with another process team.

Figure 5-1
Supply Chain Management:
Integrating and Managing Business Processes Across the Supply Chain

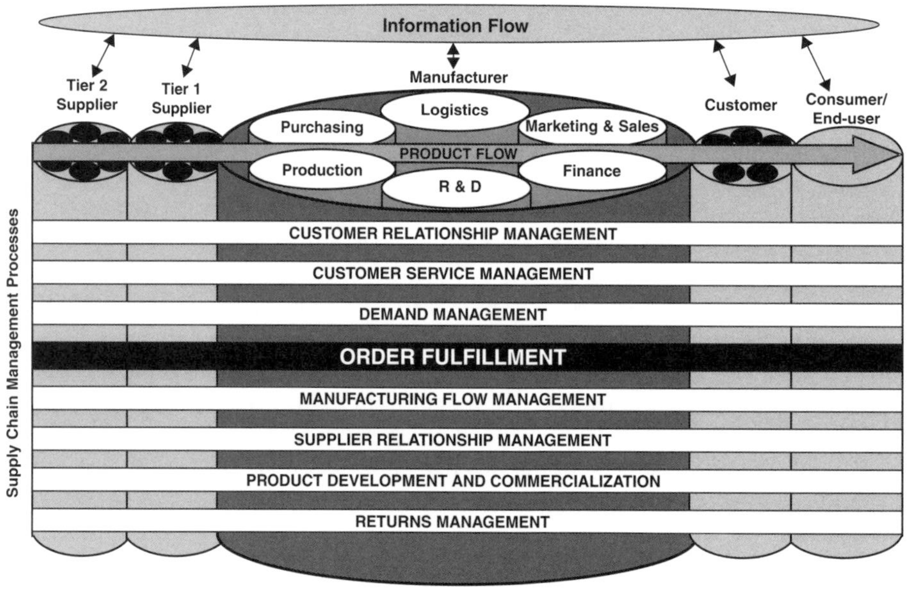

Source: Adapted from Douglas M. Lambert, Martha C. Cooper, and Janus D. Pagh, "Supply Chain Management: Implementation Issues and Research Opportunities," *The International Journal of Logistics Management,* Vol. 9, No. 2 (1998), p. 2.

Figure 5-2
Order Fulfillment

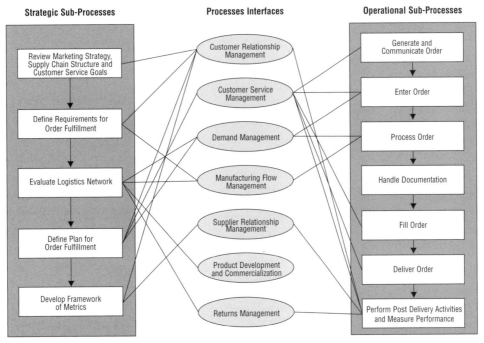

Source: Adapted from Keely L. Croxton, Sebastián J. García-Dastugue, Douglas M. Lambert and Dale S. Rogers, "The Supply Chain Management Processes," *The International Journal of Logistics Management,* Vol. 12, No. 2 (2001), p. 21.

A cross-functional process team comprised of managers from several functions, including logistics, marketing, finance, purchasing and production, leads both the strategic and operational processes. The team might also include members from outside the firm. For example, the team might include representatives from a key customer or a third-party provider. The team is responsible for developing the procedures at the strategic level and seeing that they are implemented. This team also has day-to-day responsibility for managing the process at the operational level. Firm employees outside of the team might execute parts of the process, but the team still maintains managerial responsibility.

The Strategic Order Fulfillment Process

At the strategic level, the process team designs the operational order fulfillment process. This includes designing the network, establishing policies and procedures, and determining the role of technology in the process. This requires interfacing and communicating with multiple functional areas within the firm, and can be enhanced by working with suppliers and customers to develop a network and a process that meets the customers' requirements in a cost effective manner. Although many managers consider order fulfillment to fall within the role of the logistics function, it is the integration with other functions in the firm and other firms in the supply chain that becomes key in defining order fulfillment as a supply

Figure 5-3
The Strategic Order Fulfillment Process

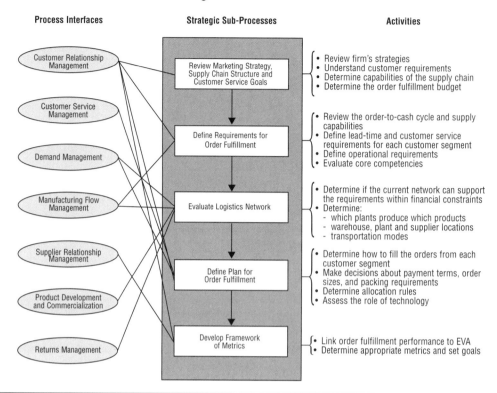

Process Interfaces	Strategic Sub-Processes	Activities

chain process. Figure 5-3 shows the sub-processes, activities and interfaces for the strategic order fulfillment process.

Review Marketing Strategy, Supply Chain Structure and Customer Service Goals

In this first sub-process the process team reviews the marketing strategy, supply chain structure, and customer service goals. By examining the marketing strategy and customer service goals, they are seeking to understand the requirements of the customer and the role that customer service plays in the overall strategy of the firm. To fully understand the customers, the team should interface with the customer relationship management team to understand what is most important to the customer. Often this information is identified through a customer service audit.[3] Together, the two teams will determine which services are necessary to achieve and maintain corporate/supply chain goals.

The order fulfillment process needs to be designed around the customer, but within the limits of the firm's business and marketing strategy. The team also needs to understand the firm's order fulfillment budget. That is, determining how much is acceptable to spend on fulfilling the order. A firm might be able to most quickly

The order fulfillment process needs to be designed around the customer, but within the limits of the firm's business and marketing strategy.

---

[3] Stock, James R. and Douglas M. Lambert, *Strategic Logistics Management*, New York, NY: McGraw-Hill, 2001, pp. 110-126.

deliver a product to the customer with an express air shipment, but the costs associated with that policy erodes profits and could be unacceptable. Likewise, financial issues might dictate a minimum order size or something about the selling terms. Throughout the design of the fulfillment process, the team needs to trade-off the costs of the solution with the benefits to the customer and the impact on the financial performance of the firm, and its customers and suppliers.

Throughout the design of the fulfillment process, the team needs to trade-off the costs of the solution with the benefits to the customer and the impact on the financial performance of the firm, and its customers and suppliers.

The supply chain structure is another important input into the design of the order fulfillment process. Both the sourcing and the distribution sub-networks that are in place impose limits on the cost and the lead-time of the fulfillment process. The team needs to examine the current network to understand its limitations and how cost is added as product moves through the supply chain.

The sub-process sets the foundation for the rest of the strategic process. Teams that fail to execute this step will struggle with the rest of the process becuase they will not understand the goals nor the constraints on the system. It is imperative that the team understands the role that order fulfillment plays in attaining the corporate goals.

Define Requirements for Order Fulfillment

Once the customer requirements and the limits imposed by the network structure are understood, the team can focus on defining the requirements for the order fulfillment process. This includes reviewing the order-to-cash cycle, understanding the supply capabilities, and defining the lead-time and customer service requirements. The customer relationship management and manufacturing flow processes provide input to accomplish this. In addition, the team needs to understand the operational requirements of the order fulfillment environment, including such details as how many orders need to be filled per day and how many dock-doors will be needed. There might also be legal requirements that need to be adhered to, for instance, handling requirements for hazardous materials, or customs requirements for international shipments. The process team should get a full understanding of all the requirements and make sure that the process is designed to adhere to them.

Customer differences might require management to develop an array of order fulfillment procedures. For instance, the customer relationship management team might have identified key customers that need a shorter lead-time than others. In this case, the team would develop multiple sets of requirements and assure that the fulfillment process can meet all the variations. International Paper, the world's largest paper and forest products company, segments its customers into four categories, according to their sales and profitability. Within each segment, customer service profiles are defined. While these activities are part of the customer relationship management process, the order fulfillment team has to plan for those parts of the profile that pertain to order fulfillment such as order cut-off times and delivery times.

In addition, the team needs to evaluate the core competencies within order fulfillment and determine which aspects of the process are potentially service differentiating. For instance, Wendy's International, a quick service restaurant chain, has focused on its order delivery to drive-through customers, offering the fastest delivery among fast-food restaurants for five straight years.[4] If a firm offers

---

[4] Gereffi, Paul, *"What the Numbers Tell Us,"* QSR, October 2002.

guaranteed service levels, the order fulfillment team needs to consider how the process can be structured to accommodate these expectations. The team should determine what value-added services will be provided, to whom those services will be offered, who will pay for them, and their impact on the profitability of the firm and the supply chain. At Shell, a global energy company, the salesperson is responsible for the cost the firm incurs for the services offered to customers. Each salesperson then decides whether to pass these costs along to the customer.

After completing this sub-process, the team should understand what the order fulfillment process will need to accomplish at the operational level. They should be able to articulate the specific order fulfillment goals for each customer segment and know the degree to which the process can be customized for specific customers or customer segments.

Evaluate Logistics Network

After the first two sub-processes, the team knows the capabilities of the supply chain and the requirements of the customers. If the capabilities cannot support the requirements, the next step is to evaluate the supply chain network to determine if the network could be redesigned to resolve the gaps.

The design and operation of the network has a significant influence on the cost and performance of the system. One study showed that network modeling projects identify cost reductions of an average of 11.6% of controllable logistics costs,[5] but the structure of the network affects more than logistics costs. It can affect customer service levels, lead times and part component costs. Network design tools can be used to determine which plants will produce which products, where warehouses, plants, and suppliers should be located, and which transportation modes should be used. In addition, customers need to be efficiently assigned to networks of supply. These decisions affect the capabilities, the cost, and the timeframe of the order fulfillment process. In some cases, these decisions can have significant impact on other members of the supply chain. For example, Dowbrands, which at the time was the consumer products affiliate of Dow Chemical Company, found that they could reduce transit-time variability by designing the distribution system so that less-than-truckload shipments avoided break-bulk terminals.[6] This variability reduction allowed customers to hold less inventory. In a supply chain management environment, they could work with key customers to see if the increase in distribution cost would be offset by the reduction in inventory cost in the supply chain.

Historically, managers have focused their network design efforts on the internal portion of their supply chain;[7] that is, where the facilities they manage should be located. Increasingly, managers are broadening the scope of their network design projects to include a greater portion of the supply chain, such as

Network design tools can be used to determine which plants will produce which products, where warehouses, plants, and suppliers should be located, and which transportation modes should be used.

---

[5] Jimenez, Sue, Tim Brown and Joe Jordan, "Network modeling tools: Enhancing supply chain decision making," *Strategic Supply Chain Alignment,* John Gattorna, Editor; Gower, 1998.

[6] Robinson, E. Powell, Li-Lian Gao and Stanley D. Muggenborg, "Designing an Integrated Distribution System at DowBrands, Inc." *Interfaces,* Vol. 23, No. 3 (1993), pp. 107-117.

[7] Pooley, John, "Integrated Production and Distribution Facility Planning at Ault Foods," *Interfaces,* Vol. 24, No. 4 (1994), pp. 113-121; Camm, Jeffrey D., et. al, "Blending OR/MS, Judgment, and GIS: Restructuring P&G's Supply Chain," *Interfaces,* Vol. 27, No. 1 (1997), pp. 128-142.

first and second tier suppliers and customers.[8]

These network models require data from every functional area within the firm. Obtaining accurate data often involves gathering data from upstream and downstream members of the supply chain. Particularly important input to this sub-process comes from the demand management, manufacturing flow, product development and commercialization, and returns management processes. Likewise, the resulting network has implications throughout the firm and the supply chain. The order fulfillment team is responsible for assuring that the new network is communicated and implemented appropriately.

While developing a formal network design model is time-consuming and requires expertise, many managers have found that once the model is developed, they can use it to monitor their network and identify potential issues early. This allows them to proactively modify their network structure before problems arise. Models can also be used to study the impact of high-level business decisions on the firm's ability to continue to meet order fulfillment needs.

Define Plan for Order Fulfillment

The next strategic sub-process defines the plan for order fulfillment, determining how orders from various customers or segments of customers will be taken and filled. This is largely where the operational order fulfillment process is defined. The team also determines which portions of the process will be outsourced to a third party.

The team needs to make decisions about payment terms, allowable order sizes, and picking and packing operations. Increasingly, customers are requesting customized packing; for instance, the size of the pallet, or the way the pallets are configured. The team needs to consider these customer requirements.

An important consideration in designing the order fulfillment system is to determine what will be done when an order cannot be filled. The order fulfillment team needs to develop rules about how demand is allocated, or possibly when an order should not be accepted at all.

The team also needs to consider the impact of their decisions on demand variability.[9] The effectiveness of the order fulfillment process can be strained by demand that is highly variable. During this sub-process, the team should work with the demand management process team, as they are responsible for finding ways to reduce demand variability.[10] For instance, payment terms might lead customers to place orders at certain times of the month, creating lumpy demand. Large order sizes could have similar effects. Smoothing out demand will make it easier to manage the operational order fulfillment process efficiently.

An important consideration in designing the order fulfillment system is to determine what will be done when an order cannot be filled. The order fulfillment team needs to develop rules about how demand is allocated, or possibly when an order should not be accepted at all. At Colgate-Palmolive, a consumer packaged goods company, the team develops "Risk and Opportunity Grids" that provide operational guidelines about what to do in the case that demand cannot be met.

---

[8] Arntzen, Bruce C., Gerald G. Brown, Terry P. Harrison and Linda L. Trafton, "Global Supply Chain Management at Digital Equipment Corporation," *Interfaces,* Vol. 27, No. 1 (1997), pp. 69-93.

[9] Bolton, Jamie, "Effective demand management: Are you limiting the performance of your own supply chain?" *Strategic Supply Chain Alignment,* John Gattorna, Editor; Gower, 1998.

[10] Croxton, Keely L., Douglas M. Lambert, Sebastián J. García-Dastugue, and Dale S. Rogers, "The Demand Management Process," *The International Journal of Logistics Management,* Vol. 13, No. 2 (2002), pp. 51-66.

For instance, which customers should receive priority, when to short a customer's order, etc? International Paper has rules in place that will only allow safety stock to be used to fill orders from its key customers. In another example, the management at Dell, a global computer manufacturer, takes a revenue management approach to order fulfillment.[11] They implemented a "sell what you have policy" where order-takers are encouraged to sell configurations that are readily available. They are given the flexibility to adjust the price on these available configurations to encourage customers to buy products that would be "easy" on the supply chain rather than ones that would incur extra costs and erode profitability.[12] For Dell, this has been an appropriate way to balance supply and demand through its order fulfillment process.

Before deciding to implement any allocation system, management needs to understand the customer service and customer satisfaction implications. The team should work with the customer relationship management team in developing these policies. Once the team determines the procedures, it is important to communicate them to the customer service management team, who addresses the concerns of the customers when these events occur. There is also a close interface with the demand management process at this point because these allocation rules need to be aligned with the contingency management system developed in the strategic demand management process.[13]

An important component of designing an order fulfillment process is determining the flow of order information; in other words, how the order information will be captured and fed to the demand management process. For instance, manufacturing is outsourced at Lucent Technologies, a global communications network provider, so orders are sent directly to suppliers. At Moen Inc., a manufacturer of plumbing products, customers can place orders directly into Moen's SAP system, bypassing the traditional, and very manual, order entry process. At Taylor Made-adidas Golf Company, a manufacturer of golf equipment, sales people carry handheld computer units which allow them to enter orders from the customer site and download them into the Taylor Made-adidas order management system. In some supply chains, point-of-sale data are communicated between firms to allow suppliers to place orders with distributors. Each of these examples requires a unique information flow that needs to be developed by the order fulfillment process team. Because this usually involves data transfer between firms, which is increasingly accomplished with technology, the team should consider the role of technology in order fulfillment and how it should be used to aid each step of the process and integrated with other members of the supply chain. Although decisions regarding technology need to be made at the strategic level, the technological options and issues will be explored later in this chapter, in the section on the operational order fulfillment process, since the technology supports the operational activities.

An important component of designing an order fulfillment process is determining the flow of order information; in other words, how the order information will be captured and fed to the demand management process.

---

[11] Harris, Frederick H. deB. and Jonathan P. Pinder, "A revenue management approach to demand management and order booking in assemble-to-order manufacturing," *Journal of Operations Management,* Vol. 13 (1995), pp. 299-309.

[12] Byrnes, Jonathan, "The Bottom Line: Who's Managing Profitability?" *HBS Working Knowledge,* September 2, 2002.

[13] Croxton, Keely L., Douglas M. Lambert, Sebastián J. García-Dastugue, and Dale S. Rogers, "The Demand Management Process," *The International Journal of Logistics Management,* Vol. 13, No. 2 (2002), pp. 51-66.

Develop Framework of Metrics

As with all the supply chain management processes, metrics should be tied back to the firm's economic value added (EVA).

In the final sub-process a framework of metrics must be developed to measure and monitor the performance of the process. As with all the supply chain management processes, metrics should be tied back to the firm's economic value added (EVA).[14] Figure 5-4 shows how improvements in the order fulfillment process can affect the firm's EVA by influencing sales, cost of goods sold, total expenses, inventory investment, other current assets and fixed assets. A streamlined order fulfillment process can reduce expenses such as handling, freight and overhead. However, the execution of the order fulfillment process has less obvious implications. For example, improved product availability increases sales and market share. Efficient supply chain design can reduce component costs which can reduce the cost of goods sold, and reduce inventory levels throughout the supply chain. If the order-to-cash cycle is reduced, payments are made more quickly, which reduces the current assets on the books. The process team needs to understand these implications and understand how the process affects financial performance.

Once the team has an understanding of the impact that order fulfillment can have on the financial performance of the firm, metrics need to be developed for the activities performed. Typical process measures include order-to-cash cycle time, order fill rate, and order completeness. Many companies measure perfect orders,

Figure 5-4
How Order Fulfillment Affects Economic Value Added (EVA®)

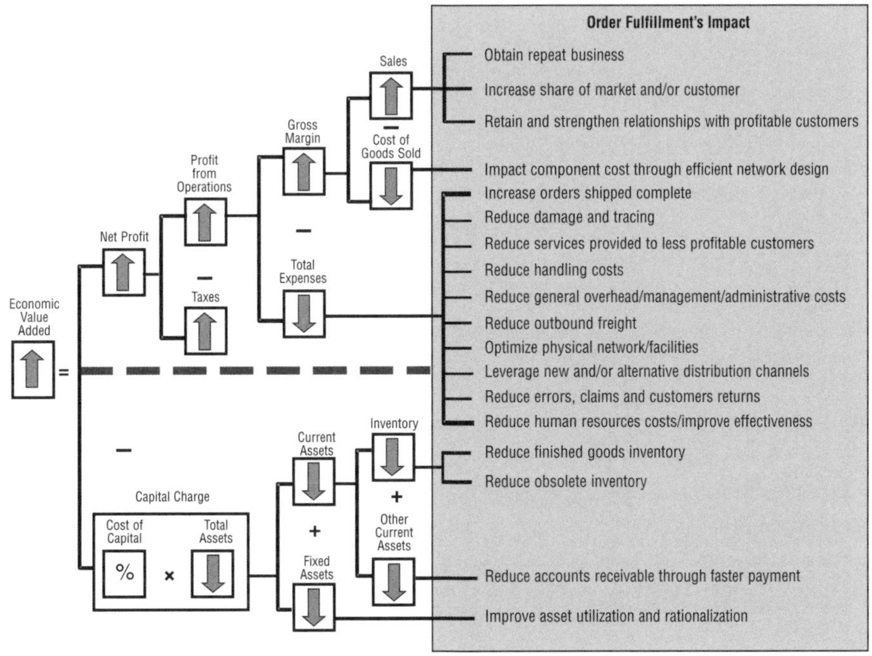

Source: Adapted from Douglas M. Lambert and Terrance L. Pohlen, "Supply Chain Metrics," *The International Journal of Logistics Management*, Vol. 12, No. 1 (2001), p.13.

---

[14] Lambert, Douglas M. and Terrance L. Pohlen, "Supply Chain Metrics," *The International Journal of Logistics Management*, Vol. 12, No. 1 (2001), pp. 1-19.

which usually incorporate the accuracy, the condition upon arrival, and the punctuality of orders. Some companies, like Hewlett-Packard, a global provider of technology products and services, track the number of order-touches to measure the efficiency of the order fulfillment process.

The team should work with the customer relationship management process team to make sure that they are not only aligning the order fulfillment metrics with the other metrics used throughout the firm, but that they are measuring what the customers deem important. It is important to assure that the firms in the supply chain implement processes that positively affect the EVA of the supply chain, not just an individual firm within it. It is the goal of supply chain management to drive behavior that benefits the entire supply chain while sharing the risks and rewards incurred. The team should share the framework of metrics with the customer relationship management and supplier relationship management processes and set goals for process improvement.

It is important to assure that the firms in the supply chain implement processes that positively affect the EVA of the supply chain, not just an individual firm within it.

Developing the metrics is the last sub-process at the strategic level, but this does not mean that the work is done. The team should review the execution of the order fulfillment process periodically to assure that it is as effective and efficient as possible. Shapiro et. al. recommend that management "staple themselves to an order" to look for horizontal and vertical gaps in the process.[15] The team should map the order flow and then follow several orders through the system. The average and variability in the time it takes to execute each step should be measured. This will help the team understand where orders might get stuck or where the process needs more standardization. This careful examination of the process once it is being executed at the operational level might lead the team back to the strategic sub-processes to re-design the network, the plan for order fulfillment, or the metrics.

The Operational Order Fulfillment Process

Figure 5-5 shows the seven sub-processes and activities that comprise the operational order fulfillment process. At the operational level, order fulfillment is very transactional. It is focused on managing the customer order cycle and the specific activities are executed primarily within the logistics function. In fact, a customer order is said to serve "as the communications message that sets the logistics process in motion".[16] However, managers need to focus attention on managing the interfaces with the other supply chain management processes and with other functional areas within the firm, and finding opportunities to integrate with other members of the supply chain.

Because order fulfillment begins with the customer's order, it is natural to integrate with key customers to streamline the order-to-cash cycle and make it as cost-effective for the supply chain as possible. The growth of technology in the supply chain environment has had significant impact on the order fulfillment process. Much of what used to be very manual steps has been automated by the advent and adoption of technology such as electronic data interchange (EDI), the

Because order fulfillment begins with the customer's order, it is natural to integrate with key customers to streamline the order-to-cash cycle and make it as cost-effective for the supply chain as possible.

[15] Shapiro, Benson P., V. Kasturi Rangan, and John J. Sviokla, "Staple Yourself to an Order," *Harvard Business Review,* Vol. 40, No. 4 (1992), pp.113-122.

[16] Stock, James R. and Douglas M. Lambert, *Strategic Logistics Management,* New York NY: McGraw-Hill, 2001, p. 146.

Figure 5-5
The Operational Order Fulfillment Process

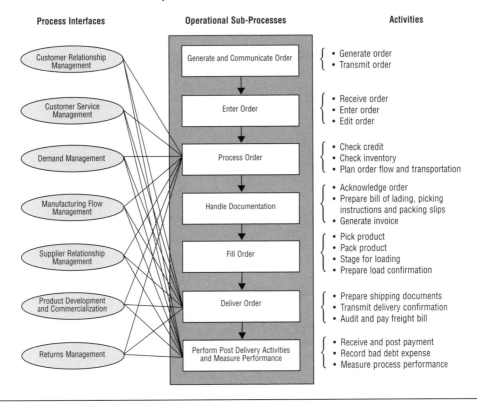

Internet, available-to-promise (ATP) and capable-to-promise (CTP) systems, and enterprise resource planning (ERP) and advanced planning and scheduling (APS) systems. These technologies, along with others such as transportation management systems (TMS) and inventory visibility tools, can provide managers information that can be used throughout the supply chain to streamline the order fulfillment process.

The implementation of these technologies has had two significant effects on the order fulfillment process. One is the streamlining of the operational process which has taken days out of the order-to-cash cycle. Ingram Macrotron Distribution, a subsidiary of Ingram Micro, implemented an electronic ordering system that reduced order processing costs by 60%, reduced order processing time by 30%, and decreased the average order fulfillment time by 60%.[17] In addition to the faster order fulfillment, it reduced the ordering costs of its customers by 12%, thereby providing benefit to other members of the supply chain.

The other effect that technology has had is on improving the ability for companies in the supply chain to integrate more effectively. Within order fulfillment, this integration usually takes place between the focal-firm and its customers. For instance, with the use of integrated technologies, the first two sub-processes can often

[17] "Ingram Macrotron Increases Electronic Sales and Decreases Order Processing Costs Using Microsoft Solution," 2002. See: www.microsoft.com/resources/casestudies/

be handled in one step. At Colgate-Palmolive, approximately 90% of orders are accepted through either EDI or the Internet and dropped directly into the SAP system for processing, where the order-flow and transportation planning is automatically executed. This not only reduces steps in the process, but reduces order entry errors which can be costly and time consuming to correct. Giving trace-and-track capabilities to customers is another way to integrate them into the process and reduce the workload on the customer service team. Streamlining the process improves customer service, allows inventory reductions, and improves cash flow. Implementing these technologies can be win-win for multiple members in the supply chain.

However, technology comes with a price, often not only for the focal firm but for other members of the supply chain. For instance, in the case of Colgate-Palmolive, the customers' technology needs to be integrated with Colgate-Palmolive's to streamline the transfer of data. It is paramount that management understands the financial impact of implementing these systems. Many companies faced failure after rushing into the e-commerce business because management believed that the internet would revolutionize order fulfillment. In determining which technologies to adopt, the order fulfillment team needs to weigh the costs against the value added by each technology. The technology should be judged by its ability to streamline the process and integrate the supply chain.

In determining which technologies to adopt, the order fulfillment team needs to weigh the costs against the value added by each technology. The technology should be judged by its ability to streamline the process and integrate the supply chain.

Generate and Communicate Order

As we trace an order through the operational order fulfillment process, the first step is to generate and communicate the order. Orders generally come through customer service, the sales organization, or directly from the customer. In some cases this is automated, for instance in an EDI or VMI environment, or other systems in which orders are automatically placed when the inventory level reaches a pre-set level. For other companies, the sales process is very labor intensive. Firms often lose valuable time in this sub-process and can reduce its duration by days using technology and automated information sharing.

The key functional interfaces for this sub-process are between the logistics, marketing and sales areas. At Herman Miller, a leading manufacturer of office furniture, management redesigned the sales process so that customers can lay-out a design for an office space on a salesperson's laptop. The customer can see how everything will fit and how colors will look together, and view it from any angle. Once the customer has the design as they want it, the software creates an order list and provides a final price. The order can be easily downloaded over the Internet into the order system. This software application was designed primarily as a sales and marketing tool, but it also streamlined the order generation and order entry processes and reduced errors. Errors were reduced from more than 20% to near zero, and customers received order confirmation with shipping and installation dates within two hours of placing the order, as opposed to the old process where this would take over a week.[18] The integration of the sales process into the order fulfillment process yielded Herman Miller substantial benefits to their operational performance.

---

[18] Sucher, Sandra J. and Stacy E. McManus, "Herman Miller (A): Innovation by Design," Harvard Business School Case Study, 2002; and, David Rocks, "Reinventing Herman Miller," Business Week Online, April 3, 2000.

Enter Order

Once received, the order needs to be entered and edited, if necessary. Errors in receiving and entering an order can be very costly. The process team should measure and track error levels and look for root causes of the errors. Often, orders that are received do not contain all the required information. This might be due to an issue with the sales process or with the customers. For instance, it might be that orders are incomplete because the sales people are providing customers with incomplete quotes.[19] If this is the case, the process team should work with the sales force to improve order quotes and give customers complete information for their orders.

The team might work directly with customers to help streamline the process to reduce errors, perhaps by integrating technologies. Some companies have found that while giving customers the capability to enter orders directly into their system has streamlined the process, it has also increased the number of errors, perhaps because the customers are not as well trained as the firm's internal people. The process team should carefully monitor this and perhaps employ more checks and balances in the system.

Data regarding the orders are transmitted to the customer service management and demand management processes. The customer service management process needs to have data on order status to help customers. The demand management process uses the order entry information as input for generating future forecasts. Both process teams benefit if the information is received in a timely and error-free fashion.

Process Order

The first step to processing the order is to check the customer's credit. The credit check requires an interface with finance and is another common source of delay in the process. If orders are getting to this stage and not passing the credit check, the process team should work with the sales force to make sure they have information on which customers have credit problems. Also, a system should be put in place so that customers can easily determine how much credit they have available.[20] In some cases, systems can be designed so that this credit check occurs before orders are placed. For instance, if customers are placing orders over the internet, the system could prevent them from ordering if their credit situation is not good. New customers could establish credit on-line before being allowed to place orders.

For orders that are not filled directly from inventory, the DRP process will determine where the order will be manufactured or assembled and how it will be shipped to the customer by the due date.

Once the credit issue is resolved, inventory levels are checked and the order flow is planned. It is determined how the order will be routed through the supply chain which is commonly referred to as the distribution requirements planning (DRP) process. If the order will be filled from inventory, the inventory location is determined, inventory levels are updated, and the distribution plan is executed. If the order is composed of several products from different locations, the shipments will have to be coordinated.[21] For orders that are not filled directly from inventory, the DRP process will determine where the order will be manufactured or assembled and how it will be shipped to the customer by the due date. This

---

[19] Waller, Matthew A., Dennis Woolsey and Robert Seaker, "Reengineering Order Fulfillment," *The International Journal of Logistics Management*, Vol. 6, No. 2 (1995), pp. 1-10.

[20] Waller, Matthew A., Dennis Woolsey and Robert Seaker, "Reengineering Order Fulfillment," *The International Journal of Logistics Management*, Vol. 6, No. 2 (1995), pp. 1-10.

[21] Croxton, Keely L., Bernard Gendron and Thomas L. Magnanti, "Models and Methods for Merge-in-Transit Operations," Transportation Science, Vol. 37, No. 1 (2003), pp. 1-22.

information is important input for the demand management and manufacturing flow processes.

Handle Documentation

Once the order has been processed and planned, the documentation related to that order is prepared, including order acknowledgement, bill of lading, picking instructions, packing slips and the invoice. If the order will be shipped internationally, the customs and duty forms will be prepared. Note that in some warehouse management systems (WMS), the documentation is prepared after the order is filled, reversing the order of this sub-process and the following one.

Many firms are providing customers with order visibility and tracking capabilities. In this case, part of the documentation is electronic in nature and needs to be updated throughout the remainder of the order fulfillment process.

Fill Order

The next stage of the order fulfillment process is filling the order. Usually, order filling occurs on the plant floor or in a warehouse and involves picking, packing, staging, and load configuration. It is important for the personnel who fill the orders to know if there are customer-specific specifications, such as particular packing requiremwents or pallet configurations. This information should be part of the picking instructions that were generated in the previous sub-process. Once the order is filled and confirmed, the order status is communicated to the customer service management team so that they can provide information to the customer if requested.

Key issues in this sub-process are the accuracy and timeliness with which these activities are performed. The adoption of warehouse technologies, particularly bar code and wireless radio frequency technology, has improved the accuracy of filling orders. Warehouse layout and material handling can have significant impact on timeliness. Changes to the physical layout, racking system, or item locations can make the process more efficient.[22] Therefore, the process team should continuously examine the potential impact of new technologies and layout changes.

The adoption of warehouse technologies, particularly bar code and wireless radio frequency technology, has improved the accuracy of filling orders.

Deliver Order

The final step in the order-to-delivery process is to arrange delivery of the order. In this sub-process, shipping documents are prepared, the transportation plan is executed, delivery is confirmed, and the freight bill is audited and paid. In order to help the customer plan, advance shipping notices (ASN) should be sent.

Delays and errors in these steps can be costly, because there is little chance to make-up for the mistakes without impacting the customer. For most firms, it is also the point in the order fulfillment process where control of the order is relinquished, as it is usually handed over to a transportation company. Effective

---

[22] Ackerman, Kenneth, "Designing Tomorrow's Warehouse: A Little Ahead of the Times," *Journal of Business Logistics*, Vol. 20, No. 1 (1999), pp. 1-4; Che-Hung Lin and Iuan-Yuan Lu, "The Procedure of Determining the Order Picking Strategies in Distribution Center," *International Journal of Production Economics*, Vol. 60/61, Issue 3 (1999), pp. 301-307; and, Simon J. Dennis, "Order Picking: An Overlooked Option?" *Logistics Focus*, Vol. 7, No. 3 (1999), pp. 3-8.

relationships with transportation companies can play an important role in executing the delivery sub-process.

As part of the information flow, trace-and-track documentation is made available to the customer service team who will use this information when a customer inquires about an order. Alternatively, it might be sent directly to customers so that they can track their orders themselves.

Perform Post-Delivery Activities and Measure Performance

In the final steps of the order fulfillment process, payment is received and posted, discrepancies are addressed, and bad debt expense is recorded. The process of receiving and posting payment can often be labor intensive. If, for example, a customer sends in payment of an invoice but subtracts out deductions without explanation, the customer service management team needs to call the customer and follow-up on what the issues are and how they can be resolved. This becomes time-consuming for both parties. If firms can work with customers to minimize these types of issues, the total cost of delivery will be reduced.

An ongoing part of the order fulfillment process is to measure the process and communicate the results throughout the firm and to key members of the supply chain.

An ongoing part of the order fulfillment process is to measure the process and communicate the results throughout the firm and to key members of the supply chain. Because the order fulfillment process has such direct impact on the customer, it is important to track the timeliness of the process. Two important metrics of the order fulfillment process are the order-to-cash cycle time and the customer cycle time. The order-to-cash cycle time measures the elapsed time from the receipt of the customer's order to the time that the proper payment is posted, while the customer cycle time is a measure of the elapsed time from the order being placed to the receipt of the order into the customer's inventory. It is important to examine not only the average duration of these cycles, but also the variability. The variability of the customer cycle time is particularly important to the customer, as they need to hold more safety stock when there is high variability. For the customer, reduction in the variability has more financial impact than a reduction in the average cycle time[23]. Measuring both the average and the variation in the time required to complete each operational sub-process will allow the team to see where they should focus their attention.

Conclusions

The order fulfillment process is often viewed as transactional and part of the logistics function within a firm. However, it is important that managers recognize its strategic components, its cross-functional needs, and its role within the management of the supply chain.

At the strategic level, the order fulfillment process involves understanding the internal and external requirements and assuring that the system has adequate capabilities. This includes understanding the business strategy and the customer service requirements, and designing a supply chain network to meet customers' needs efficiently. Another important component of the process is to have a

---

[23] Stock, James R. and Douglas M. Lambert, *Strategic Logistics Management*, New York NY: McGraw-Hill, 2001; Tomkins, James A., et. al., Facilities Planning, New York, NY: John Wiley and Sons, Inc., 1996.

responsive system in place for when demand exceeds supply and some orders cannot be filled. Assuring that this system still manages to meet at least the minimum needs of customers is critical to achieving good customer service even in the face of adversity. The other very important strategic piece comes in designing the metrics. There are numerous examples of bad metrics driving misguided behavior. The process team needs to examine the effects of order fulfillment on the financial performance of the firm and assure that the metrics used are consistent with improving the financial performance of the entire supply chain.

While the order fulfillment process is often viewed as a logistics activity, the process cannot be designed without input from other functional areas including marketing, finance, purchasing, and production, as well as support groups like information technology. Therefore, it is important that the process team be cross-functional. To achieve strong performance, the requirements of all functional areas must be met.

Although it is possible to implement many portions of the order fulfillment process without going outside the four walls of the firm, the real opportunities come when a firm reaches out to other members of the supply chain. Integrating key customers and suppliers can help streamline and improve the order fulfillment process. Whether it is through idea sharing or information sharing, the role of the other supply chain members takes the order fulfillment activities from a single-firm process to a supply chain management process.

While the order fulfillment process is often viewed as a logistics activity, the process cannot be designed without input from other functional areas including marketing, finance, purchasing, and production, as well as support groups like information technology.

The Manufacturing Flow Management Process

Thomas J. Goldsby and Sebastián J. García-Dastugue

Overview

Manufacturing flow management is the supply chain management process that includes all activities necessary to obtain, implement, and manage manufacturing flexibility in the supply chain and to move products through the plants.[1] Manufacturing flexibility reflects the ability to make a variety of products in a timely manner at the lowest possible cost. To achieve the desired level of manufacturing flexibility, planning and execution must extend beyond the four walls of the factory. In this chapter, we describe the manufacturing flow management process in detail to show how it can be implemented within a company and managed across firms in the supply chain. We examine the activities of each sub-process; evaluate the interfaces with corporate functions, processes, and firms; and provide examples of successful implementation.

Introduction

Firms that perform the manufacturing activities in a supply chain face several challenges, one of which is to produce products in varieties and quantities that are in synch with the marketplace. Connecting production management to actual demand represents a sizable opportunity for most organizations. For example, the potential savings from Efficient Consumer Response, an effort to connect production management with the market in the grocery industry, have been estimated at $30 billion.[2] Firms that integrate procurement, manufacturing and logistics activities might achieve cost reductions of between three and seven percent of revenues,[3] depending on the industry. Extending this integration beyond a single firm represents an opportunity for all members of the supply chain involved in the initiative.

Connecting production management to actual demand represents a sizable opportunity for most organizations.

---

[1] This chapter is based on Thomas J. Goldsby and Sebastián J. García-Dastugue, "The Manufacturing Flow Management Process," *The International Journal of Logistics Management*, Vol. 14, No. 2 (2003), pp. 33-52.

[2] Poirier, Charles C., *Supply Chain Optimization: Building the Strongest Total Business Network*, San Francisco: Berrett-Koehler Publishers, 1996.

[3] Hoover, William E. Jr., Eero Eloranta, Jan Holmström and Kati Huttunen, *Managing the Demand-Supply Chain: Value Innovations for Customer Satisfaction*, New York: Wiley, 2001.

The costs and expertise required to match market dynamics can be prohibitive, leading some manufacturers to rely on outsourced production activities. Contract manufacturing services provided about 10 percent of all global output in the electronics industry in 1998, totaling approximately $60 billion. It is forecasted that by the year 2008, the figure will reach $1.3 trillion - a 2,167 percent increase.[4] In pharmaceutical chemicals and agrochemicals, contract manufacturing represents approximately half of the manufacturing capacity.[5] The medical device industry outsourced roughly $8 billion, or 18 percent of its cost of goods sold, in 2002, and this is expected to increase to 42 percent by 2005.[6]

In large part, outsourced manufacturing is growing as a result of the need for manufacturing flexibility.[7] Manufacturing flexibility enables greater responsiveness to changes in customers' product preferences and quantities demanded.[8] Determining the right degree of flexibility is important to virtually any company involved in the supply, production, distribution or sales of goods, and is at the center of the manufacturing flow management process. While manufacturing activities might be outsourced to suppliers, the commitment to quality and the managerial responsibility has to be retained at the firm.

Determining the right degree of flexibility is important to virtually any company involved in the supply, production, distribution or sales of goods, and is at the center of the manufacturing flow management process.

The manufacturing flow management process team coordinates all activities necessary to obtain, implement, and manage manufacturing flexibility in the supply chain and to move products through the plants. The process involves much more than production. For example, the efficiency of the product flow through the plants depends on the reliability of the inbound logistics processes as well as the suppliers' ability to deliver orders on time and complete. Therefore, the logistics and procurement functions should work closely with production. Similarly, the degree of manufacturing flexibility partly depends on the flexibility of all suppliers. There are several ways to provide flexibilty, including reserving available capacity, and standardizing components while maintaining inventory of subcomponents. Suppliers need to be involved because they will be affected by these tactics. In sum, several factors both internal and external to the firm affect the firm's ability to achieve the desired degree of manufacturing flexibility.

In this chapter, a framework for implementing an efficient and effective manufacturing flow management process is presented. Because manufacturing flow management is one of the eight supply chain management processes, it requires interfaces with the other seven (see Figure 6-1). We describe the strategic and operational processes that comprise manufacturing flow management, including the sub-processes and their activities. In addition, we identify the interfaces with the corporate functions, the other supply chain management processes, and other firms. Finally, conclusions are presented.

---

[4] Meeks, Paul, "Heard From the Buy Side," *Red Herring,* (September 1999), p. 4.

[5] Van Arnum, Patricia, "Bulls or Bears? Outlook in Contract Manufacturing," *Chemical Market Reporter,* (February 14, 2000), pp. 3-6.

[6] "How Contract Manufacturing is Reshaping the Device Industry: A Roundtable Discussion," *Medical Device & Diagnostic Industry,* (October 2002), pp. 60-63.

[7] Panchuk, Patricia, "The Future of Manufacturing: An Exclusive Interview with Peter Drucker," *Industry Week,* (September 21, 1998), pp. 36-42.

[8] Christopher, Martin and Denis R. Towill, "Developing Marketing Specific Supply Chain Strategies," *The International Journal of Logistics Management,* Vol. 13, No. 1 (2002), pp. 1-14.

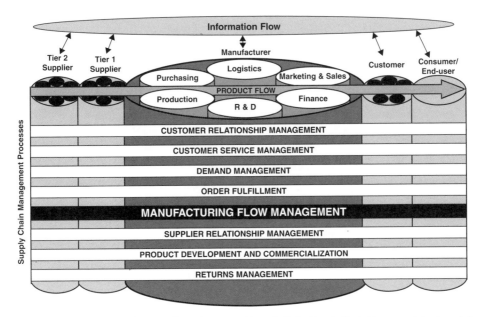

Figure 6-1
Supply Chain Management:
Integrating and Managing Business Processes Across the Supply Chain

Source: Adapted from Douglas M. Lambert, Martha C. Cooper, and Janus D. Pagh, "Supply Chain Management: Implementation Issues and Research Opportunities," *The International Journal of Logistics Management,* Vol. 9, No. 2 (1998), p. 2.

Manufacturing Flow Management as a Supply Chain Management Process

The manufacturing flow management process deals with establishing the manufacturing flexibility needed to serve the target markets and making the products.

The manufacturing flow management process deals with establishing the manufacturing flexibility needed to serve the target markets and making the products. Manufacturing flexibility is defined as "the ability to respond to environmental changes with less time and cost".[9] The concept and significance of flexibility, broadly defined and as it applies to manufacturing operations, receive treatment in a subsequent section of the chapter. Flexibility is important to most operations and particularly so when the manufacturer faces demand variation across a wide assortment of products. Less stable demand environments place a premium on flexible accommodation. The challenge is determining the right degree of flexibility to build into the manufacturing system given that increased flexibility is typically accompanied higher costs or increased investment.

Manufacturing flow management, like the other supply chain management processes, relies on external connectivity to accomplish its objectives. While it initially might appear relevant only to the finished goods manufacturer (or assembler), the process is significantly influenced by the up- and downstream members of the supply chain. Downstream members influence the process through the demand for product assortments that meet expectations in terms of

[9] Upton, D.M., "The Management of Manufacturing Flexibility," *California Management Review,* Vol. 96, No. 2 (1994), pp. 72-89.

specific attributes, quality, cost, and availability as well as through changes to plans. Upstream members affect the manufacturer's ability to fulfill the customers' expectations. It might be argued that the potential of the manufacturing capabilities of the firm is limited by the capabilities of upstream suppliers. It is important to view the manufacturing flow management process as one that extends beyond the four walls of the final assembler.

It is important to view the manufacturing flow management process as one that extends beyond the four walls of the final assembler.

The process presented here is not industry- or context-specific but rather provides guidance to companies that influence, or are influenced by, the process. For example, a grocery retailer that offers private label products should consider formalizing the manufacturing flow management process with its manufacturers. In this sense, a retailer may not perform manufacturing itself but rely on the manufacturing capabilities of suppliers to ensure its success. This example illustrates that the manufacturing flow management process is not the domain of manufacturers alone.

The manufacturing flow management process has both strategic and operational elements (see Figure 6-2). The strategic portion of manufacturing flow management provides the structure for managing the process within the firm and across key supply chain members. The operational portion of the process represents the actualization of manufacturing flow management. Developing the strategic process is a necessary to integrate the firm with other members of the supply chain. It is at the operational level that the day-to-day activities are executed.

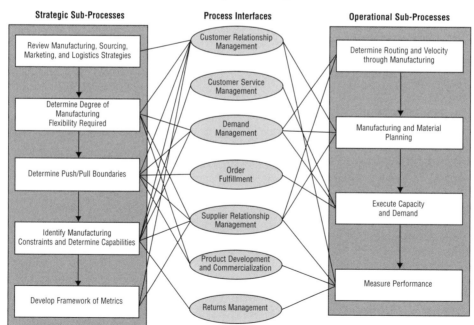

Figure 6-2
Manufacturing Flow Management

Source: Adapted from Keely L. Croxton, Sebastián J. García-Dastugue, Douglas M. Lambert, and Dale S. Rogers, "The Supply Chain Management Processes," *The International Journal of Logistics Management*, Vol. 12, No. 2 (2001), p. 22.

Much of the richness associated with the framework is found in the interfaces among processes for it is here that the processes extend to other functions within the firm and other key members of the supply chain.

Much of the richness associated with the framework is found in the interfaces among processes for it is here that the processes extend to other functions within the firm and other key members of the supply chain. These interfaces might take the form of data transfer, or the sharing of information and ideas with another process team during regular planned or ad hoc meetings.

A process team comprised of managers from several corporate functions, including production, purchasing, logistics, marketing, and finance, leads both the strategic and operational processes. The team also might have representation from outside the firm, including key customers, suppliers, and/or third-party service providers. The process team is responsible for developing the procedures at the strategic level and seeing that they are implemented at the operational level. Involvement on the operational level is typically limited to addressing exceptions or problems in execution. While employees outside of the process team might execute parts of the process, the team maintains managerial control.

The Strategic Manufacturing Flow Management Process

The strategic portion of manufacturing flow management consists of five sub-processes that collectively represent the decision-making infrastructure for the process. This infrastructure embodies the development of the manufacturing plan, the means of execution, limits to execution, and the appropriate measures of performance. We address each of the five sub-processes in order as depicted in Figure 6-3. This figure includes the activities within each of the sub-processes as

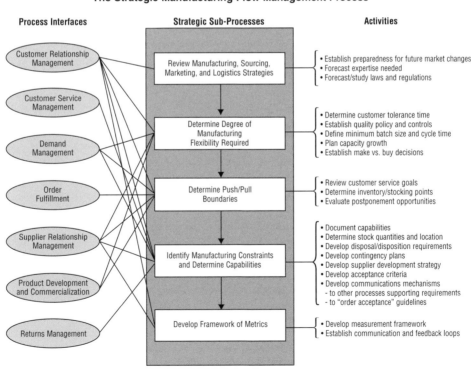

Figure 6-3
The Strategic Manufacturing Flow Management Process

well as the important interfaces between manufacturing flow management and the other supply chain management processes.

Review Manufacturing, Sourcing, Marketing, and Logistics Strategies

In this sub-process, the manufacturing flow management process team reviews the functional strategies that might have an effect on manufacturing flexibility and on the flow of products through the plants. The functional strategies that are reviewed include the manufacturing, sourcing, marketing, and logistics. This review dictates the priorities of the production function and the roles of its suppliers and supporting service providers.[10] In this sub-process, the strategy starts to be translated into required capabilities and deliverables. If these deliverables are below the customers' expectations, the firm will lose some business opportunities. On the other hand, if these deliverables exceed what the customers actually expect, the firm might be consuming resources for which the customer will fail to offer commensurate reward.

This marks an important shift in mentality from "We sell what we make," to, "We make what we sell." This important distinction leads to an assortment of products that satisfy the needs of distinct market segments. The production capabilities of the firm play an important role in the determination of a firm's competitive basis, whether that basis is cost, quality, service, or time.[11] When competitive advantage is to be gained by adopting a unique manufacturing strategy or by employing a common strategy more effectively, it is even more critical that the manufacturing strategy and corporate strategy are aligned. The key is to ensure that the strategy results in value to customers and, ultimately, shareholders.

The production capabilities of the firm play an important role in the determination of a firm's competitive basis, whether that basis is cost, quality, service, or time.

Strategy determination may be driven, in part, by the manufacturing philosophy of the firm. Two manufacturing philosophies that have gained much interest in recent years are lean manufacturing and agility. These two philosophies, while distinct, share a common objective: to satisfy customer demand at the least total cost. It is in the means by which this objective is accomplished that the two philosophies differ. Leanness embodies the relentless elimination of "muda" (the Japanese term for "waste") and is modeled primarily after the Toyota Production System developed by Taiichi Ohno. Ohno identified seven critical wastes to eliminate; these include mistakes, overproduction, overprocessing, unnecessary transport, unnecessary movement by employees, waiting, and defective offerings.[12] Meanwhile, agility is oriented toward mass customization or quick, responsive accommodation of varied demand in terms of volume, variety, and mix through flexible operations.[13] Dell Computer is a commonly cited example of agile manufacturing. The company employs a rapid configuration system for its custom-built computer products in support of its consumer-direct marketing strategy.

---

[10] Demeter, Krisztina, "Manufacturing Strategy and Competitiveness," *International Journal of Production Economics,* Vol. 81-82 (2003), pp. 205-213.

[11] Naylor, J. Ben, Mohamed M. Naim, and Danny Berry, "Leagility: Integrating the Lean and Agile Manufacturing Paradigms in the Total Supply Chain," *International Journal of Production Economics,* Vol. 62 (1999), pp. 107-118.

[12] Womack, James P. and Daniel T. Jones, *Lean Thinking,* New York, NY: Simon & Schuster, 1996.

Lean principles tend to be favored when products are standard (i.e., offer low variety) and demand is somewhat stable over long product life cycles. This allows extensive planning and a focus on efficient, defect-free production.[14] An agile approach is preferred when there is a large amount of product variety, demand is highly unpredictable, and product life cycles are short.

Situations arise where a combination of the two philosophies is appropriate. This hybrid is referred to as "leagile". Appropriate situations for "leagile" manufacturing might include products as they proceed through their life cycle (i.e., agile in infancy, lean in growth and maturity, and agile in decline), diverse products made of standard components or sub-assemblies (i.e., lean production of components with agile assembly of finished goods), or across product lines (i.e., fast-moving products produced in a lean manner and slow-moving products are produced using agility). Therefore, it is not wise to identify oneself as a "lean" or "agile" manufacturer given that either philosophy (or a combination of the philosophies) might be embraced as the situation evolves.[15] It is important that the manufacturing strategy fits the corporate strategy and the strategies of key supply chain members.

Looking beyond paradigms of lean and agile manufacturing are five generic manufacturing strategies. These five strategies from most rigid to most flexible are described briefly below:

- Ship to Stock (STS). Products are standardized and pre-positioned in the market; customers' expectations of immediate availability support the maintenance of speculative safety stock at all points of distribution.
- Make to Stock (MTS). Products are standardized but not necessarily allocated to specific locations; demand is anticipated to be stable or readily forecasted at an aggregate level.
- Assemble to Order (ATO). Products can be customized within a range of possibilities, usually based upon a standard platform; final form of the product is postponed until demand is known.
- Make to Order (MTO). Raw materials and components are common but can be configured into a wide variety of products.
- Buy to Order (BTO). Products can be unique right down to the raw material level; product variety is virtually limitless, though lead time is long as materials are procured, processed into finished goods, and delivered.[16]

...it is not wise to identify oneself as a "lean" or "agile" manufacturer given that either philosophy (or a combination of the philosophies) might be embraced as the situation evolves.

---

[13] Naylor, J. Ben, Mohamed M. Naim, and Danny Berry, "Leagility: Integrating the Lean and Agile Manufacturing Paradigms in the Total Supply Chain," *International Journal of Production Economics,* Vol. 62 (1999), pp. 107-118; and, Martin Christopher and Denis R. Towill, "Developing Market Specific Supply Chain Strategies," *The International Journal of Logistics Management,* Vol. 13, No. 1 (2002), pp. 1-14.

[14] Mason-Jones, Rachel, Ben Naylor, Denis R. Towill, "Engineering the Leagile Supply Chain," *International Journal of Agile Management Systems,* Vol. 2, No. 1 (2000), pp. 54-61.

[15] To read more about lean, agile and leagile philosophies, see J. Ben Naylor, Mohamed M. Naim, and Danny Berry, "Leagility: Integrating the Lean and Agile Manufacturing Paradigms in the Total Supply Chain," *International Journal of Production Economics,* Vol. 62 (1999), pp. 107-118; Rachel Mason-Jones, Ben Naylor, Denis R. Towill, "Engineering the Leagile Supply Chain," *International Journal of Agile Management Systems,* Vol. 2, No. 1 (2000), pp. 54-61; and, Martin Christopher and Denis R. Towill, "Developing Market Specific Supply Chain Strategies," *The International Journal of Logistics Management,* Vol. 13, No. 1 (2002), pp. 1-14.

[16] These five strategies are identified and described in J. Ben Naylor, Mohamed M. Naim, and Danny Berry, "Leagility: Integrating the Lean and Agile Manufacturing Paradigms in the Total Supply Chain," *International Journal of Production Economics,* Vol. 62 (1999), pp. 107-118.

Figure 6-4 illustrates the relationship among these five generic strategies. Selection of the best strategy depends largely upon the perceived levels of demand variability across the assortment of products offered by the manufacturer and the ability to forecast long-, medium-, and near-term demand accurately. If demand is certain and stable, there is very little need to employ flexibility to delay activities in order to learn from the behavior of the demand and, consequently, make more accurate decisions. Rather, the manufacturer can buy materials in large batches and enjoy long production runs, recognizing that inventories will be depleted at a known rate. However, given the shrinking product life cycles experienced by many products, greater flexibility is necessary to accommodate uncertainty in demand. Determining the appropriate degree of manufacturing flexibility will be described further in the next sub-process.

...given the shrinking product life cycles experienced by many products, greater flexibility is necessary to accommodate uncertainty in demand.

In addition to monitoring current market conditions is the need to develop preparedness for foreseeable changes that might affect the market. These changes might include the advent of radically new products that make current offerings obsolete, or the development of new materials or technologies that revolutionize a manufacturing process. One such example is found in the common usage of carrageenan, a seaweed extract used by toothpaste manufacturers to thicken and stabilize the toothpaste formula. It is believed that a substitute for carrageenan is being developed. The substitute will cost half of what carrageenan costs per unit of finished product. Carrageenan suppliers face the challenge of reacting to the impending threat in order to retain their customers. Should the threat become

Figure 6-4
Five Generic Manufacturing Strategies

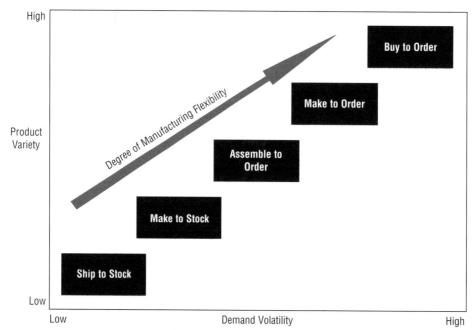

Source: Adapted from J. Ben Naylor, Mohamed M. Naim, and Danny Berry, "Leagility: Integrating the Lean and Agile Manufacturing Paradigms in the Total Supply Chain," *The International Journal of Production Economics*, Vol. 62, (1999), pp. 107-118.

imminent, the suppliers will have to invest heavily in either a new process or product to retain the relationships with their customers.

Thus, the team needs to predict the technological changes expected for the medium- and long-term future. Changes in technology might be accompanied with new expertise needed. These changes, depending on their impact, might not only be regarded as a strategic manufacturing decision, but also as a shift in business strategy. Forces that affect the manufacturing strategy might stem from competitive forces, but also from environmental policies and other regulations. For instance, government support for the advancement of hydrogen fuel cell technology can invigorate an industry. However, regulations can extinguish an industry just as easily - as has been seen with asbestos-based products, lead-based paints, and R-12 refrigerant, among others.

In reviewing the corporate and functional strategies, the manufacturing flow management team works in close collaboration with the customer relationship management team to ensure that production capabilities match market demands.

In reviewing the corporate and functional strategies, the manufacturing flow management team works in close collaboration with the customer relationship management team to ensure that production capabilities match market demands. In fact, it is the responsibility of the customer relationship manager team to communicate market conditions and opportunities that establish the competitive priorities for the marketing, purchasing, and logistics functions as well as manufacturing.

Determine Degree of Manufacturing Flexibility Required

The second strategic sub-process builds upon the first by determining the degree of manufacturing flexibility required to accommodate demand. Manufacturing flexibility ensures the company's ability to manage resources and uncertainty to meet various customer requests. Flexibility can have different meanings in different contexts. Table 6-1 summarizes types of flexibility and provides the definition for each. The most frequently cited views of flexibility are those that refer to the production function, such as mix, volume, and expansion flexibility. However, the supply chain management processes are both cross-functional and cross-firm. Within this cross-functional context, other organizational aspects need to be considered and will influence the firm's degree of flexibility. Therefore, we have included in Table 6-1 a broader view of flexibility that transcends the production function.

There are several factors that drive the need for manufacturing flexibility. As previously noted, demand characteristics factor prominently in the determination of manufacturing flexibility.   Demand volume, variation, and predictability of the variation are at the top of the list of considerations. Also important to consider is the customer's tolerance for waiting and reaction to an out-of-stock situation by either switching to a substitute product, back-ordering, delaying the purchase, or getting the item from an alternative supplier/store.[17] Characteristics associated with the product itself include the variety (i.e., the level of standardization or differentiation), stage and expected duration of the product life cycle, complexity of the product, and profit margin of the product. Finally, the lead times that can be achieved in different levels of the supply chain will influence the degree of manufacturing flexibility that will be required to satisfy demand. For example, a

---

[17] Zinn, Walter, and Peter C. Liu, "Consumer Response to Retail Stockouts," *Journal of Business Logistics,* Vol. 22, No. 1 (2001), pp.49-72.

Table 6-1
Types of Flexibility

Type of Flexibility	Definition
Organizational Flexibility	
Manufacturing or Operations	The ability of the organization to manage production resources and uncertainty to meet various customer requirements
Market	The ability to mass-customize and build close relationships with customers, including designing new products and modifying existing ones
Supply	The ability to reconfigure the supply chain (geographically) as sources of supply and customers change
Information Systems	The ability to align information systems with changing customer demands
Production Flexibility	
Mix	The ability to change over to a different product quickly and economically without changes in capacity
Volume	The ability to operate at various batch sizes and/or at different production volumes economically and effectively
Expansion	Modular building and expanding capacity
Material Handling	The ability to effectively transport different work pieces between various processing centers over multiple paths
Process (routing)	The ability to process a given set of part types using multiple routes effectively
Machine	The ability of a machine to perform different operations economically and efficiently
Work-center (labor)	The ability of the workforce to perform a broad range of tasks economically and effectively

Source: adapted from Duclos, Leslie K., Robert J. Vokurka and Rhonda R. Lummus, "A Conceptual Model of Supply Chain Flexibility," *Industrial Management & Data Systems*, Vol. 103, No. 6 (2003), pp. 446-456; and Zhang, Qingyu, Mark A. Vonderembse and Jeen-Su Lim, "Manufacturing Flexibility: Defining and Analyzing Relationships among Competence, Capability, and Customer Satisfaction," *Journal of Operations Management*, Vol. 21, No. 2 (2003), pp. 173-191.

flexible manufacturing system might be required to offset deficiencies in suppliers' lead times or outbound delivery times.

Quality policies and required degrees of control add to the lead times. Some controls such as inspection upon receiving a shipment might be removed by assigning control to the source, or removing inspections altogether by developing quality protocols jointly with suppliers, certifying their processes. In some cases, quality controls are mandated such as tests required by the Food and Drug Administration. For example, baby-food products require an incubation period before they are released to the market. This incubation-time requirement limits some aspects of flexibility by forcing the manufacturer to maintain higher inventories than would be necessary in the absence of such a mandate.

Generally, more flexibility is preferred. However, there is a cost associated with developing manufacturing flexibility. The targeted type and degree of flexibility should fit the overall business strategy.[18] Management may pursue the implementation of higher degrees of flexibility and/or specific types of flexibility for key customers.

---

[18] Gaimon, Cheryl and Vinod Singhal, "Flexibility and the Choice of Manufacturing Facilities under Short Product Life Cycles," *European Journal of Operational Research*, Vol. 60, No. 2 (1992), pp. 211.

Additionally, managers must be confident that the firm will be rewarded by its customers for providing heightened degrees of manufacturing flexibility. The ability of the demand management process to recognize demand volatility and to manage it effectively, might reduce the need for manufacturing flexibility.

Once the desired degree of manufacturing flexibility has been determined, attention turns to how best to achieve it. Batch sizes and cycle times, which can vary by product, market, or life-cycle phase, must be defined. The customer relationship management team provides critical input toward these determinations. Avery Dennison's Graphics division has established distinct approaches to accommodate fast-moving and slow-moving products. Fast-moving products are produced in large batches in a lean manner - knowing that demand will exist for them. Slower-moving products are produced on an as-needed or MTO basis. Prior to implementing this mixed-mode strategy, Avery struggled to achieve next-day service (from order receipt to shipping). Today, the business achieves same-day service across the product line at a very high level. This improved accommodation of demand has helped a market contender become the market leader.[19]

The TaylorMade-Adidas Golf Company employs mixed-mode approach to create a made-to-order, custom golf club deliverable in 24 hours. While make-to-stock clubs still represent the primary share of the company's business, demonstrating that custom clubs can be produced quickly and at a reasonable cost has reinforced the company's reputation as a best-in-class manufacturer.[20] Further reinforcement was found in 2002 when the United States Golf Association (USGA) revised its standards for clubs' coefficient of restitution (or "springiness"). The USGA extended the acceptable limit only to revert to its original level less than three months later, thereby making the company's top-selling product a non-compliant club in USGA-sanctioned events. By working closely with the product development and commercialization team and involving suppliers in the process, the manufacturing flow management team enabled TaylorMade to market a redesigned, compliant club within twelve days of the USGA's reversed decision.[21]

Beyond consideration of the manufacturer's current capabilities, there must be consideration of the manufacturing strategy's complete time horizon to determine whether current capacity is sufficient to support sales objectives. Incorporating information developed by the customer relationship management team and the marketing function regarding market growth, penetration of new markets, and sustained growth, the manufacturing flow management team will develop capacity and ability to respond to anticipated growth.

A final, critical consideration in this sub-process is whether the manufacturer can and should perform the value-added processing in-house. As indicated in the Introduction to this chapter, companies often will hire an external, contract manufacturer to fulfill specific manufacturing needs or to supplement supply during rapid growth or seasonal demand. In other instances, however, the company may choose to outsource its traditional manufacturing responsibilities entirely. More firms

---

[19] Roche, Terry, Manufacturing and Supply Chain Consultant, Avery Dennison, personal interview, conducted at Montgomery, Ohio on May 21, 2003.

[20] Bowman, Robert J., "TaylorMade Drives Supply-Chain Efficiency with 24-Hour Club," *Global Logistics & Supply Chain Strategies* (October 2002), pp. 38-43.

[21] Bowman, Robert J., "TaylorMade Drives Supply-Chain Efficiency with 24-Hour Club," *Global Logistics & Supply Chain Strategies* (October 2002), pp. 38-43.

today are choosing to build brands rather than physical products, outsourcing the full scope of manufacturing responsibilities to one or more contract manufacturers who can provide desired products at a lower cost. Companies such as The Limited, Nike, Lucent Technologies, Sara Lee, Ericsson, and Alcatel rely extensively on outsourced manufacturing to focus on new product development, marketing, and distribution.[22]

Determining when and what to outsource is a challenge. Masterfoods USA outsources production when the company either lacks a production capability or simply prefers not to own the technology. Masterfoods also employs contract manufacturers for temporary capacity during peak sales seasons. The 3M Company employs a similar logic but refuses to outsource manufacturing activities for which it has a competitive advantage. Given the importance of this decision, input should be received from purchasing, logistics, finance, and senior executives in the company.

Even when management chooses to "buy" rather than "make" key components or finished goods, it is important that the strategic planning responsibilities remain in the firm.[23] When outsourcing production, significant responsibilities shift from manufacturing flow management to the supplier relationship management process. Manufacturing expertise must remain in the company to ensure that the supplier operates in a manner consistent with the company's competitive priorities and within legal and social boundaries. The manufacturing flow management process team remains an important voice, protecting the company's interests when outside sources provide critical manufacturing services.

Even when management chooses to "buy" rather than "make" key components or finished goods, it is important that the strategic planning responsibilities remain in the firm.

The process team will interact frequently with the supplier relationship management process team even when no manufacturing activities are outsourced. The manufacturing flexibility of a firm will be influenced by the flexibility of key suppliers. Therefore, the supplier relationship management process team will provide assessment of suppliers' flexibility. They will also use this interaction with the manufacturing flow management process team to identify opportunities for improvement among the suppliers.

Determine Push/Pull Boundaries

The degree of manufacturing flexibility of each member of the supply chain influences the placement of push/pull boundaries. Push/pull boundaries refer to the positioning of decoupling points in the supply chain — up to which supply is pushed forward as make-to-stock but beyond which demand drives make-to-order execution.[24] The key to determining a push/pull boundary is recognizing the stage of value-added processing in which differentiation from a standard configuration

---

[22] Lynch, Grahame, "Telecom's New Role Model: Nike," *America's Network*, Vol. 105, No. 14 (2001), p. 58; Serant, Claire, "Selectron Opts to Lease Lucent Plant in Three-Year, $2B Ousourcing Deal," EBN, No. 1273 (2001), p.10; Susan Reda, "Customer Service, Brand Management Seen as Key spects of On-Line Fulfillment," *Stores Magazine*, Vol. 82, No. 10 (2000), pp. 40-43; and, Gretchen Morgenson, "Been There, Tried That," *Forbes*, Vol. 106, No. 9 (1997), pp.60-61.

[23] Singhal, Jaya and Kalyan Singhal, "Supply Chains and Compatibility among Components in Product Design," *Journal of Operations Management*, Vol. 20 (2002), pp. 289-302.

[24] Frequently, the push/pull boundaries are presented as determining the location of *"the"* decoupling point. This view of a single decoupling point is a conceptual simplification that, in practice, will be found only when the focus is internal to a firm or to a limited section of the product flow. When multiple members of a supply chain are involved, it is likely that more than one decoupling point is needed; see: Graves, Stephen C. and Sean P. Willems, "Optimizing Strategic Safety Stock Placement in Supply Chains," *Manufacturing and Service Operations Management*, Vol. 2, No. 1 (2000), pp. 68-83.

takes place. In a buy-to-order arrangement, manufacturing flexibility is at a premium and the primary decoupling point is upstream from the manufacturer given that raw materials are unique to the individual finished good. At the other extreme, ship-to-stock strategies generate a standardized product, allowing the decoupling point inventories to reside in the manufacturer's distribution channel.[25]

In ship-to-stock and make-to-stock arrangements, the customer can usually enjoy immediate satisfaction of an in-stock product (even though the product may not exactly match the customer's specific needs). If longer lead times can be negotiated with customers through the product and service agreement (PSA) developed by the customer relationship management team, greater opportunities for postponement become possible. Postponement reduces speculation and risks associated with finished goods inventories.[26] Should short or immediate lead times be set forth in the PSA, the manufacturer will have little choice but to pursue a speculative arrangement, position goods in the marketplace in advance of demand, and hope that the goods sufficiently meet customers' expectations in terms of appearance, performance, and quantity.

Supply chains that lack the ability to respond quickly to changes in customer demand incur the costs of oversupply and the opportunity costs of undersupply common with the bullwhip effect.

Supply chains that lack the ability to respond quickly to changes in customer demand incur the costs of oversupply and the opportunity costs of undersupply common with the bullwhip effect.[27] The primary responsibility for ensuring that the manufacturer responds to customer demand rests with the customer relationship management team in collaboration with the demand management process team. The product development and commercialization process is also involved to the extent that different product designs can be developed to accommodate manufacturing better and perhaps make postponement opportunities viable. Meanwhile, the supplier relationship management team is responsible for ensuring that suppliers understand their roles in the manufacturing flow management process.

Once the primary decoupling point is determined, the order fulfillment process must act in support of the push-pull decision to ensure that customers' expectations are fulfilled appropriately. In fact, the postponement of manufacturing activities might shift processing responsibilities typically performed by production to the logistics function of the business. Responsibilities would be limited ordinarily to light processing, such as packaging, labeling, and assembling display units. For instance, Hewlett-Packard (HP) has long performed the bundling of power supplies and users' manuals with print-imaging equipment in the distribution operation to support international sales. This effort is critical given that users in different nations will have different needs. Delaying the bundling of these items until demand is recognized by region prevents HP from speculating the nations from which demand originates. General Mills employs a similar strategy by bundling promotional items such as children's coloring books with breakfast cereals at the company's distribution centers throughout the U.S. By performing

---

[25] For more information regarding decoupling point determination, see J. Ben Naylor, Mohamed M. Naim, and Danny Berry, "Leagility: Integrating the Lean and Agile Manufacturing Paradigms in the Total Supply Chain," *International Journal of Production Economics*, Vol. 62 (1999), pp. 107-118.

[26] Cooper, Martha C. and Janus D. Pagh, "Supply Chain Postponement and Speculation Strategies: How to Choose the Right Strategy," *Journal of Business Logistics*, Vol.19, No. 2 (1998), pp. 13-33.

[27] Lee, Hau L., V. Padmanabhan and Seungjin Whang, "The Bullwhip Effect in Supply Chains," *Sloan Management Review*, Vol. 38, No. 3 (1997), pp. 93-102.

these activities closer (in terms of time and proximity) to the retail customer, General Mills experiences less uncertainty in short-term demand and reduces its risks of inventory obsolescence.[28]

Identify Manufacturing Constraints and Determine Capabilities

After the push-pull boundaries are determined, the strategic process team addresses the roles and responsibilities of the supply chain members to identify manufacturing constraints and requirements for desired performance. Recognizing bottlenecks in the manufacturing process is critical in achieving this objective. Among the more common constraints are labor and equipment resources. Ensuring that existing resources meet current and future demand ranks among the greatest difficulties for manufacturers.

Products that experience significant demand seasonality are particularly susceptible to periods of substantial under- and over-capacity. Manufacturers often hire temporary workers to offset the problem of insufficient labor on a short-term basis. With regard to equipment and facility resources, manufacturers will outsource excess production, build in advance, or use overtime capacity to ensure ready inventory availability when demand peaks. The ability to forecast these changes in demand patterns accurately is essential to providing adequate supply at the lowest possible cost. Therefore, the demand management process team not only must be aware of potential bottlenecks or problems in the flow of products through the plants but also must communicate demand forecasts well in advance, with continuous updates that provide greater accuracy in the near-term.

The manufacturing flow management process team identifies the manufacturing constraints and capabilities, and translates them into deliverables to the customers. The identification of the manufacturing constraints will lead to the development of the inventory policy for each facility in the supply chain network. The inventory policy will include how much inventory is to be held in the form of raw materials, subcomponents, work-in-process, and finished goods, and how often inventory will be replenished. Also, the inventory policy will determine the appropriate actions in the event of a stockout, which will be coordinated with demand management and, eventually, incorporated with contingency plans. Contingency plan development is imperative in minimizing disruption when problem situations cannot be anticipated or avoided.[29]

The identification of the manufacturing constraints will lead to the development of the inventory policy for each facility in the supply chain network.

Manufacturing technology sometimes poses constraints to manufacturing capabilities, such as the minimum manufacturing lead times. Other limits to the lead times that a firm can promise to its customers might be set, for example, by the planning process. Consequently, these constraints need to be identified

---

[28] For more information regarding postponement strategies, see Zinn, Walter, and Donald J. Bowersox, "Planning Physical Distribution with the Principle of Postponement," *Journal of Business Logistics*, Vol. 9, No. 2 (1988), pp. 117-136; Van Hoek, Remko I., Harry R. Commandeur, and Bart Vos, "Reconfiguring Logistics Systems through Postponement Strategies," *Journal of Business Logistics*, Vol. 19, No. 1 (1998), pp. 33-54; and, Cooper, Martha C. and Janus D. Pagh, "Supply Chain Postponement and Speculation Strategies: How to Choose the Right Strategy," *Journal of Business Logistics*, Vol.19, No. 2 (1998), pp. 13-33.

[29] Croxton, Keely L., Douglas M. Lambert, Dale S. Rogers and Sebastián J. García-Dastugue, "The Returns Management Process," *The International Journal of Logistics Management*, Vol. 13, No. 2 (2002), pp. 51-66.

explicity and translated into possible deliverables for customers. These deliverables should be incorporated in the development of the customer service strategy. Furthermore, since management should identify key customers and group other customers in segments, different manufacturing capabilities might be offered to the different key customers and segments. For example, a supplier to a US-based quick-service restaurant chain will accept rush orders from this customer; even if it means delaying production of another customer's order. Obviously, this service policy cannot be adopted for all customers. In addition, the costs associated with delaying other customers' orders must be determined. Management must assess the costs of offering prioritized customer service. The manufacturing flow management and customer relationship management teams need to discuss the possible features of the PSA, and adjust infeasible features. The capabilities are communicated to the demand managment, order fulfillment, and returns management process teams. Further, the customer service management team receives the order acceptance quidelines. The team uses these guidelines every time a customer has a request. The order acceptance guidelines help to identify which requests can be fulfilled without any further evaluation. Some requests might require additional management time to evaluate their economic and technical viability though the majority can be done based solely on the order acceptance guidelines.

Manufacturing flow management is enhanced as upstream supply chain members understand their roles and engage in synchronized flow to support the manufacturer's value-added processing.

Manufacturing flow management is enhanced as upstream supply chain members understand their roles and engage in synchronized flow to support the manufacturer's value-added processing. The process team is responsible for developing communication mechanisms that make synchronization possible across companies. In addition, the team develops criteria for acceptable quality throughout the manufacturing processes. The supplier relationship management process facilitates this interaction with key suppliers. The supplier relationship management team is charged not only with coordinating responsibilities with suppliers, but also jointly developing and implementing process improvement initiatives. Opportunities for process improvement often can be more easily identified by upstream supply chain members than by the manufacturer. For example, Cargill, Inc., works closely with its food processing customers to develop better products and better processes for improved product flow.

The manufacturing flow management process team will also participate in the development of the disposition requirements and returns management strategy. The disposition guidelines are developed in the returns management process.[30] However, the manufacturing flow management team will possess know-how regarding the methods for disassembling and disposing of the manufactured products. Disposition options include sending the product to landfill but the more preferable option is recapturing value. Therefore, the manufacturing flow management team participates in the feasibility analysis of the disposition options, including the determination of materials that can be reused or recycled, as well as the development of refurbishing and remanufacturing capacity.

[30] Rogers, Dale S. , Douglas M. Lambert, Keely L. Croxton and Sebastián J. García-Dastugue, "The Returns Management Process," *The International Journal of Logistics Management,* Vol. 13, No. 2 (2002), pp. 1-18.

Develop Framework of Metrics

In the final strategic sub-process, the process team develops the framework of metrics to be used to measure and improve the performance of the process. A uniform approach should be used throughout the firm to develop these metrics.[31] The team should start by understanding how the manufacturing flow management process can directly affect the firm's financial performance, as measured by economic value added (EVA).[32] The true test of the process' effectiveness is found in the value it creates. Figure 6-5 provides a framework that shows how manufacturing flow management can impact sales, cost of goods sold, total expenses, inventory investment, other current assets, and fixed assets.

Though the financial implications of production operations typically focus on cost reduction, the manufacturing flow management process should be credited with revenue enhancement associated with successful execution as well. For example, better manufacturing flow management can result in higher sales and healthier margins through consistent availability of products that meet customers' specific needs. Manufacturing flexibility that accommodates changes in product attributes and volume allows the company to meet demand better than rivals and to do so with lower inventory investment. Together, these factors strengthen customer loyalty and support repeat business. Loyal customers are also more likely to direct a greater proportion of their business to the proven manufacturer, improving the company's "share of customer." The value provided to the customer through manufacturing flexibility should be measured and sold both to upper management and to the customer. This value should be traded-off with the cost of obtaining, developing, and managing flexibility.

Though the financial implications of production operations typically focus on cost reduction, the manufacturing flow management process should be credited with revenue enhancement associated with successful execution as well.

Cost of goods sold can be reduced as a result of reduced labor and material expenses. Improving manufacturing processes increases plant productivity. Reducing waste and rework, and increasing labor utilization are other potential sources of savings. Non-manufacturing expenses also can be reduced through improved manufacturing flow management. A responsive manufacturing process leads to better order fill rates and orders shipped complete. Not only will order fill increase but it will be achieved faster and with fewer expedited shipments. A process focused on quality in execution will reduce damage and handling expense and perhaps investment in packaging. In addition, a well designed and implemented manufacturing flow management process can reduce human resource costs and improve the effectiveness of employees.

Better manufacturing flow management increases inventory turns and reduces component, work in process, and finished goods inventories. Manufacturing flexibility accommodates demand with less inventory obsolescence. More responsive supply and improved order fill leads to fewer disputes with customers, and reductions in accounts receivable. Finally, better manufacturing flow management improves asset utilization, as well as better investment planning and deployment. It is only through

---

[31] Lambert, Douglas M. and Terrance L. Pohlen, "Supply Chain Metrics," *The International Journal of Logistics Management,* Vol. 12, No. 1 (2001), pp. 1-19; and Croxton, Keely L., Douglas M. Lambert, Dale S. Rogers and Sebastián J. García-Dastugue, "The Demand Management Process," *The International Journal of Logistics Management,* Vol. 13, No. 2 (2002), pp. 51-66.

[32] Bennett, Stewart G., III, *The Quest for Value: A Guide for Managers,* 2nd Edition, New York: Harper Collins, 1999; and Joel M. Stern, "One Way to Build Value in Your Firm, a la Executive Compensation," *Financial Executive,* November-December 1990, pp. 51-54.

Figure 6-5
How Manufacturing Flow Management Affects Economic Value Added (EVA®)

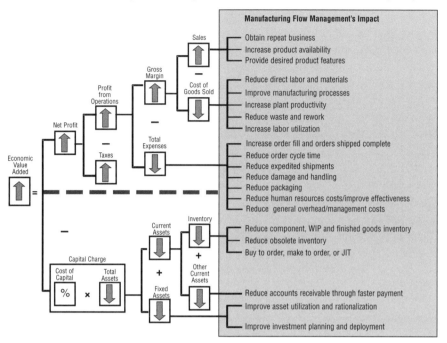

Source: Adapted from Douglas M. Lambert and Terrance L. Pohlen, "Supply Chain Metrics," *The International Journal of Logistics Management*, Vol. 12, No. 1 (2001), p. 10.

demonstrating the manufacturing flow management process' contribution to the greater success of the firm and supply chain that further investments in the process will be justified and rewards for good performance will be determined.

Upon recognizing the impact of manufacturing flow management on the firm's financial performance, as measured by EVA, the team must develop operational metrics that guide behavior in production operations and yield desired performance.

Upon recognizing the impact of manufacturing flow management on the firm's financial performance, as measured by EVA, the team must develop operational metrics that guide behavior in production operations and yield desired performance. The metrics assess efficiency and effectiveness in terms of important performance criteria such as product quality, productivity, cycle time, inventory levels, cost, and safety. The importance of these measures should correlate closely with the prioritization of competitive bases, as determined by the manufacturing strategy and must be tied back to financial measures. The manufacturing flow management team coordinates the metrics with the aid of the customer relationship management team to ensure appropriateness and importance to customers. To the extent possible, the manufacturer should gather both formal and informal input from customers (next-tier customers and end users should they not be the same). Metrics for upstream performance might also be devised for the supplier relationship management team to assess the contribution of suppliers to process performance. In the same way metrics are coordinated with customer relationship management so that the customers reward the firm, metrics are also communicated to supplier relationship management to reward suppliers' efforts to firm success. The manufacturing flow management process will generate input to guide the supplier relationship management team in seeking process improvements from the supply base.

Finally, the framework for metrics should provide the basis for aligning the efforts of the corporate functions. Traditionally, interface between functions focused on efficiency (e.g., production) and functions that are focused on the customers (e.g., marketing) has been a source of conflict. This type of conflict may be resolved through better communication, teamwork, better understanding of the other one's responsibilities, and clarification of goals.[33] The appropriate framework for metrics should facilitate internal integration; it should enable viewing the firm's activities holistically across the corporate functions.

The Operational Manufacturing Flow Management Process

The operational portion of manufacturing flow management is the realization of the process developed at the strategic level. Despite the apparent similarities between the operational sub-processes and the planning and scheduling activities of the production function internal to most manufacturers, key differences exist. These differences include the guidance provided by the infrastructure developed at the strategic level and the interfaces that link the operational sub-processes in a structured way to the other seven supply chain management processes. There are four sub-processes that represent the operational flow. Each is depicted in Figure 6-6.

Determine Routing and Velocity through Manufacturing

The first operational sub-process establishes the execution of the plan set forth in the strategic portion of the process. Determining the routing and velocity of materials and goods through manufacturing is the first step. The demand management process provides critical input to this sub-process, primarily though sharing the aggregate production plan. This plan is based on historical demand, marketing and sales strategies, and general market intelligence and is developed at the product family or group level.

Upon reviewing the aggregate production plan, production management assesses the volume capacity across the manufacturing network and allocates volume to each plant. To the extent that production is outsourced to third parties, the supplier relationship management team will be instrumental in communicating with these external service providers. Each plant then develops its own master production schedule (MPS) that dictates which products to produce, when, and in what quantities. The MPS reflects the manufacturing priorities set forth at the strategic level, recognizing the products and customers that are most important to the manufacturer's profitability by granting them higher priorities. In addition, it reflects the manufacturing strategy among the range of possibilities (buy to order, make to order, assemble to order, make to stock, and ship to stock). Factors such as capacity limitations, manufacturing constraints, production setup time and costs, and inventory carrying costs are considered when developing the MPS.[34] There is communication with the supplier relationship management team to ensure that the

To the extent that production is outsourced to third parties, the supplier relationship management team will be instrumental in communicating with these external service providers.

---

[33] Shaw, Vivienne , Christopher T. Shaw and Margit Enke, "Conflict Between Engineers and Marketers: the Experience of German Engineers," *Industrial Marketing Management,* Vol. 32, No. 6 (2003), pp. 489-499.

[34] Krajewski, Lee J. and Larry P. Ritzman, *Operations Management: Strategy and Analysis,* Reading, MA: Addison-Wesley, 1996.

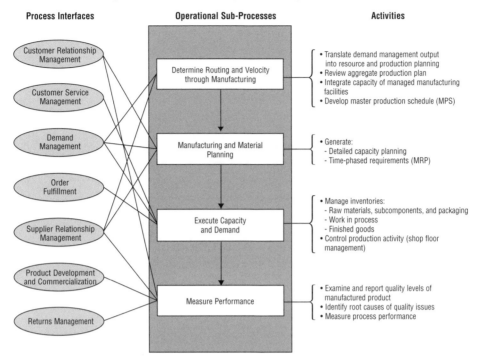

Figure 6-6
The Operational Manufacturing Flow Management Process

Process Interfaces	Operational Sub-Processes	Activities

Process Interfaces:
- Customer Relationship Management
- Customer Service Management
- Demand Management
- Order Fulfillment
- Supplier Relationship Management
- Product Development and Commercialization
- Returns Management

Operational Sub-Processes:
- Determine Routing and Velocity through Manufacturing
- Manufacturing and Material Planning
- Execute Capacity and Demand
- Measure Performance

Activities:
- Determine Routing and Velocity through Manufacturing:
  - Translate demand management output into resource and production planning
  - Review aggregate production plan
  - Integrate capacity of managed manufacturing facilities
  - Develop master production schedule (MPS)
- Manufacturing and Material Planning:
  - Generate:
    - Detailed capacity planning
    - Time-phased requirements (MRP)
- Execute Capacity and Demand:
  - Manage inventories:
    - Raw materials, subcomponents, and packaging
    - Work in process
    - Finished goods
  - Control production activity (shop floor management)
- Measure Performance:
  - Examine and report quality levels of manufactured product
  - Identify root causes of quality issues
  - Measure process performance

As manufacturing firms gain greater flexibility in their operations, less reliance will be placed on advanced planning.

supply base is committed to the accommodation of the manufacturing priorities.

As manufacturing firms gain greater flexibility in their operations, less reliance will be placed on advanced planning. Rather, agility will be emphasized where rapid accommodation of varied customer demands proves both efficient and valued in the marketplace. While flexibility is regarded among the most promising opportunities in manufacturing, most operations remain driven by sales forecasts that subsequently determine routing and velocity.

Manufacturing and Material Planning

Once the MPS is determined, orientation shifts to the detailed planning of capacity and inbound materials necessary to "feed" the production schedule sufficiently. The material requirements plan (MRP) identifies the quantities and timing of all subassemblies, components, and raw materials needed to support production of the end-items.[35] The MRP, therefore, serves as the prime operational interface between manufacturing flow management and supplier relationship management. Along with the MPS, product-specific bills of materials and on-hand inventories drive the MRP explosion that yields the desired quantities of input materials required at any given time to support product flow. The MRP includes not only material inputs for the product but also packaging material.

Next, production management develops the capacity resource plan, which

---

[35] Krajewski, Lee J. and Larry P. Ritzman, *Operations Management: Strategy and Analysis,* Reading, MA: Addison-Wesley, 1996.

represents a time-phased plan of the capacity needed from each resource. Should a capacity or materials shortage be identified, the team will interact, on the one hand, with the demand management team to find possible solutions to the bottleneck from the demand side. On the other hand, the process team will interact with the supplier relationship management process team to work with materials suppliers or with third-party providers, if manufacturing activities are outsourced.

The supplier relationship management team not only prepares suppliers for future material needs but keeps manufacturing informed of any potential hazards or disruptions that might be encountered upstream in the supply chain. Similarly, supplier relationship management will coordinate changes to the MRP in response to changes of demand, rush orders, or capacity-related issues. Management should be aware of other types of contingencies that are not related to daily operational activities. For instance, many North American manufacturers were affected by the West Coast port closures of October 2002, essentially cutting off supply from Asia for a period of several weeks. During such times, customer relationship management may be involved to the extent that problems arise in fulfilling demand. Should capacity prove insufficient to meet the needs of all customers, the demand management team will designate the order of manufacturing priorities.

Execute Capacity and Demand

Execution follows the completed planning process. This sub-process involves frequent interface with the demand management and order fulfillment process teams to maintain efficient flow of materials, work-in-process, and finished goods. Daily verification ensures that schedule attainment is achieved - providing adjustments as necessary. In addition, the supply of packaging materials must be sufficient to ensure that shortages do not disrupt the flow of inbound materials and outbound goods. This is particularly challenging for manufacturers using returnable packaging in a closed-loop system.

Synchronizing available capacity and demand represents the on-going effort to provide sufficient, timely supply with minimal inventories, asset and labor productivity consistent with established standards, and high quality. Timely execution relies on well developed plans and an ability to adapt to variation in the process. Quality programs such as Six Sigma and its associated blackbelt training are popular means to reduce process variance. To the extent that processing time can be lessened and the variance minimized, the manufacturer can better meet customers' changing needs with less disruption and lower costs.[36]

Timely execution relies on well developed plans and an ability to adapt to variation in the process.

Beyond demand management and order fulfillment, the synchronization of capacity and demand calls for interaction with customer service management. This primarily will take the form of executing the order acceptance guidelines established in the strategic sub-process associated with manufacturing capabilities. Customer service failures will be minimal in number and severity if customer service management personnel are prepared to make reasonable promises that affect manufacturing and its support functions. Problems only worsen when unreasonable promises are extended or when problem resolution requires time and resources already dedicated to existing orders. The extension of "reasonable" orders can be

---

[36] George, Michael L., *Lean Six Sigma: Combining Six Sigma Quality with Lean Production Speed,* New York: McGraw-Hill, 2002.

facilitated through order promising, a common feature of manufacturing resource planning (MRP II) systems. MRP II is an expansion of closed-loop MRP to include information to all corporate functions, and order promising is a way to tie customers' orders to product availability.[37] Order acceptance guidelines, developed at the strategic level of manufacturing flow management, should extend beyond product availability and include other order parameters such as required lead time, order size, or changes to existing orders. These guidelines might change based on situational factors. For example, if working below capacity it is likely that the firm may behave more flexibly than if working at full capacity.

Measure Performance

The final operational sub-process involves process assessment and identification of improvement opportunities. The manufacturing flow management process, like all of the other supply chain management processes, spans beyond the four walls of the company. Therefore, the manufacturing flow management team not only must measure performance within the firm's manufacturing plants but also must relate this performance to the broader supply chain.

The manufacturing flow management team regularly tracks performance measures and conveys these metrics to the customer relationship management and supplier relationship management teams.

The manufacturing flow management team regularly tracks performance measures and conveys these metrics to the customer relationship management and supplier relationship management teams. Recognition of improvement opportunities may only be possible through external measurement of performance. With regard to customer satisfaction, for instance, internal measures alone will not capture the disparity between what a customer expects and what is actually delivered. This information can only be obtained by communicating with the customer. The customer relationship management team is well positioned to gather this information on behalf of manufacturing flow management and order fulfillment. The same might be true of problems on the inbound side of the manufacturing operation. For this reason, regular conversation with suppliers through the supplier relationship management team ensures that inbound materials flow with minimal disruption. The customer relationship management and supplier relationship management teams can then use these metrics to generate cost and profitability reports. These reports are valuable when negotiating services with key material and service providers, and when determining rewards for customers and suppliers who have positively influenced the performance of the manufacturing flow management process.[38]

The manufacturing flow management process team must interact with other process teams. For instance, product design flaws or inconsistencies between product design and manufacturing would require the imput of the product development and commercialization process team. In addition, the returns management process can provide important indications of design or manufacturing problems based upon the unfortunate situation of customers recognizing flaws before they can be reconciled internally. Once a root cause is determined, the process teams resolve the problem and informs those within and outside the company that are affected.

---

[37] Markland, Robert E., Shawnee K. Vickery and Robert A. Davis, *Operations Management: Concepts in Manufacturing and Services*, 2nd ed., Cincinnati, Ohio: South-Western College, 1998.

[38] Lambert, Douglas M. and Terrance L. Pohlen, "Supply Chain Metrics," *The International Journal of Logistics Management*, Vol. 12, No. 1 (2001), pp. 1-19.

Conclusions

The manufacturing flow management process deals with establishing and implementing the capabilities for the management of the conversion of materials and components into finished goods demanded by the market. The areas of operations management, operations research, and industrial engineering are well versed in recognizing new, better ways to perform the conversion activities within the four walls of the manufacturer. Supply chain management, on the other hand, seeks ways to improve performance by leveraging the capabilities of not only the production function within the firm but also the capabilities of supply chain members. While manufacturing flow management represents only one of the eight supply chain management processes, it is a critical driver of success for all supply chain members.

Successful implementation requires the involvement of customers and suppliers in the manufacturing flow management process. This involvement is coordinated through the customer relationship management and supplier relationship management teams, respectively. In fact, customer relationship management interfaces with all five of the strategic sub-processes and two of the four operational sub-processes. Supplier relationship management is involved in four of five strategic sub-processes and three of four operational sub-processes. It is not only through internal efforts of the manufacturer but through the efforts of material and service providers that the desired degree of manufacturing flexibility is achieved.

Capturing demand information and better managing demand is critical to the manufacturing flow management process. The close relationship between manufacturing flow management and demand management is characterized by the many interfaces between these two processes. The ability of the demand management process to anticipate demand with precision alleviates the need of the manufacturing system to be flexible. However, the trend in most industries is one of frequent and often dramatic change, driving the need for greater flexibility.

Economic value added analysis was introduced as a way to help sell the value of manufacturing flow management as a supply chain management process. The financial benefits must be clear within the firm and with other members of the supply chain to gain buy-in and long-term commitment. When value can be demonstrated, management wants to know how quickly the benefits can be achieved.

When value can be demonstrated, management wants to know how quickly the benefits can be achieved.

7 The Supplier Relationship Management Process

Douglas M. Lambert

Overview

The supplier relationship management process provides the structure for how relationships with suppliers are developed and maintained. Close relationships are developed with a small set of key suppliers based on the value that they provide to the organization over time, and more traditional relationships are maintained with the others. In this chapter, detailed descriptions of the strategic and operational sub-processes that comprise supplier relationship management are provided. Also, there are descriptions of the interfaces that are necessary with the other seven supply chain management processes identified by The Global Supply Chain Forum and each of the corporate functions. Guidelines for successful implementation are provided.

Introduction

The cost of materials as a percentage of sales has been estimated at approximately 53 percent for all types of manufacturing in the United States. These costs range from a low of 27 percent for tobacco products to a high of 83 percent for petroleum and coal products but most industries are in the 45 – 60 percent range.[1] For wholesalers and retailers, the cost of goods sold is higher than the materials costs of manufacturers. These numbers indicate the magnitude of the benefits that are possible through better management of the supplier network.

Supplier relationship management is the supply chain management process that provides the structure for how relationships with suppliers are developed and maintained.

Supplier relationship management is the supply chain management process that provides the structure for how relationships with suppliers are developed and maintained. As the name suggests, it is a mirror image of customer relationship management. Just as close relationships need to be developed with key customers, management should forge close relationships with a small number of key suppliers, and maintain more traditional relationships with the others.[2] Management

---

[1] Stock, James R. and Douglas M. Lambert, *Strategic Logistics Management*, 4th Ed,. New York, NY: McGraw Hill/Irwin, 2001.

[2] Dyer, Jeffery H., Dong Sung Cho and Wujin Wu, "Strategic Supplier Segmentation: The Next 'Best Practice' in Supply Chain Management," *California Management Review*, Vol. 40, No. 2 (1998), pp. 57-77.

identifies those suppliers and supplier groups to be targeted as part of the firm's business mission. Supplier relationship management teams work with key suppliers to tailor product and service agreements (PSA) to meet the organization's needs, as well as those of the selected suppliers. Standard PSAs are crafted for segments of other suppliers. Supplier relationship management is about developing and managing the PSAs. Teams work with key suppliers to improve processes, and eliminate demand variability and non-value-added activities. The goal is to develop PSAs that address the major business drivers of both the organization and the supplier. Performance reports are designed to measure the profit impact of individual suppliers as well as the firm's impact on the profitability of suppliers.

Supplier relationship management teams work with key suppliers to tailor product and service agreements (PSA) to meet the organization's needs, as well as those of the selected suppliers.

Supplier relationship management has become a critical business process as a result of: competitive pressures; the need to achieve cost efficiency in order to be cost competitive; and, the need to develop closer relationships with key suppliers who can provide the expertise necessary to develop innovative new products and successfully bring them to market. Supplier relationship management is one of the eight processes and it must interface with each of the other seven (see Figure 7-1). A description of the strategic and operational processes that comprise supplier relationship management is provided along with the sub-processes and their activities. Also, there are descriptions of the interfaces with functions, the other supply chain management processes and other firms. Finally, conclusions are presented.

Figure 7-1
Supply Chain Management:
Integrating and Managing Business Processes Across the Supply Chain

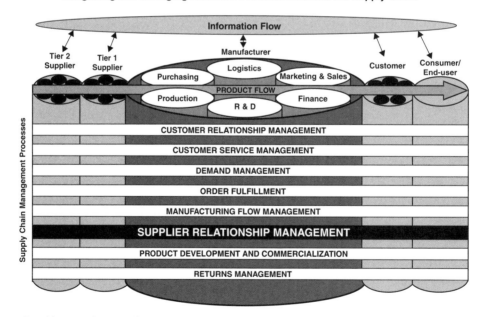

Source: Adapted from Douglas M. Lambert, Martha C. Cooper, and Janus D. Pagh, "Supply Chain Management: Implementation Issues and Research Opportunities," *The International Journal of Logistics Management,* Vol. 9, No. 2 (1998), p. 2.

Supplier Relationship Management as a Supply Chain Management Process

Supplier relationship management and customer relationship management provide the critical linkages throughout the supply chain (see Figure 7-2). For each supplier, the ultimate measure of success for the customer relationship management process is the change in profitability of the customer. For each customer, the measure of success for the supplier relationship management process is the impact that the supplier has on the firm's profitability. The supplier relationship management process has both strategic and operational elements. Therefore, we have divided the process into two parts, the strategic process in which the firm establishes and strategically manages the process, and the operational process which is the actualization of the process once it has been established (see Figure 7-3). Implementation of the strategic process within the firm is a necessary step in integrating the firm with suppliers, and it is at the operational level that the day-to-day activities take place. The strategic process is led by a management team. At the operational level, there will be teams established for each key supplier and for each segment of non-key suppliers. The teams are comprised of managers from several functions, including marketing, finance, production, purchasing and logistics. At the strategic level, the team is responsible for developing the strategic process, and seeing that it is implemented. At the operational level, supplier teams have the day-to-day responsibility for managing the process. Firm employees outside of the teams might execute parts of the process, but the teams still maintain managerial control.

Figure 7-2
Customer Relationship Management (CRM) and Supplier Relationship Management (SRM):
The Critical Supply Chain Management Linkages

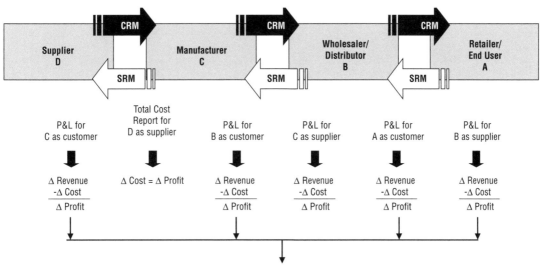

Source: Adapted from Douglas M. Lambert and Terrance L. Pohlen, "Supply Chain Metrics," *The International Journal of Logistics Management,* Vol. 12, No. 1 (2001), p. 14.

Figure 7-3
Supplier Relationship Management

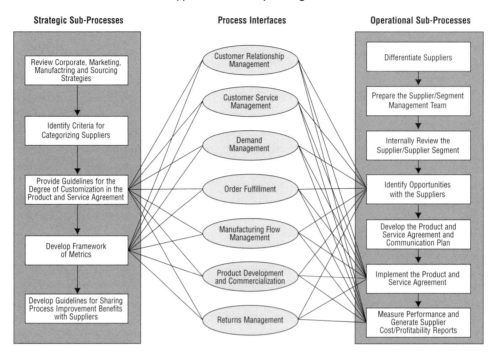

Source: Adapted from Keely L. Croxton, Sebastián J. García-Dastugue, Douglas M. Lambert and Dale S. Rogers, "The Supply Chain Management Processes," *The International Journal of Logistics Management,* Vol. 12, No. 2 (2001), p. 15.

The Strategic Supplier Relationship Management Process

At the strategic level, the supplier relationship management process provides the structure for how relationships with suppliers will be developed and managed. It is comprised of five sub-processes (see Figure 7-4) and includes a key supplier component.

Review Corporate, Marketing, Manufacturing and Sourcing Strategies

The supplier relationship management process team reviews the corporate strategy, and the marketing, manufacturing and sourcing strategies, in order to identify supplier segments that are critical to the organization's success now and in the future. The supplier network is a key part of profitable business development since it will impact: the quality of products, product availability, the time to market for new products, and access to critical technology. By reviewing these strategies, management identifies the supplier types with whom the firm needs to develop long-term relationships. For example, at Colgate-Palmolive Company stretch financial goals led management in the oral care business to the conclusion that closer, partnership type, relationships were necessary with key suppliers. Management believed that these relationships would result in product innovations that would enable the business to achieve the financial goals.

The supplier relationship management process team reviews the corporate strategy, and the marketing, manufacturing and sourcing strategies, in order to identify supplier segments that are critical to the organization's success now and in the future.

Figure 7-4
The Strategic Supplier Relationship Management Process

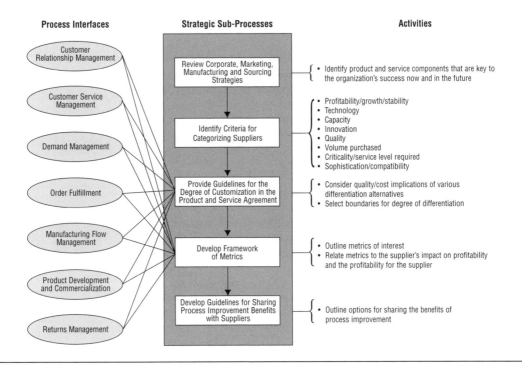

Identify Criteria for Categorizing Suppliers

In the second sub-process, the team identifies the criteria that can be used to categorize suppliers. This includes providing guidelines for determining with which suppliers the firm should develop tailored PSAs and which suppliers will be grouped and offered a standard PSA that is developed to meet the firm's goals as well as generate a reasonable profit for the supplier. Potential criteria include: profitability; growth and stability; the criticality of the service level necessary; the sophistication and compatibility of the supplier's process implementation; the supplier's technology capability and compatibility; the volume purchased from the supplier; the capacity available from the supplier; the culture of innovation at the supplier; and, the supplier's anticipated quality levels.[3]

The team determines which criteria to use and how suppliers will be evaluated on each criterion. A categorization scheme is developed that will be used at the operational level to identify key suppliers and segments of other suppliers. At Wendy's International, a matrix is used to compare suppliers on the basis of the complexity of the commodity for Wendy's and the volume of the spend (see Figure 7-5).

Items that are low in complexity and low in terms of the expenditure are *non-critical* items such as straws. *Bottlenecks* are items for which Wendy's does not spend much money but are very complex such as cooking oil. *Leverage* items are

A categorization scheme is developed that will be used at the operational level to identify key suppliers and segments of other suppliers.

[3] Burt, David, N., Donald W. Dobler and Stephen L. Starling, *World Class Supply Management,* New York, NY: McGraw-Hill/Irwin, 2003.

Figure 7-5
Comparing Suppliers on Complexity and Volume

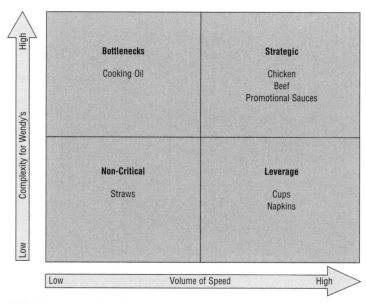

Source: Judy Hollis, Vice President, Wendy's Internatonal

those for which Wendy's spends a lot of money but the items are not complex or strategic to the business. The goal for these items is to improve service by such things as reducing lead times. Finally, *strategic* items are those that are both high in complexity and high in the amount spent per year. These items for Wendy's include chicken, beef and promotional sauces. Generally, Wendy's management tries to move items from the bottleneck quadrant to the non-critical or to the leverage quadrant. Management's goal was to move cooking oil from the bottleneck category to the leverage category, but it was actually moved to the strategic category as a result of product innovation with Cargill, a key supplier.

Masterfoods USA uses a matrix that is similar to Wendy's, but substitutes "supply risk" for "complexity" and "contribution potential" for "volume of spend". The fewer the number of suppliers the more Masterfoods moves up on the low to high scale for supply risk. The mid point on the low to high "contribution potential" scale is $500,000. The savings potential must exceed $500,000 for the supplier to be in either of the categories on the right side of the matrix (Strategic and Leverage quadrants).

Provide Guidelines for the Degree of Differentiation in the Product and Service Agreement

In the third sub-process, the team develops guidelines for the degree of differentiation in the PSA. This involves developing the differentiation alternatives and considering the revenue and cost implications of each. To do this, the team considers the quality and cost implications of various differentiation alternatives, and selects the boundaries for the degree of customization. The team must

...the team develops guidelines for the degree of differentiation in the PSA. This involves developing the differentiation alternatives and considering the revenue and cost implications of each.

interface with each of the other processes in order to understand the degree of differentiation that is desirable as well as be ready to design supporting systems to aid in implementation. For example, the demand management process team may want to share with key suppliers demand information from Collaborative Planning, Forecasting and Replenishment implementations with customers. Investments in technology may be necessary for this to be successful.[4] At Masterfoods USA, the PSA represents a letter of intent that covers five key areas: cost, innovation, supply chain, quality, and environment.

Develop Framework of Metrics

Developing the framework of metrics involves outlining the metrics of interest and relating them to the supplier's impact on the firm's profitability as well as the firm's impact on the supplier's profitability. The supplier relationship management process team has the responsibility for assuring that the metrics used to measure supplier performance do not conflict with the metrics used in the other processes. Management needs to insure that all internal and external measures are driving consistent and appropriate behavior.[5]

Figure 7-6 shows how the supplier relationship management process can affect the firm's financial performance as measured by economic value added (EVA). It illustrates how supplier relationship management can impact sales, cost of goods sold, total expenses, inventory investment, other current assets, and the investment in fixed assets. For example, supplier relationship management can lead to higher sales volume by improving the quality of materials and the service obtained from suppliers. Higher quality products will enable the firm to charge higher prices and/or increase unit sales. Improved service from suppliers might enable the firm to provide better service to its customers and thus lead to increased sales.

Cost of goods sold can be reduced as a result of better planning and fewer last minute production changes, less expediting of materials as well as lower costs for direct materials. In Wendy's case, these savings occur in suppliers' operations and they share the savings with Wendy's through price reductions.

A number of expenses can be reduced as a result of: increased productivity; lower freight and receiving costs; realignment of network facilities; lower order management costs; lower information system costs; improved management of human resources; and, lower general overhead and administrative costs.

Supplier relationship management can lead to lower inventories of purchased materials, in-process inventories and finished goods inventories. Improvement in suppliers' order fulfillment and on-time delivery performance will result in lower safety stock needs for all three types of inventory. Finally, better supplier relationship management can lead to lower fixed assets as a result of improved asset utilization and rationalization (warehousing and plant facilities), and improved investment planning and deployment.

> *The supplier relationship management process team has the responsibility for assuring that the metrics used to measure supplier performance do not conflict with the metrics used in the other processes.*

---

[4] Skjoett-Larsen, Tage, Christian Thernoe and Claus Andresen, "Supply Chain Collaboration: Theoretical Perspectives and Empirical Evidence", *International Journal of Physical Distribution & Logistics Management*, Vol. 33, No. 6 (2003), pp. 531 – 549; and, Gene Fliedner, "CPFR: An Emerging Supply Chain Tool", *Industrial Management and Data Systems*, Vol. 103, No. 1 (2003), pp.14-21.

[5] Lambert, Douglas M. and Terrance L. Pohlen, "Supply Chain Metrics", *The International Journal of Logistics Management*, Vol. 12, No. 1 (2001), pp.1-19.

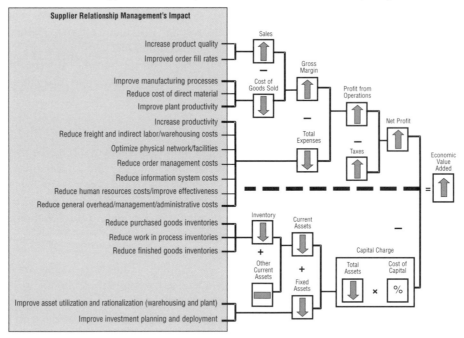

Source: Adapted from Douglas M. Lambert and Terrance L. Pohlen, "Supply Chain Metrics," *The International Journal of Logistics Management,* Vol. 12, No. 1 (2001), p. 11.

Once the team has an understanding of how supplier relationship management can impact the firm's financial performance as measured by EVA, metrics must be developed for each of the individual activities performed and these metrics must be tied back to financial performance. Management should implement initiatives that increase the profitability of the total supply chain not just the profitability of a single firm. It is the goal of supply chain management to encourage actions that benefit the whole supply chain while at the same time equally sharing in the risks and rewards. If the management of a firm makes a decision that positively affect that firm's EVA at the expense of the EVA of a supplier or a customer, every effort should be made to share the benefits in a manner that improves the financial performance of each firm involved and thus gives each one an incentive to improve supply chain performance.

At the wholesale and retail level, the development of supplier profitability reports enables the process team to track performance over time. If calculated as shown in Table 7-1, these reports reflect all of the cost and revenue implications of the relationship. Cost of good sold is deducted from net sales to calculate a gross margin. Then, revenue adjustments such as discounts and allowances, market development funds, slotting allowances and co-operative advertising allowances must be added to achieve a net margin. Next, variable marketing and logistics costs are deducted to calculate a contribution margin. Assignable non-variable costs, such as salaries, advertising, and inventory carrying costs less a charge for accounts payable, are subtracted to obtain a segment controllable margin. These

Once the team has an understanding of how supplier relationship management can impact the firm's financial performance as measured by EVA, metrics must be developed for each of the individual activities performed and these metrics must be tied back to financial performance.

Table 7-1
Supplier Profitability Analysis:
A Contribution Approach With Charge for Assets Employed

	Supplier A	Supplier B	Supplier C	Supplier D
Sales				
Cost of Goods Sold				
Gross Margin				
Plus: Discounts and Allowances				
Market Development Funds				
Slotting Allowances				
Co-operative Advertising Allowances				
Net Margin				
Variable Marketing and Logistics Costs:				
Transportation				
Receiving				
Order Processing				
Order Costs (will depend on situation)				
Controllable Margin				
Assignable Nonvariable Costs				
Salaries				
Advertising				
Inventory Carrying Costs Less:				
Charge for Accounts Payable				
Other Costs (will depend on situation)				
Segment Controllable Margin				

statements contain opportunity costs for investment in inventory. Consequently, they are much closer to cash flow statements than a traditional profit and loss statement. They contain revenues minus the costs (avoidable costs) that disappear if the revenue disappears.

Supplier profitability reports can be constructed by wholesalers and retailers but it might not be possible for manufacturers to develop these reports for the suppliers of undifferentiated components and materials. In this case, total cost reports are used along with calculations of the total delivered cost per unit purchased. Total cost reports should include the purchase price plus transportation costs, inventory carrying costs, financial impact of terms of sale, ordering costs, receiving costs, quality costs and administrative costs.

Develop Guidelines for Sharing Process Improvement Benefits with Suppliers

The goal is to make process improvements win-win solutions for both the firm and the supplier.

In the final sub-process, the team develops the guidelines for sharing process improvement benefits with suppliers. The goal is to make process improvements win-win solutions for both the firm and the supplier. If both parties do not gain from the relationship, it will be difficult to gain the supplier's full commitment to the firm's goals. The supplier relationship management team must find ways to quantify the benefits for process improvements in financial terms. At Masterfoods USA, suppliers are given a 100% of the benefits derived from cost savings projects until they recover the entire investment that has been made and make an agreed upon level of profit. After that point has been reached, 100% of the benefits go to Masterfoods USA. The goal is to encourage suppliers to keep improving and to avoid becoming complacent.

At Wendy's International, the following description of cost savings initiatives and gain sharing is attached to the terms and conditions of every PSA:

Supplier shall in good faith endeavor, throughout the term of this Agreement, to continually reduce the cost of the services and products it provides hereunder and be responsible to present to Wendy's potential cost savings initiatives on a semi-annual basis. Cost savings may occur in specification changes (as agreed upon by both parties), changes in manufacturing capabilities or other potential cost efficiency areas to be agreed upon by the parties. Wendy's and Supplier agree to review, not less than semi-annually, Supplier's satisfaction of Wendy's reasonable cost and efficiency standards and to reasonably and in good faith improve the cost and efficiency of the Approved Products if and to the extent reasonable in light of the then applicable requirements as set forth by Wendy's, acting reasonably. Supplier shall use its commercially reasonable and good faith efforts to satisfy any such heightened or more stringent standards that the parties agree to pursuant to such semi-annual reviews.

Gain sharing arrangement for multi-year Agreements:

- Supplier will deliver 2% minimum annual cost savings on controllable portion of costs.
- 1st year – cost savings generated in year 1 as a result of supplier idea or joint development will be retained by the supplier.
- 2nd year – cost savings generated in year 2 as a result of supplier idea or joint development will be shared between Wendy's and the supplier at a ratio of 50% : 50%.
- 3rd year – cost savings generated in year 3 as a result of supplier idea or joint development will be passed along to Wendy's.
- Any cost savings generated by an idea proposed exclusively by Wendy's that does not require capital investment by supplier will be immediately passed along to Wendy's.[6]

In summary, the objective of supplier relationship management at the strategic level is to identify supplier segments, provide criteria for categorizing suppliers, provide supplier teams with guidelines for customizing the product and service offering, develop a framework of metrics, and provide guidelines for the sharing of process improvement benefits with the suppliers.

The Operational Supplier Relationship Management Process

At the operational level, the supplier relationship management process deals with writing and implementing the PSAs. It is comprised of seven sub-processes: differentiate suppliers; prepare the supplier/segment management team; internally review the supplier/supplier segment; identify opportunities with the suppliers; develop the product/service agreements and communication plans; implement the product/service agreements; and, measure performance and generate supplier cost/profitability reports (see Figure 7-7).

At the operational level, the supplier relationship management process deals with writing and implementing the PSAs.

---

[6] Wendy's International, "Additional Terms and Conditions".

Figure 7-7
The Operational Supplier Relationship Management Process

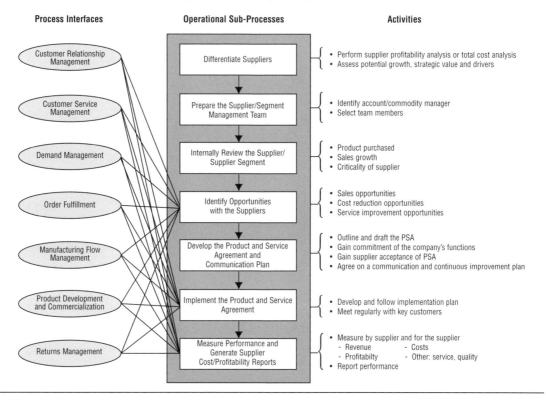

Process Interfaces	Operational Sub-Processes	Activities
Customer Relationship Management	Differentiate Suppliers	• Perform supplier profitability analysis or total cost analysis • Assess potential growth, strategic value and drivers
Customer Service Management	Prepare the Supplier/Segment Management Team	• Identify account/commodity manager • Select team members
Demand Management	Internally Review the Supplier/ Supplier Segment	• Product purchased • Sales growth • Criticality of supplier
Order Fulfillment	Identify Opportunities with the Suppliers	• Sales opportunities • Cost reduction opportunities • Service improvement opportunities
Manufacturing Flow Management	Develop the Product and Service Agreement and Communication Plan	• Outline and draft the PSA • Gain commitment of the company's functions • Gain supplier acceptance of PSA • Agree on a communication and continuous improvement plan
Product Development and Commercialization	Implement the Product and Service Agreement	• Develop and follow implementation plan • Meet regularly with key customers

Returns Management	Measure Performance and Generate Supplier Cost/Profitability Reports	• Measure by supplier and for the supplier
		  - Revenue - Costs
		  - Profitabilty - Other: service, quality
		• Report performance

Differentiate Suppliers

In the first sub-process, suppliers are differentiated based on the criteria that were established in the strategic process. A key measure is how each supplier contributes to the firm's profitability both current and potential. Other criteria might include: growth, stability, technology, capacity, innovation, quality, volume purchased, criticality, service level required, sophistication, and compatibility.

At Masterfoods USA, individual packaging suppliers are categorized using the framework shown in Figure 7-8. The four categories are niche, core, assessment and potential. *Niche* suppliers provide a unique offering. *Core* suppliers are categorized as such based on the percentage of spend with the supplier, the supplier's focus on the company's business (similar thinking around quality, innovation, commitment, etc), the potential for a long-term relationship (two suppliers have been associated with the company for 50 years), and the ability to have an open relationship. *Assessment* refers to suppliers who are under development. They can be a niche or core supplier that has the potential to grow, one that requires intensive care, or one that is temporary. *Potential* suppliers are not current suppliers but there are reasons for having interest in them such as size, technology, innovation or diversity.

At Wendy's International, management performs an industry analysis including consideration of strengths, weaknesses, opportunities and threats that helps differentiate among suppliers. For example, no single supplier can fill all of

Figure 7-8
Categorizing Packaging Suppliers of Masterfoods USA

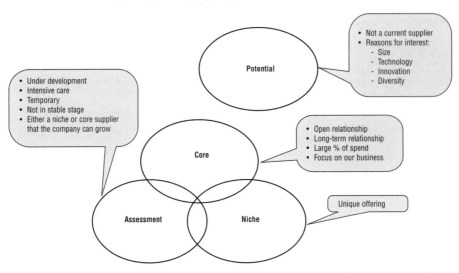

Wendy's needs for chicken. One supplier is a low cost supplier who gets 60 percent of Wendy's volume and guides Wendy's in its dealing with all chicken suppliers in terms of where there are opportunities for cost reduction. Another supplier, who has 30 percent of the volume, is a leader in research and development and generates new products for Wendy's. But, this supplier cannot meet all of Wendy's needs, and must share these innovations with Wendy's other suppliers. Since this supplier conducted the research, it will receive 40 percent of the first year volume of the new products. The final 10 percent of the volume goes to a minority supplier to satisfy Wendy's corporate goal to encourage diversity. The output of this sub-process is the identification of which suppliers are key to the firm and which suppliers are grouped into segments.

Prepare the Supplier/Segment Management Team

In this sub-process, the account or segment management teams are formed, including the buyer who will be supplier or supplier segment relationship manager. The teams are cross-functional with representation from each of the functional areas. In the case of key suppliers, each team is dedicated to a specific supplier and meets regularly with a team from the supplier organization. In the case of supplier segments, a team manages a group of suppliers and develops and manages the standard PSA for the segment. Each supplier/segment team is comprised of a team manager and a cross-functional group of members. At Wendy's International, the criteria that are used to identify the key suppliers are also used to identify critical team members. For an example, Marzetti's is a supplier of promotional sauces which Wendy's management views as strategic. The development of new sauces is a critical component of this relationship which means that research and development personnel must be part of the Wendy's supplier relationship management team and the Marzetti's customer relationship management team.

In the case of key suppliers, each team is dedicated to a specific supplier and meets regularly with a team from the supplier organization.

Internally Review the Supplier/Supplier Segment

Each supplier/segment team reviews their supplier or segment of suppliers to determine the role that the supplier or segment of suppliers plays in the supply chain. A supplier team works with each supplier or segment of suppliers to identify improvement opportunities. The team examines each of the other supply chain management processes, both at the firm and at the supplier or supplier segment to identify opportunities for improvement.

Identify Opportunities with the Suppliers

Once the teams have an understanding of the supplier(s), they work with each supplier or segment of suppliers to develop improvement opportunities. These opportunities might arise from any of the supply chain management processes, so the account teams need to interface with each of the other processes. Wendy's uses the partnership model, described in Chapter 10, to structure relationships with key suppliers. Out of these partnership sessions both Wendy's and the supplier gain knowledge about the business drivers for the other firm. This leads to goal setting that becomes an ongoing part of the quarterly business review between the firms. Also, the Wendy's buyers prepare a scorecard for each of their suppliers in which the drivers are included. Masterfoods USA and Colgate-Palmolive Company are also using the partnership model with key suppliers. In fact, Masterfoods USA has used it with a Tier 1 supplier and also with the Tier 2 supplier who provides the key ingredient to the Tier 1 supplier.

Develop the Product and Service Agreement and Communication Plan

For key suppliers, the team negotiates a mutually beneficial PSA, and then gains commitment from the supplier's internal functions.

In the fifth sub-process, each team develops the PSA for their supplier or segment of suppliers. For key suppliers, the team negotiates a mutually beneficial PSA, and then gains commitment from the supplier's internal functions. They work with the suppliers until agreement has been reached. It is important that the PSA for key suppliers include a communication and continuous improvement plan. For segments of non-key suppliers, a standard PSA is developed for each segment. These represent the minimum requirements to be a supplier and they are not negotiable. At Wendy's, supplier relationship management teams prepare a negotiation plan for meetings with key suppliers to develop the PSAs. What does Wendy's want to have versus what does it need to have? It is important to prioritize initiatives and negotiate the best solution if all of them are not possible. Items that Wendy's includes in the PSA include the cost savings initiative described earlier as well as goals for spending with minority-owned business.

> Suppliers will make a good faith effort to competitively purchase goods and/or services directly related to the goods covered in this Agreement from Historically Underutilized Businesses (HUB's), also commonly referred to as minority-owned business. Supplier shall report all HUB sending on a quarterly basis to Wendy's.[7]

Additional items that may included in Wendy's PSA with suppliers are the following:

- **Open-book Costing.** Supplier shall provide a monthly detailed

---

[7] Wendy's International, Exhibit B, "Additional Terms and Conditions".

breakdown of all applicable actual costs as they relate to pricing and costs affecting Wendy's business and the Approved Products.

- **Key Business Review.** Supplier and Wendy's shall meet regularly for the purpose of conducting business reviews to review the plans and expectations as outlined in the Agreement.
- **Diversity Clause.** Supplier agrees to seek out first and second-tier diversity suppliers where applicable to the Wendy's business.
- **Written Contingency Plans.** Supplier shall provide, in writing, detailed and executable contingency plans applicable for Supplier to insure continuity of supply.
- **Weekly Volume and Pricing Reports.** Supplier shall provide to Wendy's in writing at such time periods and in a form as reasonably required by Wendy's, volume and applicable prices sold to Wendy's Approved Distributors and restaurants.[8]

At Masterfoods USA the PSAs include an eight step vendor assurance program (shown in Table 7-2) that is described in company documents as follows:

Vendor Assurance requires that we seek and develop relationships with those suppliers who have the ability, currently or potentially, to meet Masterfoods USA standards and specifications consistently. This confidence building process is a joint activity between Masterfoods and the Supplier, and is grounded on the Mutuality Principle. As our partners, vendors need a thorough knowledge of the specific way in which we will use their product. Open communications will help them to understand our reasons to increasing conformance. Masterfoods' goal is a vendor certification of quality achievement which requires a minimum auditing by ourselves and which assures that materials will perform reliably over time.[9]

Implement the Product and Service Agreement

In the sixth sub-process, the team implements the PSA, which includes holding regular planning sessions with key suppliers. The supplier relationship management teams provide input to each of the other supply chain management processes that are affected by the customizations that have been made in the PSAs. Supplier relationship management teams must work with other processes to assure that the PSA is being implemented as determined, and meet with suppliers on a regular basis to monitor progress and performance. At Wendy's, the PSAs are reviewed at the quarterly business meetings to ensure that implementation is taking place as planned. Depending on the supplier involved, as many as 50 people can participate in these quarterly business reviews.

The supplier relationship management teams provide input to each of the other supply chain management processes that are affected by the customizations that have been made in the PSAs.

Measure Performance and Generate Supplier Cost/Profitability Reports

In the last operational sub-process, the team captures and reports the process performance measures. Metrics from each of the other processes also are captured in order to generate the supplier cost/profitability reports. These reports provide information for measuring and selling the value of the relationship to each supplier

---

[8] Wendy's International, "Additional Terms and Conditions".

[9] Masterfoods USA.

Table 7-2
Vendor Assurance: The Eight Steps

Step 1	**Specifications.** The concept of Vendor Assurance is explained to the vendor and the mutual commitment to Vendor Assurance established. The specifications of the goods or service to be purchased are explained and their content discussed.
Step 2	**Process Description.** Good manufacturing practices and environmental responsibility are demonstrated by the vendor. A detailed description of the vendor's normal process is provided in confidence and forms the basis of the Vendor File.
Step 3	**Risk Assessment.** Jointly, hazards are identified, risks are quantified, and Critical Control Points associated with the vendor's process are located.
Step 4	**Quality Management.** Existing quality systems to minimize risks are assessed and documented. Where necessary, additional methods to monitor and control key areas are implemented. A commitment and positive attitude to quality improvement are demonstrated by the vendor.
Step 5	**Conformance.** The vendor provides data that demonstrates his process is capable of consistently meeting his customers' requirements.
Step 6	**Review.** The periods' activities are reviewed, confirming that the customers' requirements are met, assuring incoming materials can be accepted based on vendor data, and identifying areas for improvement.
Step 7	**Mutual Development.** Exchanged visits between Mars, Incorporated and the vendor by relevant personnel from all parts of both companies occur, as appropriate, to better understand one another's processes, needs, limitations, specifications and quality performance.
Step 8	**Continue Commitment to Quality.** Enduring business relationships are established which motivate vendors to continuously improve quality, costs, and responsiveness to our mutual benefits. This will be assured by regular audits as part of normal communications between partners.

Source: Masterfoods USA

and internally to upper management. The value provided should be measured in terms of costs, impact on sales, and associated investment, otherwise the efforts incurred will go unrewarded.[10]

The other process teams communicate supplier-related performance to the supplier teams who tie these metrics back to the profitability of the firm and the profitability of its suppliers. Wendy's regularly schedules comprehensive performance reviews with key suppliers at quarterly business meetings. Less critical suppliers might have less frequent review meetings but all suppliers meet with Wendy's personnel at least once per year to review performance.

Conclusions

The ultimate measure of success of each relationship is the impact that it is having on the financial performance of the firms involved.

Supplier relationship management provides the structure for how relationships with suppliers are developed and maintained, including the establishment of PSAs between the firm and its suppliers. It is a key supply chain management process which along with the customer relationship management process combines to form the critical linkages that connect firms in the supply chain. Supply chain management is about relationship management and the supply chain is managed link-by-link, relationship-by-relationship. The ultimate measure of success of each relationship is the impact that it is having on the financial performance of the firms involved. Consequently, it is necessary for each

[10] Lambert, Douglas M. and Terrance L. Pohlen, "Supply Chain Metrics", *The International Journal of Logistics Management*, Vol. 12, No. 1 (2001), pp.1-19.

firm to have the capability of measuring the performance of both supplier relationship management and customer relationship management in terms of their impact on incremental revenues and costs. With this knowledge, it will be possible to develop programs that improve supply chain performance and negotiate sharing of benefits and costs so that all of the involved players have the incentive to participate.

The Product Development and Commercialization Process

Dale S. Rogers, Douglas M. Lambert and A. Michael Knemeyer

Overview

Product development and commercialization is the supply chain management process that provides structure for developing and bringing to market new products jointly with customers and suppliers.[1] Effective implementation of the process not only enables management to coordinate the efficient flow of new products across the supply chain, but also assists supply chain members with the ramp-up of manufacturing, logistics, marketing and other related activities to support the commercialization of the product. In this chapter, the product development and commercialization process is described in detail to show how it can be implemented. To do this, the process is described in terms of its sub-processes and associated activities, and the interfaces with business functions, other supply chain management processes and other firms. Examples of successful implementation are provided.

Developing products rapidly and moving them into the marketplace efficiently is important for long-term corporate success.

Introduction

The product development and commercialization process requires effective planning and execution throughout the supply chain, and if managed correctly can provide a sustainable competitive advantage. Developing products rapidly and moving them into the marketplace efficiently is important for long-term corporate success.[2] In many markets, 40 percent or more of revenues come from products introduced in the prior year.[3]

While the creation of successful products is a multidisciplinary process,[4]

---

[1] This chapter is based on Dale S. Rogers, Douglas M. Lambert and A. Michael Knemeyer, "The Product Development and Commercialization Process," *The International Journal of Logistics Management*, Vol. 15, No. 1 (2004), pp. 43-56.

[2] Cooper, Robert G., Scott J. Edgett, and Elko J. Kleinschmidt, *Protfolio Management for New Products*, Reading, MA: Perseus Books, 1998.

[3] Handfield, Robert B. and Ernest L. Nichols, Jr., *Supply Chain Redesign*, Upper Saddle River, NJ: Financial Times Prentice Hall, 2002.

[4] Olson, Eric M., Orville C. Walker, Jr., Robert W. Ruekert, and Joseph M. Bonner, "Patterns of Cooperation During New Product Development Among Marketing, Operations and R&D: Implications for Project Performance," *The Journal of Product Innovation Management*, Vol. 18, No. 4 (2001), pp. 258-271.

product development and commercialization from a supply chain management perspective integrates both customers[5] and suppliers[6] into the process in order to reduce time to market. The ability to reduce time to market is key to innovation success and profitability[7] as well as the most critical objective of the process.[8] As product life cycles shorten, the right products must be developed and successfully launched in ever-shorter time frames in order to remain competitive[9] and achieve differentiation in the market place.

The product development and commercialization process requires the integration of customers and suppliers and the alignment of their activities. Successful implementation requires metrics that measure the financial impact on the firm and on other members of the supply chain.

Product development and commercialization is one of the eight supply chain management processes and it requires interfaces with the other seven (see Figure 8-1). In this chapter, we review the different types of product development and relevant definitions. Then, we describe the strategic and operational processes that comprise the product development and commercialization process. Finally, we present conclusions.

...product development and commercialization from a supply chain management perspective integrates both customers and suppliers into the process in order to reduce time to market.

Types of Product Development Projects

Product development projects can be classified as one of the following four types:[10]

- **New product platforms:** This type of project involves a major development effort to create a family of products based on a new, common platform. The product family addresses familiar markets and product categories. Moen Incorporated's project involving the Revolution Massaging Showerhead is an example. This product offers several features not available with any of their other products

- **Derivatives of existing product platforms:** These projects extend an existing product platform to better address familiar markets with one or more new products. Sony Corporation, by using common components in successive generations of the Sony Walkman, achieved higher quality throughout the platform life.[11]

---

[5] Karkkainen, Hannu and Petteri Piippo, "Ten Tools for Customer-driven Product Development in Industrial Companies," *International Journal of Production Economics*, Vol. 69, No. 2 (2001), pp. 161-176.

[6] Schilling, Melissa A. and Charles W. L. Hill, "Managing the New Product Development Process: Strategic Imperatives," *Academy of Management Executive*, Vol. 12, No. 3 (1998), pp. 67-82.

[7] Dröge, Cornelia, Jayanth Jayaram and Shawnee K Vickery, "The Ability to Minimize the Timing of New Product Development and Introduction: An Examination of Antecedent Factors in the North American Automobile Supplier Industry," *The Journal of Product Innovation Management*, Vol. 17, No. 1 (2000), pp. 24-37.

[8] Schilling, Melissa A. and Charles W. L. Hill, "Managing the New Product Development Process: Strategic Imperatives," *Academy of Management Executive*, Vol. 12, No. 3 (1998), pp. 67-82.

[9] Zacharia, Zach G., "Research and Development in Supply Chain Management," in *Supply Chain Management*, ed. John T. Mentzer., Thousand Oaks, CA: Sage Publications, Inc., 2001.

[10] Ulrich, Karl T. and Steven D. Eppinger, *Product Design and Development- 3rd Edition*, New York, NY: McGraw-Hill/Irwin, 2004.

[11] Sanderson, S. and M. Uzumeri, "A Framework Model and Product Family Competition," *Research Policy*, (1995), pp. 24.

Figure 8-1
Supply Chain Management:
Integrating and Managing Business Processes Across the Supply Chain

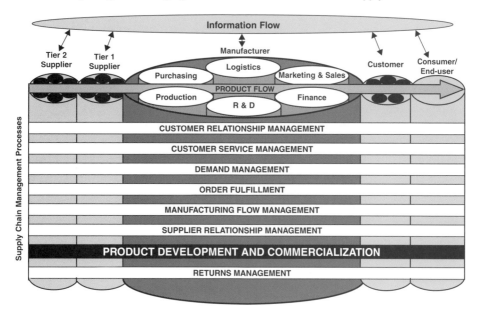

Source: Adapted from Douglas M. Lambert, Martha C. Cooper, and Janus D. Pagh, "Supply Chain Management: Implementation Issues and Research Opportunities," *The International Journal of Logistics Management,* Vol. 9, No. 2 (1998), p. 2.

- **Incremental improvements to existing products:** These projects might only involve adding or modifying some features of existing products in order to keep the product line current and competitive. As an example, TaylorMade-adidas Golf, has introduced, in its Rossa putters brand, two new versions of its popular mallet-style Monza putter: the Monza Long and Monza Mid. While the new products maintain the features of the original Monza putter, the heads of both of these new putters are engineered to work best with a long and mid-length shaft respectively.
- **Fundamentally new products:** These projects involve radically different product or production technologies and might help to address new and unfamiliar markets. In late 2001, Apple Computer rolled out the iPod, a small digital music player weighing just 6.5 ounces and capable of holding about 1,000 songs.[12] This product was quite different than anything Apple had previously sold.

> *Product development and commercialization may include the integration of services. The combination of a physical product with services makes the product more valuable.*

Product development and commercialization might include the integration of services. The combination of a physical product with services makes the product more valuable. Services such as maintenance or training might be integrated into the product development process. For example, the product development and commercialization process at Lucent Technologies includes specific review criteria relating to the development of customer documentation and training plans. Supply chain considerations might drive innovative customer-focused solutions which

---

[12] Walker, Rob, "The Guts of a New Machine," *The New York Times Magazine,* (November 30, 2003), pp. 78.

differentiate the product from competitors' offerings, particularly in saturated markets. Physical products might include intangible services which means that many solutions now include varying proportions of products or services.

Product Development and Commercialization as a Supply Chain Management Process

Each of the eight supply chain processes defined by The Global Supply Chain Forum contains strategic and operational elements. The strategic portion of the product development and commercialization process establishes a structure for developing a product and moving it to the market, providing a template for implementation within the firm. The operational portion is the realization of the process that has been established at the strategic level. Figure 8-2 shows the sequence of sub-processes that comprise the strategic and operational product development and commercialization processes. The lines connecting the sub-processes to the other seven supply chain management processes in the center of the diagram depict the interfaces between each sub-process and the other processes.

Both the strategic and operational processes are led by cross-functional teams. The teams are comprised of managers representing product engineering, research and development, marketing, finance, production, purchasing and logistics. The teams should include members from outside the firm such as representatives

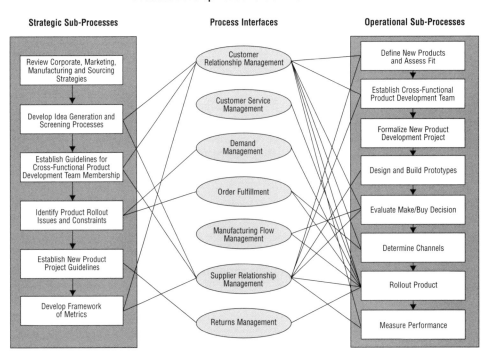

Figure 8-2
Product Development and Commercialization

Source: Adapted from Keely L. Croxton, Sebastián J. García-Dastugue, Douglas M. Lambert, and Dale S. Rogers, "Supply Chain Management: Implementation Issues and Research Opportunities," *The International Journal of Logistics Management*, Vol. 12, No. 2 (2001), p. 27.

from key customers and/or suppliers. For example, Visteon, a supplier of automotive components, is a key player on the product development and commercialization team of the Ford Motor Company. Similarly, a user advocate is part of the product development and commercialization team at Lucent Technologies. The user advocate helps identify the customer value proposition for the product during the early stages of development and assists with the formulation of appropriate documentation and training as the product reaches commercialization.

At the strategic level, a process team is responsible for developing the framework for product development and commercialization within the firm. Multiple operational teams have day-to-day responsibility for managing the process for specific development projects. While these various teams have project responsibility, the strategic team maintains control of the overall process.

The Strategic Product Development and Commercialization Process

The objective of the strategic portion of the product development and commercialization management process is to construct a formalized structure through which the operational process is executed. The strategic process provides the blueprint for the implementation and is composed of six sub-processes, as shown in Figure 8-3.

Review Corporate, Marketing, Manufacturing and Sourcing Strategies

The first sub-process in the strategic portion of the product development and commercialization process is to review the corporate, marketing, manufacturing and sourcing strategies to determine how they will impact products to be developed and sold. The marketing strategy contains the key customer segment needs assessment.

Corporate and marketing strategies should influence idea generation for products.

Corporate and marketing strategies should influence idea generation for products. These strategies guide budget priorities that are examined to determine specific product development and commercialization objectives. General business strategies are honed into explicit plans that define how the firm's strategy translates into product development and commercialization requirements. The time frames of these strategies are aligned with expected product development cycle times. This gives the product development and commercialization team detailed objectives that are aligned with overall firm strategies and budgets, and include time to market objectives. Research has shown that managers in successful firms clearly communicate the organization's overall strategic direction, and then implement the product development and commercialization process in a manner consistent with their business strategies.[13] For example, a review of a firm's marketing strategy should allow the product development and commercialization team to more effectively identify projects that address customer needs. While the marketing strategy identifies customers, the product development and commercialization process implements the activities to meet the needs of those customers.[14]

---

[13] Schilling, Melissa A. and Charles W. L. Hill, "Managing the New Product Development Process: Strategic Imperatives," *Academy of Management Executive*, Vol. 12, No. 3 (1998), pp. 67-82.

[14] O'Dwyer, Marie and Tom O'Toole, "Marketing-R&D Interface Contexts in New Product Development," *Irish Marketing Review*, Vol. 11, No. 1 (1998), pp. 59-68.

Figure 8-3
The Strategic Product Development and Commercialization Process

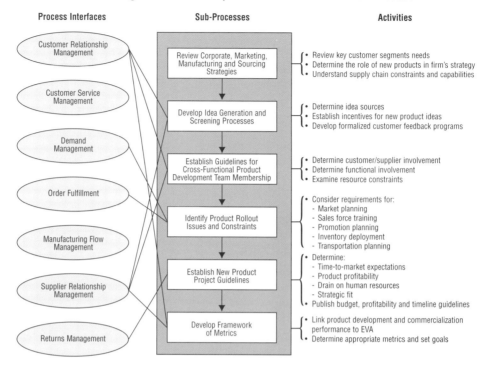

The review of corporate, marketing, manufacturing and sourcing strategies is particularly relevant as management establishes the objectives for the product development and commercialization process and examines how resources and competencies support achievement of these objectives. For example, the product development and commercialization team at Moen Incorporated is driven by a corporate edict that SKU growth will be proportional to sales growth. Therefore, as the team reviews the organization's three-year product strategy to identify and prioritize new product opportunities, they rank the revenue potential and operational complexity of the opportunities. The revenue potential is provided by the marketing function and is based on market intelligence. Market intelligence is largely driven by gap analyses of the current product portfolio which management uses to identify style and/or price point gaps within the current product mix. The operational complexity rankings are developed through consultations among the sourcing, manufacturing and engineering functions. These complexity rankings reflect the ability of the organization to source, make and deliver the desired product. The product design can simplify or complicate the execution of the other supply chain management processes. A proliferation of products and product variations might cause complications with little or no payoff.

In addition to reviewing of the overall product strategy, the product development and commercialization team reviews the sourcing, manufacturing and marketing strategies in order to assess the fit of the product development objectives with current capabilities. Then, the team provides feedback of future

The product design can simplify or complicate the execution of the other supply chain management processes.

product development requirements to the sourcing, manufacturing and marketing functional areas so that the acquisition of needed capabilities can be integrated into their future strategies.

Develop Idea Generation and Screening Procedures

The idea generation and screening procedures are developed next. The outputs of the first sub-process are objectives that will drive the idea generation and screening procedures. This can include determining sources for ideas, considering incentives for developing products for the focal firm, for the suppliers, and for customers. In addition, this sub-process will begin to develop formalized customer feedback programs. At this point in the product development and commercialization process, there needs to be an interface with the customer relationship management process to determine how new products will impact key customers and whether those products will be accepted.

Ideas for new products may come from several sources, including:[15]
- Marketing and sales personnel.
- Research and technology development teams.
- Product development and commercialization teams.
- Manufacturing and operations organizations.
- Customers and potential customers.
- Suppliers and third parties.
- Competitors and potential competitors.

The product development and commercialization process team should explicitly develop a methodology for generating these opportunities. As an example, 3M has implemented the lead user methodology to generate new ideas. Lead users are defined as users of a given product that expect attractive innovation related benefits and whose needs for a given innovation are typically earlier than the majority of the target market.[16] The lead user method as conducted at 3M involves identifying and learning from lead users both within the target market and in advanced analog markets that have similar needs in a more extreme form.[17] Lead users provide information on both needs and ideas for solutions.

It is critical to have the right people from the internal functions along with key customers and suppliers involved in the product development and commercialization process.

Establish Guidelines for Cross-Functional Product Development Team Membership

Next, the process team establishes guidelines for the membership of the cross-functional product development team. It is critical to have the right people from the internal functions along with key customers and suppliers involved in the product development and commercialization process. The involvement of the process teams from customer relationship management and supplier relationship management is central to managing the relationships across the supply chain. Business rules related to the product development and commercialization process

---

[15] Ulrich, Karl T. and Steven D. Eppinger, *Product Design and Development*, 3rd Edition, New York, NY: McGraw-Hill/Irwin, 2004.

[16] von Hippel, Eric, *The Sources of Innovation*, New York, NY: Oxford University Press, 1988.

[17] Lilien, Gary L., Pamela D. Morrison, Kathleen Searls, Mary Sonnack, and Eric von Hippel, "Performance Assessment of the Lead User Idea-Generation Process for New Product Development," *Management Science*, Vol. 48, No. 8 (2002), pp. 1042-1059.

should be included in the product and service agreements (PSAs).

While the strategic product development and commercialization process team is a standing team, the operational level teams are formed on a project by project basis.[18] There are two basic types of operational product development teams. Operating and innovating teams[19] are identified based on the underlying objectives of their project. The operating teams are concerned with evolutionary development of current product and service offerings. Operating teams span boundaries, but tend to be more internally focused. Innovating teams, which pursue new business opportunities that are distinct from existing offerings, span organizations and have a wider perspective. Innovating teams interact with consumers, retailers, wholesalers and suppliers. Guidelines established by the strategic level team should take these differences into consideration in terms of establishing the guidelines for team membership.

The strategic product development and commercialization process team works to determine the extent of involvement from key customers and suppliers. Partnerships might be formed with customers and suppliers to complement internal knowledge as well as to learn about new markets and technologies, and reduce overall risk.[20] Relative strengths, weaknesses and roles of personnel within the internal functions are assessed to determine their involvement. Resource constraints are examined to determine which resources can be utilized on specific new product projects.

As part of the product development and commercialization process at Lucent Technologies, specific involvement guidelines by functional areas are established for each stage of the process. Functional representatives on the team are identified as either deliverable owner, input provider, or consultant. Functional representatives might include corporate, legal/contract management, development, sales, marketing, services, finance, product management, logistics, intellectual property and standards, quality management as well as an advocate for the user.

Identify Product Rollout Issues and Constraints

The fourth sub-process is the identification of product rollout issues and constraints. Pinch points that will hamper the product development or commercialization process are determined. This sub-process includes considerations of market and promotion planning, sales force training, inventory deployment planning, transportation planning and capacity planning. Each of the internal business functions needs to be involved to avoid poor product rollouts. In addition, the team should get input from the order fulfillment process to assess how new products will impact this process.

It is critical to identify potential commercialization problems and think about solutions to these problems. As part of this sub-process, the team works with the

It is critical to identify potential commercialization problems and think about solutions to these problems.

---

[18] Pitta, Dennis A., Frank Franzak and Lea P. Katanis, "Redefining New Product Development Teams: Learning to Actualize Consumer Contributions," *Journal of Product & Brand Management*, Vol. 5, No. 6 (1996), pp. 48-60.

[19] Barczak, Gloria and David Wilemon, "Leadership Differences in New Product Development Teams," *Journal of Product Innovation Management*, Vol. 6, No. 4 (1989), pp. 259-267.

[20] McDermott, Richard, "How to Build Communities of Practice in Team Organizations: Learning Across Teams," *Knowledge Management Review*, Vol. 2, No. 2 (1999), pp. 32-37.

supplier relationship management and manufacturing flow management teams to determine if there are constraints related to components for the new product. In the case of completely outsourced manufacturing, the manufacturing flow management team helps to identify problems with scheduling or production. A linkage to order fulfillment assists in the consideration of rollout issues. Typical decisions to be made at this point are initial inventory levels and the positioning of the inventory.

Unisys has standardized product rollout procedures because of the complexity and high cost of their products and the difficulties and expenses associated with sourcing, manufacturing and distribution. Utilizing project management tools that allow all of the key issues to be considered is important when the price of a computer can be greater than $1,000,000. Anticipating pinch points and developing a solution in advance can determine a product's success.

Anticipating pinch points and developing a solution in advance can determine a product's success.

As part of their product development and commercialization process, Lucent Technologies produces a detailed financial assessment, product description and execution plan for a successful rollout. This enables management to examine rollout issues and constraints when making the business decision to commit significant resources to the project.

Establish New Product Project Guidelines

Next, new product project guidelines are established. In this sub-process, expectations for time to market are developed. Product profitability scenarios are developed and the implications for human resources resulting from new product projects are determined. The guidelines for evaluating the strategic fit of new products are established. Ritchey Bicycle Components, a high-end bicycle parts company, provides an example of establishing new product project guidelines. Before a new product is approved, the team must submit a detailed plan that includes budgets and project guidelines to the Chief Operating Officer. If it does not appear that the project will be a strategic fit and successful in the marketplace, the proposed project will not move forward without changes. Finally, budget, profitability, and timeline guidelines are published.

At Unisys after the customer need is identified, the product management process (PMP) begins, encompassing the feasibility, design, development, qualification, support and termination stages of the identified product. To ensure that supply chain requirements are defined and included, Unisys generates detailed documents and provides them to engineering to be embedded in the marketing statement of requirements, the starting point of the PMP process.

Develop Framework of Metrics

The final sub-process is to develop the framework of metrics. Typical process metrics might include time to market, time to profitability and initial sales. As with the other processes, the metrics that are chosen need to be coordinated with the customer relationship management and the supplier relationship management process teams to assure that they do not conflict with other metrics or the firm's overall objectives.

As part of this sub-process, the team develops procedures for analyzing the total cost of product development and commercialization and the impact of new products on current ones. Product development and commercialization can be a key driver of profitability. At Colgate-Palmolive, the development of innovative products with key suppliers has been identified as a strategy for achieving their stretch financial goals.

Figure 8-4 depicts the relationship between product development and commercialization management and the firm's financial performance as measured by EVA. EVA considers revenues, costs and profit, as well as the cost of assets required to generate the profits. For example, better management of the product development and commercialization process can lead to sales increases as a result of rolling out successful new products, improving product availability, retaining existing customers, and attracting new customers. Cost of goods sold can be reduced by lowering material requirements, reducing production setup and changeover costs, increasing labor utilization, and reducing packaging requirements.

Expenses can be reduced by increasing productivity, optimizing the physical network of facilities, leveraging new and/or alternative distribution channels. Management can leverage product development and commercialization to help reduce the costs of freight and warehouse labor, customer service, order management, information, human resources, overhead and/or administrative costs. In many companies, managers not only focus the product development and commercialization activities on developing products to take to market, but find ways to more effectively and efficiently perform supporting processes.

Better management of product development and commercialization can result in reductions in component, work-in-process and finished goods inventories.

At Colgate-Palmolive, the development of innovative products with key suppliers has been identified as a strategy for achieving their stretch financial goals.

Figure 8-4
How Product Development and Commercialization Affects Economic Value Added (EVA®)

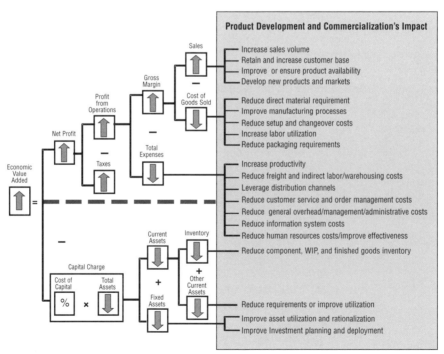

Source: Adapted from Douglas M. Lambert and Terrance L. Pohlen, "Supply Chain Metrics," *The International Journal of Logistics Management,* Vol. 12, No. 1 (2001), p. 10.

Other current assets also can be reduced as a result of better new product planning and introduction. Finally, better management of new product development and commercialization can lead to lower fixed assets as a result of improved asset utilization and rationalization, and better investment planning and deployment.

The product development and commercialization process can have a significant impact on the profitability of customers.

The product development and commercialization process can have a significant impact on the profitability of customers. For this reason, every attempt should be made to identify and report the revenue, cost, and asset implications of this process on the profitability of key customers and segments of customers. The cost of customer specific assets can be reflected in customer profitability reports by incorporating a charge for assets employed.

The Operational Product Development and Commercialization Process

The operational portion of the product development and commercialization process is the implementation of the structure developed at the strategic level. It is a template for the synchronization of product development and commercialization activities and consists of eight sub-processes as shown in Figure 8-5.

Define New Products and Assess Fit

The objective of this sub-process is to define new products and assess their fit. New product ideas are generated and screened. A market assessment is completed, key customers and suppliers are consulted, and the fit with existing channels, manufacturing, and logistics is determined. This sub-process involves interfaces with customer relationship management and supplier relationship management, as well as with the business functions in the firm.

As an example, Moen Incorporated utilizes various forms of customer input in the product development and commercialization process. Moen has used retailer input as a means for identifying new product opportunities. Retail buyers along with their Moen sales representative have identified new product opportunities while reviewing current products within the store aisle. The retail buyer requested a product that was similar to a previously successful product but had certain stylistic adjustments that reflected changes in consumer preferences. The Moen sales representative and the retail buyer contacted a product development and commercialization process team to determine the potential feasibility of the request.

Establish Cross-Functional Product Development Team

Using the guidelines developed at the strategic level, the cross-functional product development and commercialization teams are established. Internal and external parties such as suppliers or customers whose input is necessary for the success of the new product need to be included on the team as early as possible. These teams will be responsible for formalizing the new product development project.

One of the barriers to including suppliers and customers on the product development and commercialization team is the geographical separation of the potential members. Virtual teaming has been proposed as a model and practice

Figure 8-5
The Operational Product Development and Commercialization Process

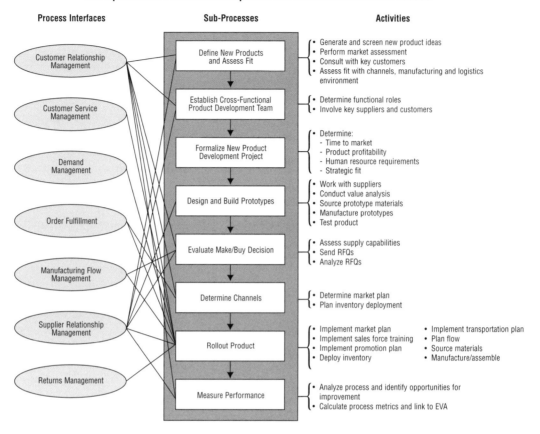

Process Interfaces	Sub-Processes	Activities

that can overcome this geographical barrier.[21] This approach utilizes technology to form collaborative relationships, unconstrained by geography that can quickly apply knowledge and expertise that affect the product development and commercialization process.

Differences in corporate culture represent another barrier that affects the involvement of suppliers and customers on the team. A culture must exist in each of the organizations involved on the team that facilitates and encourages joint problem solving and decision making across organizational boundaries. The internal functions of the individual organizations must be willing to pursue collaborative relationships. This requires a culture permeating each organization that encourages and values collaboration.[22]

At Unisys, the product development and commercialization team has the involvement of marketing, engineering, sales, operations, logistics, procurement, field service, and external suppliers. The establishment of cross-functional,

Differences in corporate culture represent another barrier that affects the involvement of suppliers and customers on the team.

[21] Bal, Jay, Richard Wilding, and John Gundry, "Virtual Teaming in the Agile Supply Chain," *The International Journal of Logistics Management*, Vol. 10, No. 2 (1999), pp. 71-82.

[22] McIvor, R. and P. Humphreys, "Eary Supplier Involvement in the Design Process: Lessons from the Electronics Industry," Omega: *The International Journal of Management Science*, Vol. 32, No. 3 (2004), pp. 179-199.

boundary spanning teams at Unisys is driven by the dedication to the principles of supply chain management and concurrent engineering. When they adhere to these principles, design time and cost is reduced while maintaining product quality and reliability.

Formalize New Product Development Project

Using the guidelines established at the strategic level, the cross-functional product development teams examine the strategic fit of the new product within the organization's current product portfolio.

Using the guidelines established at the strategic level, the cross-functional product development teams examine the strategic fit of the new product within the organization's current product portfolio. The team works with key suppliers to formalize time to market expectations, product profitability goals, and budget requirements. Any potential implications for human resources are identified and addressed.

The formation of budget and resource needs within this sub-process are particularly relevant given that 75 percent of new product development programs fail commercially,[23] while 55 percent of managers report that product development efforts in their companies failed to meet its sales and profit objectives.[24] The reasons for failure include lack of market information, a failure to listen to the voice of the customer, poor up-front pre-development homework, unstable product definition, poor quality of execution of key product development tasks, and poorly structured, ineffectual project teams.[25] A closer examination of these reasons combined with recent benchmarking studies suggests that many problems are interlinked, and traceable to resource deficiencies.[26] Devoting adequate resources to the project is important for increasing the likelihood of success.

Design, Build and Test Prototypes

The team manages the process of designing, building and testing prototypes of the product ideas. For example, auto companies develop concept cars to test new product ideas. In this phase, teams work with suppliers and perform a value analysis to determine what portions of the product design and rollout process truly add value. Then, they source prototype materials and manufacture product samples. The final step of this sub-process is to test the product.

Ford Motor Company invested in a prototype optimization model with its related expert systems to budget, plan and manage prototype test fleets, and to maintain testing integrity. The model reduced annual prototype costs by more than

---

[23] Griffin, A. and Albert L. Page, "PDMA Success Measurement Project: Recommended Measures for Product Development Success and Failure," *Journal of Innovation Management*, Vol. 13, No. 6 (1996), pp. 478-496.

[24] Cooper, Robert G., Scott J. Edgett, and Elko J. Kleinschmidt, "Best Practices for Managing R&D Portfolios," *Research Technology Management*, Vol. 41, No. 4 (1998), pp. 20-33.

[25] See drivers of new product development success in: Mitzi M. Montoya-Weiss, and Roger Calantone, "Determinants of New Product Performance: A Review and Meta Analysis," *Journal of Product Innovation Management*, Vol. 11, No. 5 (1994), pp. 397-417; Sanjay Mishra, Dongwook Kim, and Dae Hoon H. Lee, "Factors Affecting New Product Success: Cross Country Comparisons," *Journal of Product Innovation Management*, Vol. 13, No. 6 (1996), pp. 530-550; and, Robert G. Cooper, "New Products: What Separates the Winners from the Losers," in *PDMA Handbook for New Product Development*, ed. Milton D. Rosenau Jr., New York, NY: John Wiley & Sons, 1996.

[26] Cooper, Robert G. and Scott J. Edgett, "Overcoming the Crunch in Resources for New Product Development," *Research Technology Management*, Vol. 46, No. 3 (2003), pp. 48-58.

$250 million.[27] This has shortened the planning process, established global procedures for prototype development, and created a common structure for communication between budgeting and engineering.[28]

At Harley-Davidson, suppliers that only provide prototypes have been eliminated. Harley-Davidson works exclusively with ultimate production suppliers for the supply of prototypes. While these suppliers will either build prototypes or contract them out to an outside organization, they nonetheless are directly involved in this stage of the process. Management believes that product development success has been improved by having direct design input and oversight from suppliers at the prototype stage.[29]

Evalute Make/Buy Decision

Once the prototypes have been evaluated, the team needs to determine whether the product should be manufactured in-house, or purchased from suppliers. Part of the make/buy decision is to determine how much of the new product should be made in-house and how much by different portions of the supply base. In many firms, management has a short-term perspective for make/buy decisions that erodes long-term profitability. These decisions might have strategic implications for the firm and should be formulated from a strategic perspective with senior management involvement.[30]

The decision to outsource or keep the product sourcing and manufacturing within the firms is a critical one. There might be strategic reasons for keeping the product in-house. The need to control costs or to retain product knowledge within the firm might lead management to keep the product in-house. This decision involves interfacing with other supply chain management processes including customer relationship management, manufacturing flow management and supplier relationship management. Once it is determined what will be sourced, supply capabilities are assessed and requests for quotations are sent, received and analyzed.

The need to control costs or to retain product knowledge within the firm might lead management to keep the product in-house.

Determine Channels

In the sixth sub-process, the marketing and distribution channels for the new product are determined. The customer relationship management and order fulfillment process teams provide input at this stage. Then, the market plan for the product is developed, and initial inventory planning is performed.

The team needs to consider the channel choice decision carefully. In some cases, the channel decision is the primary factor in determining a product's success. Strengths and weaknesses of various channels need to be analyzed.

---

[27] Chelst, Kenneth, John Sidelko, Alex Przebienda, Jeffrey Lockledge, and Dimitrios Mihailidis, "Rightsizing and Management of Prototype Vehicle Testing at Ford Motor Company," *Interfaces*, Vol. 31, No. 1 (2001), pp. 91-108.

[28] Chelst, Kenneth, John Sidelko, Alex Przebienda, Jeffrey Lockledge, and Dimitrios Mihailidis, "Rightsizing and Management of Prototype Vehicle Testing at Ford Motor Company," *Interfaces*, Vol. 31, No. 1 (2001), pp. 91-108.

[29] Fitzgerald, Kevin R., "Purchasing at Harley Links Supply with Design," *Purchasing*, Vol. 122, No. 2 (1997), pp. 56-58.

[30] Humphreys, P. and R. McIvor, and G. Huang, "An Expert System for Evaluating the Make or Buy Decision," *Computers and Industrial Engineering*, Vol. 42, No. 2-4 (2002), pp. 567-585.

Consumer packaged goods companies are often faced with the choice of moving product through mass-merchandise channels where price is low and vendor compliance demands are high, or through lower volume channels where price is protected and logistics requirements are lower. The products might have cost or physical requirements that necessitate specific channel characteristics. It may be useful for the team to work with the customer relationship management team to determine how current and potential customers will react to the new products that will flow through existing or new channels.

It may be useful for the team to work with the customer relationship management team to determine how current and potential customers will react to the new products that will flow through existing or new channels.

At Moen Incorporated, the channel implications of the product development and commercialization process is a critical consideration. Depending on the channel used to rollout the new product, the inventory loading curves will vary. The retail channel requires that minimum inventory levels of the new product are available in their stores at launch. The wholesale channel is characterized by a much slower ramp-up period, but demonstrates a higher level of demand volatility. Moen's retail channel is becoming more demanding with regard to new products. In order to maintain shelf space, Moen must consistently provide retailers with a flow of new product offerings that are specific to their organizations. The wholesale channel is also looking for new products that are specific to individual firms.

Rollout Product

Many products are unsuccessful because of poor product rollout. Materials need to be sourced, inbound materials positioned, and products manufactured and/or assembled. The market plan is implemented, the sales force is trained on the new product offering, and the promotion plan is executed. Inventory is deployed using methodologies developed through the transportation plan. It is important that all of the other processes are involved in planning and executing the product rollout.

In the early 1990s, Coca-Cola developed Fruitopia and Powerade which were juice-based, non-carbonated products. The group responsible for the rollout did not adequately consider the manufacturing and sales requirements for pasteurized beverages. With the majority of their other products, the bottlers would buy concentrate, use a cold-fill process, and distribute the product to stores and restaurants. For juice-based products that required pasteurization, new equipment was needed that the bottling network was not ready to purchase themselves. So, the burden of producing bottled finished product was shifted back to a group that was unfamiliar with rolling out products that did not move in tank trucks. Because they did not anticipate the complexity involved, it took longer to establish Fruitopia and Powerade as strong brands. After rethinking the rollout, they were able to relaunch the brands which have become successful.

A successful rollout can enhance the impact that a new product has in the marketplace. Having the right amount of product available at the right time in the right place are key elements of product success. No matter how much potential a new product has, if it is not moved to market efficiently and effectively, it is likely that the product development process will not be successful.

Measure Performance

In the final sub-process, performance is measured using the metrics developed at the strategic level, and communicated to the appropriate individuals both within the organization and across the supply chain. Communications with other members of the supply chain are coordinated through the customer relationship management and supplier relationship management processes.

Tracking new product performance is important at Moen Incorporated which has established three distinct product groups: core products, custom products and new products. Moen requires a 95% fill rate for three consecutive months in order to move new products into the core product category.

Conclusions

Product development and commercialization is one of the eight supply chain management processes that transcend the boundaries of the firm. Effectively implementing product development and commercialization can reduce a firm's costs, increase revenues and positively impact Economic Value Added (EVA). The need for managers to implement product development and commercialization across the supply chain is increasingly necessary for business success and value creation. By tapping into the knowledge and skills of other supply chain members, a firm can expand its information resources and gain access to ideas for product development or increased development efficiency.

By tapping into the knowledge and skills of other supply chain members, a firm can expand its information resources and gain access to ideas for product development or increased development efficiency.

The Returns Management Process

9

Dale S. Rogers, Douglas M. Lambert, Keely L. Croxton
and Sebastián J. García-Dastugue

Returns management is the supply chain management process by which activities associated with returns, reverse logistics, gatekeeping, and avoidance are managed within the firm and across key members of the supply chain.

Overview

Returns management is the supply chain management process by which activities associated with returns, reverse logistics, gatekeeping, and avoidance are managed within the firm and across key members of the supply chain.[1] The correct implementation of this process enables management not only to manage the reverse product flow efficiently, but to identify opportunities to reduce unwanted returns and to control reusable assets such as containers. In this chapter, we describe how the returns management process is implemented. The process is described in terms of its sub-processes and activities, and the interfaces with corporate functions, other supply chain management processes and other firms. Examples of successful implementation are provided.

Introduction

The management of returns is important for many firms. In the United States, retail customer returns for general merchandise are estimated to be approximately six percent of revenue.[2] At this rate, returns for the top 30 U.S. non-grocery retailers for 2001 were approximately $44 billion. Return rates can be even higher for specialty retailers. For example, one catalog apparel retailer has experienced return rates of up to 40 percent. Logistics costs associated with managing returns have been estimated at four percent of a firm's total logistics costs.[3] For 2001, this would represent about $40 billion to the U.S. economy. The magnitude of these numbers demonstrates the need for management attention to the returns process.

---

[1] This chapter is based on Dale S. Rogers, Douglas M. Lambert, Keely L. Croxton and Sebastián J. García-Dastugue, "The Returns Management Process," *The International Journal of Logistics Management,* Vol. 13, No. 2 (2002), pp. 1-18.

[2] Rogers, Dale S. and Ron S. Tibben-Lembke, *Going Backwards: Reverse Logistics Trends and Practices,* Pittsburgh, PA: Reverse Logistics Executive Council, 1999.

[3] Rogers, Dale S., Ronald S. Tibben-Lembke, Kasia Banasiak, Karl Brokmann, and Timothy Johnson, "Reverse Logistics Challenges," *Proceedings of the 2001 Council of Logistics Management Annual Conference,* Oak Brook, IL: Council of Logistics Management, 2001, p. 1.

Returns management is a critical supply chain management process that requires planning and effective execution across the firms in the supply chain. Effective implementation of returns management enables executives to identify productivity improvement opportunities. Returns management is a boundary spanning process that requires interaction between members of the supply chain. It encompasses activities such as avoidance and gatekeeping, which are central elements to effective management of the return flow. As part of implementing the process, management needs to measure the financial impact of returns on the firm and on other members of the supply chain.

Returns management is a critical supply chain management process that requires planning and effective execution across the firms in the supply chain.

The chapter is organized as follows. We review the different types of returns and relevant definitions. We then describe the strategic and operational processes that comprise returns management, and present the sub-processes and their activities. Returns management is one of the eight processes and it requires interfaces with the other seven (see Figure 9-1). Therefore, we identify the interfaces with the corporate functions, the other supply chain management processes and other firms. Finally, we present the conclusions.

Types of Returns

There are many types of returns that need to be managed within this process, each of which poses unique challenges. Based on input from The Global Supply Chain Forum, we group returns into five categories: consumer returns, marketing returns, asset returns, product recalls and environmental returns.

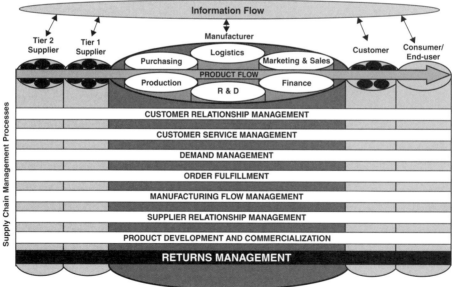

Figure 9-1
Supply Chain Management:
Integrating and Managing Business Processes Across the Supply Chain

Source: Adapted from Douglas M. Lambert, Martha C. Cooper, and Janus D. Pagh, "Supply Chain Management: Implementation Issues and Research Opportunities," *The International Journal of Logistics Management,* Vol. 9, No. 2 (1998), p. 2.

Consumer Returns

Consumer returns due to buyers' remorse or product defects are generally the largest category of returns. Many companies have liberal returns policies that make it easy for consumers to return products. This is based on the belief that consumers will continue to purchase from a retailer with liberal returns policies which increase the retailer's revenues. For the Christmas 2002 season, Circuit City, a large U.S. retailer of consumer electronics, made returns easier for the customer by not requiring receipts for credit card purchases, since they keep information of past purchases linked to each customer's credit card number. Some companies such as L.L. Bean, a large U.S. based catalog retailer, even have lifetime warranties that allow consumers to return a product after years of ownership.

Marketing Returns

Marketing returns consist of product returned from a position forward in the supply chain. These returns are often due to slow sales, quality issues, or the need to reposition inventory. Other examples of marketing returns include: close-out returns, which are first quality products that the retailer or distributor has decided to no longer carry; buy-outs or "lifts", where one manufacturer purchases a retailer's supply of a competitor's product to get access to shelf space; job-outs, where seasonal merchandise is returned after the season's end; and, surplus and overruns. In many cases, marketing returns can represent a significant percentage of sales.

In addition to returns driven by market issues, some marketing returns are driven by management practices.

In addition to returns driven by market issues, some marketing returns are driven by management practices. For example, end-of-quarter loads to the channel in order to achieve short-term financial results can produce high return rates. Management should identify the costs associated with these returns to evaluate the benefits from artificially loading the channel. Inappropriate incentive systems drive undesired behavior such as loading the channel unnecessarily by misaligning the firm's objectives and those of the sales force. For example, when sales force bonuses are linked to revenues and returns are not taken into account, the objective of some salespeople is to ship products out to the channel. This practice often results in high return rates.

Asset Returns

Asset returns consist of the recapture and repositioning of an asset. These returns are typically characterized as items that management wants to see returned. Categories that fall within asset returns are repositioning of an asset such as oil drilling equipment, and reusable containers. For example, the Ford Customer Service Division of the Ford Motor Company uses a closed-loop reusable collapsible rack system to deliver automobile parts to their dealerships. A truck driver delivers the order in a wheeled cage that collapses to facilitate shipping the cage back to the Ford Customer Service Division distribution center. The driver makes the delivery of the parts and picks up the collapsed cages from the previous order. This racking system has reduced the overall delivery cost and is also environmentally friendly.

Reusable totes are another example of a desirable return that has become a standard in many industries. At Baker and Taylor, a book, music, and video wholesaler, reusable plastic totes are used to move product between Baker and

Taylor and some of its customers such as Amazon. These totes are stackable, protect the product better than corrugated cardboard and are less expensive on a per movement basis. The use of reusable pallets, racks or totes should be coordinated with customer relationship management and/or supplier relationship management process teams.

Product Recalls

Product recalls are a form of return that are usually initiated because of a safety or quality issue. Recalls can be voluntary or mandated by a government agency. They require more up-front planning than most other return types, and this planning is central to managing them effectively.[4] Information technology and effective communications play a central roll in the management of product recalls. For industries that are susceptible to recalls, like the automotive or food industries, part of designing an effective returns management process is developing procedures for informing customers of a recall and efficiently handling the return.

Environmental Returns

Environmental returns include the disposal of hazardous materials or abiding by environmental regulations. Environmental returns are different from other types of returns because they might include regulatory compliance that limits the set of options. Additionally, there are often stringent documentation and audit requirements. For example, the Environmental Protection Agency in the United States has banned computer monitors that use cathode ray tubes from landfills since 1992 because of the lead content in the components.[5] Due to this regulation, the firms responsible for the cathode ray tubes need to have a process in place to dispose of the unusable computer monitors.

In the European Union (EU), producer responsibility regulations have been adopted. For example, the EU Packaging Waste Directive established the concept of the "polluter pays" by sharing the responsibility for waste packaging recovery across the whole supply chain. This legislation has helped to dramatically reduce packaging waste. In 2001, German firms recovered 80 percent of packaging and Dutch firms recovered 65 percent.[6]

Summary

When designing a returns management process, managers need to consider each type of return and develop procedures that are appropriate for each one. The type of return might have a different impact within the firm and on other firms in the supply chain. For instance, a return that affects a consumer could have a long lasting effect on the market's perception of the firm; thus, management might take marketing considerations into account to find the best procedure to handle the event. In contrast, for a return in which there is no direct effect on the consumer, the key

When designing a returns management process, managers need to consider each type of return and develop procedures that are appropriate for each one.

---

[4] Smith, N. Craig, Robert J. Thomas and John A. Quelch, "A Strategic Approach to Managing Product Recalls," *Harvard Business Review,* Vol. 74, No. 5 (1997), pp. 102-112.

[5] Raymond Communications, *Transportation Packaging and the Environment,* College Park, MD: Raymond Communications, 1997.

[6] Fernie, John, and Cathy Hart, "UK Packaging Waste Legislation Implications for Food Retailers," *British Food Journal,* Vol. 103, No. 3 (2001), pp. 187-199.

considerations might be limited to finding the most cost effective return flow option. Similarly, returns due to product failure might require interfaces with the supplier relationship management and/or product development and commercialization process teams, while returns due to consumer remorse might not.

Defining Returns Management

Terms such as reverse logistics, closed-loop supply chain management, and returns have been used to describe some of the activities in returns management. However, these terms do not adequately describe the returns management process.

Terms such as reverse logistics, closed-loop supply chain management, and returns have been used to describe some of the activities in returns management. However, these terms do not adequately describe the returns management process.

For example, reverse logistics has been defined to be:

> The process of planning, implementing, and controlling the efficient, cost effective flow of raw materials, in-process inventory, finished goods and related information from the point of consumption to the point of origin for the purpose of recapturing value or proper disposal.[7]

Reverse logistics is the process of moving goods from their typical final destination for the purpose of capturing value, or proper disposal. Remanufacturing and refurbishing activities also may be included in the definition of reverse logistics, as well as processing returned merchandise due to damage, seasonal inventory, salvage, recalls, and repositioning of inventory. It also includes recycling programs, hazardous material programs, obsolete equipment disposition, and asset recovery. While reverse logistics is a useful term, it does not include all activities involved in managing the return flow of materials and information through the supply chain. Reverse logistics is limited to the movement of goods or materials "backward" through the supply chain. Returns management is much broader in scope.

Another phrase that has been coined to attempt to describe these activities is closed-loop supply chain management, which has been defined as:

> Supply chains that are designed to consider the acquisition and return flows of products, reuse activities, and the distribution of the recovered products.[8]

This definition is helpful because it recognizes that both forward and backward flows need to be managed in the supply chain. However, it does not help in understanding the activities that make up the management of the return flows.

Another term often used to describe the backward flow of goods is returns. The Supply Chain Council expanded their definition of the SCOR model to include returns in 2000. The Council has defined returns to be:

> Processes associated with returning or receiving returned products for any reason. These processes extend into post-delivery customer support.[9]

This definition appears to focus on the physical movement of goods backwards in the supply chain and does not include critical activities such as gatekeeping and avoidance. Also, the SCOR returns process does not include activities required for the financial management of returns nor does it link returns

---

[7] Rogers, Dale S. and Ron S. Tibben-Lembke, *Going Backwards: Reverse Logistics Trends and Practices, Pittsburgh,* PA: Reverse Logistics Executive Council, 1999, p. 2.

[8] Guide, Jr., Daniel., "The Development of Closed-Loop Supply Chains," Presentation to CIMSO Supply Chain Forum, Insead, November 20, 2001.

[9] Supply-Chain Operations Reference-model: Overview of SCOR Version 5.0, Pittsburgh PA: Supply-Chain Council, 2001, p. 9.

to the financial performance of the firm.

The term used throughout this article to describe the process is returns management which we define as follows:

> Returns management is that part of supply chain management that includes returns, reverse logistics, gatekeeping, and avoidance.

This definition includes activities that are critical to supply chain management such as avoidance and gatekeeping. Avoidance involves finding ways to minimize the number of return requests. It can include ensuring that the quality of product and user friendliness for the consumer is at the highest attainable level before the product is sold and shipped, or changing promotional programs that load the trade when there is no realistic chance that the product shipped to the customer will be sold.

Returns management is that part of supply chain management that includes returns, reverse logistics, gatekeeping, and avoidance.

Gatekeeping means making decisions to limit the number of items that are allowed into the reverse flow. Successful gatekeeping allows management to control and reduce returns without damaging customer service. Gatekeeping eliminates the cost associated with returning products that should not be returned or the cost of products returned to the inappropriate destination. The point of entry into the reverse flow is the best point to eliminate unnecessary cost and management of materials by screening unwarranted returned merchandise.

Returns Management as a Supply Chain Management Process

Each of the eight supply chain management processes defined by The Global Supply Chain Forum contains strategic and operational elements.[10] The strategic portion of returns management establishes a structure for implementation of the process within the firm and across key members of the supply chain. The operational portion is the realization of the process that has been established at the strategic level. Figure 9-2 shows the sequence of sub-processes that comprise strategic and operational returns management. The lines connecting the sub-processes to the other seven supply chain management processes in the center of the diagram depict the interfaces between each sub-process and these processes.

Both the strategic and operational processes are led by a management team that is comprised of managers from several functions including marketing, finance, production, purchasing and logistics. In some cases, the team may include members from outside the firm such as customers, suppliers or representatives from third-party service companies. For example, Genco, a third-party provider, is a key player on the returns management team of Sears, a U.S. retailer. When management of Sears considers a change in their returns process, Genco is usually part of the team that analyzes the data and develops options.

The process team is responsible for developing the procedures at the strategic level and seeing that they are implemented. This team also has day-to-day responsibility for managing the process at the operational level. While firm employees outside of the team might execute parts of the process, the team maintains managerial control.

---

[10] Croxton, Keely L., Sebastián García-Dastugue, Douglas M. Lambert and Dale S. Rogers, "The Supply Chain Management Processes," *The International Journal of Logistics Management,* Vol. 12, No. 2 (2001), pp. 13-36.

Figure 9-2
Returns Management

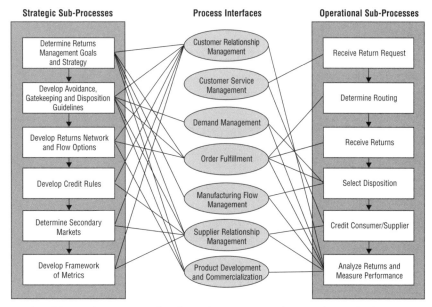

Source: Adapted from Keely L. Croxton, Sebastián García-Dastugue, Douglas M. Lambert, and Dale S. Rogers, "The Supply Chain Management Processes," *The International Journal of Logistics Management*, Vol. 12, No. 2 (2001), p. 19.

The Strategic Returns Management Process

The objective of the strategic portion of the returns management process is to construct a formalized structure through which the operational process is executed. It provides the blueprint for the implementation of returns management. The strategic process is composed of six sub-processes, as shown in Figure 9-3.

Determine Returns Management Goals and Strategy

A firm's returns management capabilities can be used strategically to enhance the overall performance of the company.

A firm's returns management capabilities can be used strategically to enhance the overall performance of the company. For example, returns policies can be used to improve customer loyalty, improve profits, and enhance the brand or firm's public image.

Returns policies can be used to improve customer loyalty by reducing risk to the customer. A buyer for a retailer will be more likely to purchase a new product if he/she knows that it can be returned if the product does not sell. For example, an electronics distributor facing a period of volatile memory chip prices used their returns policy to help resellers better control inventories. By allowing resellers to return anything within a reasonable timeframe, customers' risk is reduced.[11] Consumers are also more likely to buy a product that can be returned if they experience buyer's remorse.[12] Allowing returns is critical to the catalog apparel

[11] Rogers, Dale S. and Ron S. Tibben-Lembke, *Going Backwards: Reverse Logistics Trenus and Practices,* Pittsburgh, PA: Reverse Logistics Executive Council, 1999.

[12] Banker, Steve, "e-Business and Reverse Logistics," ebizQ, ITQuadrant, Inc. December 24, 2001 (b2b.ebizq.net).

Figure 9-3
The Strategic Returns Management Process

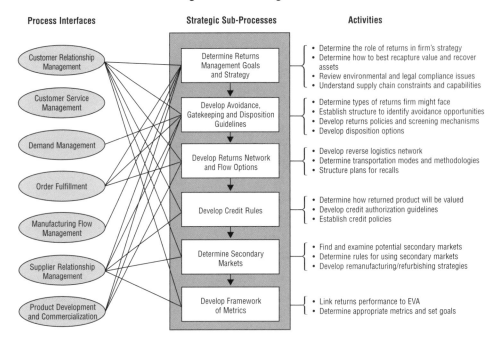

Process Interfaces	Strategic Sub-Processes	Activities

Process Interfaces:
- Customer Relationship Management
- Customer Service Management
- Demand Management
- Order Fulfillment
- Manufacturing Flow Management
- Supplier Relationship Management
- Product Development and Commercialization

Strategic Sub-Processes / Activities:

Determine Returns Management Goals and Strategy
- Determine the role of returns in firm's strategy
- Determine how to best recapture value and recover assets
- Review environmental and legal compliance issues
- Understand supply chain constraints and capabilities

Develop Avoidance, Gatekeeping and Disposition Guidelines
- Determine types of returns firm might face
- Establish structure to identify avoidance opportunities
- Develop returns policies and screening mechanisms
- Develop disposition options

Develop Returns Network and Flow Options
- Develop reverse logistics network
- Determine transportation modes and methodologies
- Structure plans for recalls

Develop Credit Rules
- Determine how returned product will be valued
- Develop credit authorization guidelines
- Establish credit policies

Determine Secondary Markets
- Find and examine potential secondary markets
- Determine rules for using secondary markets
- Develop remanufacturing/refurbishing strategies

Develop Framework of Metrics
- Link returns performance to EVA
- Determine appropriate metrics and set goals

---

business because most consumers need the assurance that they can return something if it does not fit or otherwise meet their expectations.

Management can also use returns policies to improve loyalty from small wholesalers or retailers by helping them control their inventories. Often these customers will buy large quantities of one product on a deal offered by a salesperson, but then are unable to purchase other products later from the same company because their inventory levels are too high or their credit lines are full. It may be in the best interest of the supplier to allow customers to return product that is not selling to help reduce these inventory and credit-line constraints.

In addition, return policies can be used to directly improve profits. For example, manufacturers can use returns management capabilities to protect marketing channels. They may pull product off the shelf and bring it back for refurbishment or disposal in order to make certain that the product is not sold through channels that might damage the value of the brand. For some high-end brands, it is critical for the long-term value of the brand to protect the channel and not allow leakage into inappropriate channels. For example, when Federated Department Stores rebranded some of its Florida stores as Burdines, Mitchell & Ness, a high-end manufacturer of authentic throwback sports jerseys, pulled its products from the Burdines' stores to protect its brand image. Mitchell & Ness management used the company's returns management abilities to reposition the inventory in the appropriate chanels.

In addition, return policies can be used to directly improve profits.

Recapturing value and recovering assets is another strategic use of returns that can reduce costs and improve profits. Innovative ways of reusing materials, or refurbishing and reselling products, whether through primary or secondary channels, can be an important source of revenue. In interviews, we found that firms with asset recovery programs achieve significant bottom-line profits as a result.

Another way a firm can improve profits is using returns capabilities to adjust which products are being offered to the consumer. The most important asset a retail store has is its retail space. To maximize profit per square foot of selling space, management needs the flexibility to take slow-moving items off the shelf and replace them with fast-movers. Traditionally, retailers compensated for mistakes with markdowns. Increasingly, the returns management capabilities of the supply chain are being used to keep the products fresh and other outlets are being used for the slow-moving products.[13]

Management can also use returns to enhance the firm's public image or exhibit good citizenship by doing what they believe is the right thing. For example, some companies engage in voluntary recycling programs with their products. Nike, Inc. established the Reuse-A-Shoe program where old athletic shoes are collected and sorted, and those that are in good condition are donated to charity. The remaining shoes are shipped to Nike's shredding facility. The recycled material is used to make running tracks, athletic courts and playground surfaces.[14]

In order to design a returns management system, the process team needs to first consider the role that returns play in their firm's overall customer service strategy and the ways returns management might contribute to improved profits.

In order to design a returns management system, the process team needs to first consider the role that returns play in their firm's overall customer service strategy and the ways returns management might contribute to improved profits. This should be done in conjunction with the customer relationship management process team who will best understand the needs and expectations of the customers.

Another key consideration in determining the goals of the returns management process is to understand the environmental and legal compliance issues that impact the firm and the supply chain. In many firms, environmental and legal issues are the impetus to start improving returns management. Laws that apply to used product and product planned for disposal need to be understood by team members. For example, in one U.S. state, Minnesota, it has been ruled that automotive shocks and struts cannot be placed in landfills.[15] Various computer components are banned from landfills, including circuit boards with high lead content and computer monitors with cathode ray tubes. Each member of the supply chain needs to understand and minimize the environmental impact of returned materials. This step could also include developing guidelines for measuring the environmental impact of particular modes of transport, obtaining ISO 14000 certification, reducing usage of hazardous materials and decreasing unnecessary packaging. In many cases, there will be an interface with the product development and commercialization process because the product and packaging will have to be designed with these environmental issues in mind.

Compliance with legal requirements is a minimum baseline. Firms that appear to be environmentally careless risk offending a large portion of the

---

[13] Rogers, Dale S. and Ron S. Tibben-Lembke, *Going Backwards: Reverse Logistics Trends and Practices,* Pittsburgh, PA: Reverse Logistics Executive Council, 1999.

[14] Goldfield, Robert, "Nike tests curbside recycling of shoes," *The Business Journal Portland,* June 1, 2001.

[15] Rogers, Dale S. and Ron S. Tibben-Lembke, *Going Backwards: Reverse Logistics Trends and Practices,* Pittsburgh, PA: Reverse Logistics Executive Council, 1999.

consumer base. For example, firms that wish to sell to the European market need to be aware of the Green Dot initiative. The Green Dot is the logo for the Duales System Deutschland which is a joint effort by 400 firms in Germany to try to meet the German government's quotas for recycling packaging. When the Green Dot trademark was implemented in Germany, it set a new standard for extended producer responsibility. For example, to obtain the right to place the Green Dot symbol on their product packaging, German beverage brand owners must ensure that at least 72 percent of their bottles are refillable and that deposits are charged on all non-refillable containers. A package stamped with a Green Dot indicates the brand owner is paying its fair share of waste recovery.[16]

In industries that could be subject to product recalls, the team also needs to review the legal issues that arise in the event of a recall. Product recalls can either be mandated by a government agency, or they can be initiated by one of the members of the supply chain. Either way, there are legal and ethical issues that need to be addressed. For example, in the infant care industry, product recalls occur frequently. Firms that operate in this industry need to identify and remove affected product from the supply chain quickly when a product recall issue develops.

Part of developing the returns management strategy is understanding the constraints and capabilities of the firm and the supply chain. This requires interfaces with the order fulfillment and manufacturing flow management processes. Order fulfillment assists the returns management process team in understanding the boundaries around the physical flow and the information technology capabilities and constraints of the logistics system. Manufacturing flow management provides costs and capacity available for remanufacturing and refurbishing in order to identify the best options to recapture value and recover assets.

There is also an interface with the supplier relationship management process. Firms such as large retailers determine their returns management strategy in conjunction with their buying group. The PSAs that are developed with suppliers include policies regarding returns.

Develop Return Avoidance, Gatekeeping and Disposition Guidelines

The second step in the strategic returns management process is to develop return avoidance, gatekeeping and disposition guidelines. This step includes determining the types of returns the firm might face, and developing policies and screening mechanisms to handle those anticipated returns. The team in conjuction with suppliers and customers will develop disposition options for returned items and establish the structure to identify avoidance opportunities.

The use of effective avoidance, gatekeeping and disposition procedures minimizes the cost of moving returned items back through the supply chain. Avoidance aims at reducing the number of return requests. The goal of gatekeeping is to identify as early as possible what products should be accepted as a return. The disposition procedures will enable quick routing of a return to the most appropriate destination. Interfaces with order fulfillment, demand management, supplier relationship management, and product development and commercialization facilitate the construction of these guidelines. Order fulfillment assists the returns

The use of effective avoidance, gatekeeping and disposition procedures minimizes the cost of moving returned items back through the supply chain.

---

[16] Menzies, David, "Reduce, Reuse, Reject," *Canadian Business*, Vol. 73, No. 24 (2000), pp. 135-136.

management process with developing disposition guidelines that reflect the capabilities of the distribution system. Demand management provides long-term forecasts which can be used to structure the disposition guidelines. Supplier relationship management coordinates with suppliers to determine appropriate avoidance and gatekeeping procedures. The link between this sub-process and product development and commercialization facilitates communication about product quality which is critical to return avoidance.

Return avoidance means developing and selling the product in a manner such that return requests are minimized. This is a critical part of returns management and differentiates this process from reverse logistics and the traditional view of returns.

Return Avoidance. Return avoidance means developing and selling the product in a manner such that return requests are minimized. This is a critical part of returns management and differentiates this process from reverse logistics and the traditional view of returns.

Avoidance can be accomplished in a number of ways. For example, it can be derived from improved quality by having fewer items that are defective, or by giving better instructions to the consumer regarding how to properly operate the product. In some consumer electronics categories, over half of the products returned are classified as "no-fault found." In many of these cases, the product was returned because the consumer did not know how to operate it properly. In the computer industry, return avoidance has been improved through "ease-of-use" initiatives,[17] such as a setup poster included inside a computer's shipping box. Because consumers are often intimidated by the complexity of the computer and the accompanying setup manuals, or refuse to read the setup manuals, PC manufacturers include an easy to understand poster that includes pictures and minimal text to improve the consumer's experience and reduce the number of unnecessary support calls and returns. For the TIVO tapeless video recorder and player, many consumers were unaware of the product complexity, that it required a phone line and there was a recurring monthly charge. This misunderstanding by the consumer resulted in many first quality, fully functional TIVO machines being returned to the store. The high return rate could have been reduced if retail sales personnel had been better trained to explain to the consumer how the product functioned.

Black and Decker integrates the returns process with product development to learn from the returns how to develop better products, increase ease-of-use, and minimize future returns. Most Black and Decker returns from around the U.S. flow back to the National Disposition Center in Nashville, Tennessee. The National Disposition Center includes a laboratory for product engineers so that they can evaluate the defective products and work to develop solutions to improve quality or ease-of-use. This has decreased the time it takes to make engineering changes, and reduced the amount of defective product sold.

Consistency of product can be critical in return avoidance. For the catalog business at Victoria's Secret, a lingerie retailer, many returns are a result of sizing issues. If their suppliers do not consistently size the product, consumers might order the wrong size. Victoria's Secret incurs the cost of shipping the item back to the distribution center and putting it back into stock. In order to reduce the number of returns, management works with suppliers to apply sizing guidelines across all

---

[17] Brown, Bruce, "PC Ease of Use: Getting Better ~or Worse?" *Extreme Tech*, July 10, 2001 Ziff Davis Media Inc. (www.extremetech.com).

products in a uniform manner. This reduces the costs associated with returns and improves customer satisfaction. In situations where suppliers have a direct effect on the amount of returns, the returns management team must coordinate with the supplier relationship management team so that suppliers know their role in avoidance.

Internal procedures and metrics can lead to returns. For example, if sales people engage in end-of-quarter loads, some customer firms will accept the product and return unsold product later, despite the fact that both seller and buyer anticipated that some of the product would be returned. In some cases, internal procedures that drive returns reach the end-customer. For instance, catalog retailers frequently offer free shipping if customers spend more than a set minimum. Some customers will spend more than the required amount only to get the free shipping, with intentions to return some of the items. At the strategic level, the process team develops procedures that will be used to identify avoidance opportunities. At the operational level, the team will look for sources of these unnecessary returns and try to change the internal policies to limit them.

Gatekeeping. Gatekeeping is the screening of both the return request and the returned merchandise.[18] When the return request is initiated, it might be possible to divert it to technical support to assist the customer on the appropriate use of the product to avoid the need for the return. If a product is returned, gatekeeping is the screening of the product to determine if it is a valid return. The gatekeeping guidelines include the description of returns that are allowed. Gatekeeping assures that only product that should be returned to a specific point in the returns network is allowed to enter the return flow. Preventing unwarranted returned merchandise from entering the channel improves the disposition of the warranted goods. By gatekeeping at the point of entry into the reverse flow, unnecessary costs can be eliminated. However, there might be more than one gatekeeping point in the supply chain.

Gatekeeping is the screening of both the return request and the returned merchandise.

Failure in gatekeeping can create significant friction between supplier and customer firms, not to mention lost revenue and higher costs. Store-level clerks and front-line personnel are often unwilling or unable to gatekeep returns. Once a sales associate makes a decision about a return, it is usually not overturned. Unwarranted return problems are exacerbated because items that should not be in the return flow continue to pick up additional costs as they travel back through the supply chain. Thus, the sales associates have the power and the responsibility to avoid unnecessary cost. Management has to make sure that sales associates are aware of this and have the necessary information and empowerment to make the right decisions.

Nintendo, the electronic game manufacturer, has developed a particularly innovative gatekeeping system. They encourage retailers to register the game machine at the point of sale. If the game machine is returned to the store, Nintendo and the retailer can determine if the product is covered by warranty, and if it is being returned inside the allotted time. A window was added to the package that allows the product's serial number to be scanned at the point-of-sale. This information updates a database that a retailer can access when the customer brings

---

[18] Rogers, Dale S. and Ron S. Tibben-Lembke, *Going Backwards: Reverse Logistics Trends and Practices,* Pittsburgh, PA: Reverse Logistics Executive Council, 1999.

back a Nintendo machine.[19] This gatekeeping system has become so successful for Nintendo that a spin-off firm, SiRas, has been established to sell the Nintendo gatekeeping solution commercially.

The implementation of effective gatekeeping usually involves integrating some activities with other members of the supply chain. Thus, the involvement of the customer relationship management and supplier relationship management process teams is central to managing the relationships across the supply chain. Considerations related to returns are likely to be an item to be included in the product and service agreements (PSAs).

Disposition refers to the decision about what to do with returned product, which might include resale through secondary markets, recycle, remanufacture or transfer to a landfill.

Disposition. Disposition refers to the decision about what to do with returned product, which might include resale through secondary markets, recycle, remanufacture or transfer to a landfill. The disposition guidelines define the returned items ultimate destiny. A firm forward in the supply chain should make disposition decisions quickly, particularly with products that have date codes or lose value over time. Rules need to be developed for disposition options in conjunction with other members of the supply chain, as well as with input from other processes, such as customer relationship management, product development and commercialization, and supplier relationship management. For example, returning an item to the vendor needs to be accomplished in accordance with the PSA with the supplier that was developed through the supplier relationship management process.

Develop Returns Network and Flow Options

Next, the returns network and flow options are determined. The team develops the reverse logistics network and evaluates if it is appropriate to outsource any of the returns management activities to third-party logistics providers. Transportation modes and methodologies are determined during this sub-process. For example, managers might decide that utilizing backhauls is the most efficient way of transporting returns. For some firms, a network of central return centers might be established to handle returned product separately from products moving forward toward the consumer. Rogers and Tibben-Lembke found that for many firms, distribution centers do not effectively handle both forward and reverse flows.[20]

The customer relationship management team helps assure that the returns management process meets customers' expectations.

This step in the process is completed with input from the customer relationship management, order fulfillment, and product development and commercialization process teams. The customer relationship management team helps assure that the returns management process meets customers' expectations. Input from the order fulfillment process team is important because both forward and reverse flows might use the same resources or systems. If management wants to analyze the returned product and provide feedback into the development of new products, then the product development and commercialization process team should be involved in designing the returns network.

When developing the returns network, the team must consider the different

[19] Rogers, Dale S. and Ron S. Tibben-Lembke, *Going Backwards: Reverse Logistics Trends and Practices,* Pittsburgh, PA: Reverse Logistics Executive Council, 1999.

[20] Rogers, Dale S. and Ron S. Tibben-Lembke, *Going Backwards: Reverse Logistics Trends and Practices,* Pittsburgh, PA: Reverse Logistics Executive Council, 1999.

types of returns and develop procedures that meet the needs of each one. For instance, product recalls usually require an efficient communication system with consumers, and a well thought-out process for how material will be returned and handled. Having the ability to respond to the unexpected can be critical. In 1982, cyanide was put into unopened bottles of Tylenol, poisoning several people in the Chicago area. McNeil Laboratories' response was to immediately recall approximately 31 million bottles of the pain reliever, with a retail value of more than $100 million. The company quickly took the product off the shelf, analyzed all of it for further tampering, and offered consumers incentives such as free replacement of capsules with caplets and coupons for future purchases. The recall was executed with a returns management system that immediately cleansed the channel of any possibly tainted product. Because they acted quickly and competently, long-term sales were not affected negatively and the perception of the brand was strengthened.[21]

Develop Credit Rules

The next sub-process in strategic returns management is to develop credit rules. In this sub-process, general guidelines are established with input from suppliers and customers that will determine how returned merchandise will be valued. Credit authorization guidelines will be developed and credit policies established. Since this involves customers and suppliers, the customer relationship management and the supplier relationship management process teams should be involved in determining the rules that will be included in the PSAs. Determining the value of used items that are returned and unused items that have not sold well also takes place in this sub-process.

Determine Secondary Markets

Once it has been determined where in the supply chain the returned product will be shipped, the process team can examine potential secondary markets. The team will determine which secondary markets are most appropriate. These secondary markets can include Internet-based auctions, or retailers that specialize in returned goods or "seconds." Often, manufacturers that utilize outlet malls as a secondary market will require that the store selling their second products not be located near a retailer for their first quality or new product.

Firms that choose to obtain additional value from items that have been returned must consider sales cannibalization of first quality items and the impact of secondary markets on brand image. For many years the large American automobile companies did not sell remanufactured or refurbished aftermarket parts because they did not want to damage sales of new parts. When they chose not to sell remanufactured parts, an entire industry of salvage dealers and remanufacturers grew to fill the need for less expensive auto parts. The large automobile companies recognized that selling refurbished parts could be as profitable as the new parts business and have now entered this business. If cannibalization is an issue, the team should interface with the customer relationship management and supplier relationship management processes to develop programs that benefit all concerned parties.

Firms that choose to obtain additional value from items that have been returned must consider sales cannibalization of first quality items and the impact of secondary markets on brand image.

---

[21] Roberts, Sally, "Tragedy Spurred Innovation," *Business Insurance*, Vol. 36, No. 42 (2002), pp. 1, 54.

Develop Framework of Metrics

The team should develop procedures for analyzing return rates and tracing the returns back to the root causes.

The last sub-process of strategic returns management is developing the framework of metrics. Metrics that might be used include return rates and financial impact of returns. The team should develop procedures for analyzing return rates and tracing the returns back to the root causes. Measures such as amount of product to be reclaimed and resold as is, or percentage of material recycled are examples of such metrics. For example, at Victoria's Secret Catalog, managers track the cost of returns, what items customers are returning and why, the return percentage, and the percentage of the garments that may be resold. This analysis of returns, in an industry that traditionally has high returns costs, has resulted in a more effective system. For catalog retailers, returns can be a key driver of profitability.

Key metrics should be developed in conjunction with the customer relationship management and supplier relationship management processes, and be included in the PSAs. These agreements might include policies and procedures for handling returns from the customers. Returns management can impact critical firm metrics such as economic value added (EVA). Figure 9-4 depicts the relationship between returns management and EVA. EVA considers not only revenues, costs and profit, but also the cost of assets required to earn stated profits.[22]

For example, better returns management can increase sales through removing

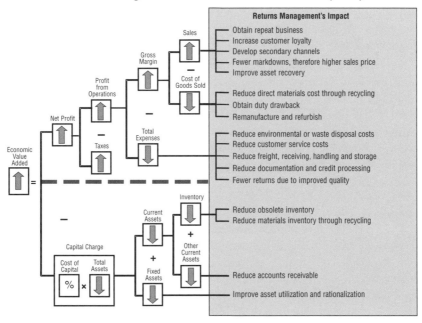

Figure 9-4
How Returns Management Affects Economic Value Added (EVA®)

Source: Framework adapted from Douglas M. Lambert and Terrance L. Pohlen, "Supply Chain Metrics," *The International Journal of Logistics Management*, Vol. 12, No. 1 (2001), p. 10.

[22] Bennett, Stewart G., III, *The Quest for Value: A Guide for Managers*, 2nd Edition, New York, NY: Harper Collins, 1999.

risk from the customer and transferring it back to the firm. This will increase customer loyalty and the probability of obtaining repeat business. Also, sales are increased by the sale of returned products through secondary channels. Returns management improves product freshness by moving slow selling items off of the sales floor and keeping the channel clear. Through avoidance efforts, policies that load the trade will be questioned which also leads to lower markdowns, as well as reduced demand variability which is an objective of the demand management process. Cost of goods sold can be reduced through recycling. The use of remanufactured and refurbished product also reduces the cost of materials. A firm might be entitled to duty drawback for imported products that are returned which reduces the cost of goods sold.

Expenses can be reduced through better management of packaging or products with less negative environmental impact and lower waste disposal costs. Using better returns management can reduce customer service costs, freight and handling costs, documentation and credit processing, and the costs of returns related to poor quality.

Better management of returns can lead to reduction of obsolete inventory both within the firm and throughout the supply chain. Sometimes recycled materials can be used in place of new raw materials so that the value of raw materials inventories can be reduced. Accounts receivable can be improved through better credit management. Better returns management can result in lower fixed assets for investments such as buildings and equipment, particularly if the volume of returns is significantly reduced or third-party providers are used.

The returns management process can have a significant impact on the profitability of customers. For this reason, every attempt should be made to identify and report the revenue, cost, and asset implications of returns management on the profitability of key customers and segments of customers. Changes in assets can be reflected in customer profitability reports by incorporating a charge for assets employed.

The returns management process can have a significant impact on the profitability of customers.

The Operational Returns Management Process

The operational portion of returns management is the realization of the process developed at the strategic level. For returns management, the operational portion is a template for managing returns transactions. It consists of six sub-processes, as shown in Figure 9-5.

Receive Return Request

The process is initiated when a return request is received from the customer who could either be a consumer or another firm downstream in the supply chain. Returns might result from consumers bringing an item back to the store, or they might be marketing returns from retailers or distributors due to slow sales, clearing credit lines, or stock rotation. In some cases, the return requests will come through the customer service management process. For firms with catalog business such as Victoria's Secret, the consumer can submit a return request through the Internet, over the phone, or simply return the item through the mail.

At Hewlett-Packard, when a customer needs to replace a used printer toner cartridge, the returns management process begins when a customer calls a local

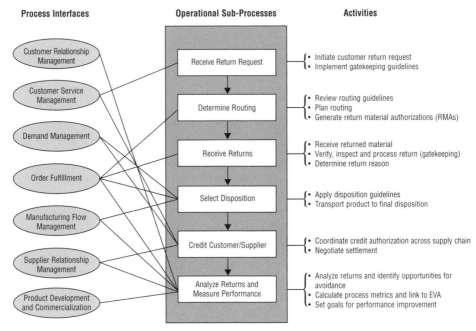

Figure 9-5
The Operational Returns Management Process

Process Interfaces	Operational Sub-Processes	Activities
Customer Relationship Management	Receive Return Request	• Initiate customer return request • Implement gatekeeping guidelines
Customer Service Management	Determine Routing	• Review routing guidelines • Plan routing • Generate return material authorizations (RMAs)
Demand Management	Receive Returns	• Receive returned material • Verify, inspect and process return (gatekeeping) • Determine return reason
Order Fulfillment	Select Disposition	• Apply disposition guidelines • Transport product to final disposition
Manufacturing Flow Management	Credit Customer/Supplier	• Coordinate credit authorization across supply chain • Negotiate settlement
Supplier Relationship Management	Analyze Returns and Measure Performance	• Analyze returns and identify opportunities for avoidance • Calculate process metrics and link to EVA • Set goals for performance improvement
Product Development and Commercialization		

phone number for collection of their boxed, empty toner cartridges. In some cases, a third-party firm handles the customer's calls and picks up the used cartridges from the customer's site. Hewlett-Packard has a 16 percent worldwide return rate on used toner cartridges and 31 percent in the United States. Since 1991, over 47 million toner cartridges have been recycled.

The first gatekeeping should occur when the return requests are received in order to identify items that should not be returned. When a customer calls seeking authorization for a return, the employees can work with the customer to determine if an option other than return may be acceptable. For example, a direct computer retailer may require the customer to speak with a technical support person to assist in determining whether the computer is defective before granting authorization for the return. Most retail stores do not perform this technical support gatekeeping function. For the manufacturer, it is much more difficult to implement gatekeeping when the consumer can bring an item back to the retail store without having to talk to a technical support person that can analyze the problem.

Determine Routing

Once a return request is received, routing is determined based on the guidelines and policies established in the strategic portion of the process.

Once a return request is received, routing is determined based on the guidelines and policies established in the strategic portion of the process. The routing activity is primarily a planning function. During this stage of the process, return material authorizations (RMA) derived from the return requests are generated and advanced ship notices are sent signaling to the receiving location that the returns are on their way. The order fulfillment process may assist in determining the routing.

In many cases, a third party performs this service. Genco, a third-party provider that specializes in reverse logistics and returns management, runs centralized return centers for several customer firms. As part of their end-to-end returns management service offerings, they can manage both the inbound and outbound transportation of the reverse flow. For a few of their large customers, Genco coordinates with carriers to pick up returned merchandise at the retail stores in consolidated milk-run shipments, and then deliver the consolidated loads to the return center at a lower cost than if the store shipped back returned products independently.

Receive Returns

If the return item is sent to a warehouse or central return center, products need to be verified, inspected, and processed. It might be that the order fulfillment process assists in managing the return flow. Generally this is a manual process that should be completed as quickly as possible to improve cash flow. Although gatekeeping is performed at the point of entry to the reverse flow, a thorough evaluation of returned goods must be performed at the warehouse or central return center.

When a product is returned, a reason code should be assigned to it. Typical reason codes developed by the Reverse Logistics Executive Council fall into the categories of repair/service codes, order processing errors, damaged/ defective product, and contractual issues.[23] Returns should be tracked by reason codes to develop more meaningful performance metrics that can provide valuable information both within the firm and to suppliers and customers. In some cases, it is not cost effective to track return reasons in great detail because it is costly to examine and track every return. However, failure to examine products carefully and establish reasons for returns may lead to even higher costs.

Returns should be tracked by reason codes to develop more meaningful performance metrics that can provide valuable information both within the firm and to suppliers and customers.

Select Disposition

The next sub-process in the operational returns management process is to examine each return and select the appropriate disposition. Rules developed in the strategic returns management process and contained in a database that is available to workers processing returns are used to determine the final disposition. The dispositioning of the product can include refurbish, remanufacture, recycle, resell as is, resell through a secondary market, or send the product to a landfill. The order fulfillment and manufacturing flow management processes can assist returns management in determining how and where the disposition is executed. In addition, information about where recoverable product is in the system needs to be communicated with the demand management process.

Short disposition cycle times are a critical element of good returns management, so the speed of disposition should be measured. For electronic items such as computers, product value decreases quickly with time, so it is imperative that the product move quickly into the returns channel. Equally important is that the disposition guidelines are clear and the employees are well-trained to assure that the correct disposition is made.

---

[23] Brothers, Jacob and Dale S. Rogers, Presentation to the Reverse Logistics Executive Council, Chicago, 1997.

It is often less expensive to refurbish returned product than it is to manufacture items from new materials. With the growth of the Internet, secondary markets for refurbished products, such as Internet-enabled auctions, have developed. Companies such as Hewlett-Packard utilize the Internet to sell remanufactured and refurbished product to derive revenues from returned items. The largest secondary market, ebay, now accounts for approximately 25 percent of the dollars spent in e-commerce in the United States and over 55 percent of the e-commerce expenditures in Germany.[24]

Credit Customer/Supplier

Once the returns have been processed, credit needs to be given to the appropriate customer, consumer or supplier. This process can be difficult and requires negotiation between members of the supply chain. Clear rules in the PSAs, will make it easier to determine the appropriate credit. Credit authorization guidelines that were developed in the strategic returns sub-processes are implemented. If the return is complex and has not been negotiated in the PSA, this portion of the process can involve the customer relationship management and supplier relationship management processes, several functions within the firm, and other firms in the supply chain.

Financial issues related to credit to customers and suppliers can impact the efficiency of the returns management process. Much like the push to increase sales near the end of the quarter, some retailers try to shift the ownership of their returned goods and slow moving inventory back to suppliers before closing their books.

Much like the push to increase sales near the end of the quarter, some retailers try to shift the ownership of their returned goods and slow moving inventory back to suppliers before closing their books.

Some downstream supply chain members use chargebacks to get credited by the supplier more quickly. Chargebacks are deductions, discounts or short payments from a supplier's invoice. A retailer may deduct from a supplier's current invoice the amount of the item that they have returned or are planning to return.

Analyze Returns and Measure Performance

The final step in the operational process is to analyze the returns and measure performance. An important component of this step is to use the data on returns to identify opportunities for avoidance in order to make improvements to the product and the other processes. This analysis might result in feedback to order fulfillment, demand management, manufacturing flow management, product development and commercialization, or supplier relationship management. It should also be used in the ongoing strategic returns process to help develop avoidance guidelines.

The rates of defective products can be given to the supplier relationship management process team so that quality can be improved, and/or to the product development and commercialization process team so that product designers can quickly identify problems with their designs. Other key measures are return rates and disposition cycle time. Costs related to returned product and the recovery of value derived from resale or recycling are also critical metrics.

Every effort should be made to document the impact of the returns management process on the financial performance of the firm as measured by EVA

---

[24] Todd Lutwak, Presentation of the Reverse Logistics Executive Council, December 11, 2003.

(see Figure 9-4). While measuring the sales implications will be more difficult than measuring cost and asset implications, potential sales increases should not be ignored since they might have the greatest impact on profitability. Cost reductions and asset reductions are usually much easier to measure and for this reason they are often the only areas where financial performance is measured.

The final activity of the sub-process is to set goals for performance improvement. Following a thorough analysis of firm performance, objectives for improvement are established and communicated within the firm and to relevant portions of the supply chain. These communications with other members of the supply chain are coordinated through the customer relationship management and supplier relationship management processes.

While measuring the sales implications will be more difficult than measuring cost and asset implications, potential sales increases should not be ignored since they might have the greatest impact on profitability.

Conclusions

Returns management as a supply chain management process includes several features that can make an individual firm more effective and efficient. However, the process will provide the most benefits when implemented across members of the supply chain. The returns management process can reduce costs, increase revenues and increase customer satisfaction.

Returns management includes the implementation of avoidance, gatekeeping, disposition guidelines, and the measurement of the financial aspects of returns. Avoidance of unnecessary returns through improved policies and better understanding of the sources and reasons behind returns can reduce the number of return requests which will reduce costs and increase customer satisfaction. Gatekeeping can reduce the cost of doing business by identifying as early as possible the products that should not be returned. Developing disposition guidelines and implementing them across the supply chain will reduce costs by increasing the speed in the reverse flow and assisting in the selection of the destination of the returned product. Linking the performance of the process with the firm's financial measures will help in the appropriate identification of the benefits from returns management which can be used internally to reward managers and, in the supply chain, to reward customers and suppliers.

Overall, the returns management process can increase customer satisfaction by avoiding returns, and in the case of unavoidable or desirable returns, by handling returns quickly and effectively.

Measuring the benefits from returns management may be used to justify investments for future improvements to the process. Returns management can be used strategically to increase switching costs and reduce risk to the customer. Overall, the returns management process can increase customer satisfaction by avoiding returns, and in the case of unavoidable or desirable returns, by handling returns quickly and effectively.

10 Developing and Implementing Partnerships in the Supply Chain

Douglas M. Lambert, A. Michael Knemeyer and John T. Gardner

Overview

An important aspect of implementing supply chain management is the formation of appropriate linkages between members of the supply chain.

An important aspect of implementing supply chain management is the formation of appropriate linkages between members of the supply chain.[1] While practitioners and academics have championed the value of partnerships for this purpose, the challenge is to find effective methods for developing the appropriate type of relationship. In this chapter, we describe a model that can be used to structure business relationships. Implementation issues are documented and direction is provided for managers interested in using this tool for tailoring key supply chain relationships.

Introduction

In an environment characterized by scarce resources, increased competition, higher customer expectations, and faster rates of change, executives are turning to partnerships to strengthen supply chain integration and provide sustainable competitive advantage. Partnering provides a way to leverage the unique skills and expertise of each partner and may also increase switching costs. According to Rosabeth Moss Kanter, "...being a good partner has become a key corporate asset...In the global economy, a well-developed ability to create and sustain fruitful collaborations gives companies a significant competitive leg up".[2] But exactly what is a partnership, and when is one appropriate? At first glance, the answers to these questions might appear straight-forward, but they are not.

---

[1] This chapter is based on Douglas M. Lambert, Margaret A. Emmelhainz and John T. Gardner, "Developing and Implementing Supply Chain Partnerships," *The International Journal of Logistics Management,* Vol. 7, No. 2 (1996), pp. 1-17; Douglas M. Lambert, Margaret A. Emmelhainz and John T. Gardner, "Building Successful Logistics Partnerships," *Journal of Business Logistics,* Vol. 20, No. 1 (1999), pp. 165-181; and, Douglas M. Lambert, A. Michael Knemeyer and John T. Gardner, "Supply Chain Partnerships: Model Validation and Implementation," *Journal of Business Logistics,* forthcoming, 2004.

[2] Kanter, Rosabeth M., "Collaborative Advantage: The Art of Alliances", *Harvard Business Review*, Vol. 72, No. 4 (1994), pp. 96 – 108.

There is considerable confusion over the definition and use of partnerships. As an example, one executive from a major manufacturer in the health care industry identified a relationship with a small-package express delivery company as a partnership. When analyzed in detail, it became apparent that the relationship was not a partnership; rather it was simply a long-term contract with volume guarantees. The reason why managers from both firms believed that they were involved in a partnership was each firm was achieving the desired outcomes from the relationship. The transportation firm received a large revenue increase as the single-source provider of the service and the manufacturer achieved the service improvement and cost reductions that were promised. The initial reaction of an executive from the manufacturer was that she ought to work to turn the relationship into a partnership. This executive's reaction is understandable and fairly common. A basic premise is that partnerships are essential elements of business strategy and managers should strive to achieve such relationships with every customer and supplier. This is not only flawed thinking, it is dangerous thinking. The lesson here is that a partnership is not necessarily a requirement for achieving business success.

When analyzed in detail, it became apparent that the relationship was not a partnership; rather it was simply a long-term contract with volume guarantees. The reason why managers from both firms believed that they were involved in a partnership was each firm was achieving the desired outcomes from the relationship.

Partnerships, while necessary and beneficial, are costly in terms of the time and effort required.[3] Consequently, a firm cannot and should not partner with every supplier, customer or third-party provider. It is important to ensure that scarce resources are dedicated only to those relationships which will truly benefit from a partnership. Yet, many organizations become involved in relationships that do not meet management expectations and/or which end in failure. How can managers determine, in advance, if a potential relationship is one which will result in competitive advantage, and is worthy of the time and resources needed to fully develop into a partnership? Further, all partnerships are not the same. How does management know what type of partnership would provide the best pay-off? These questions may be answered by utilizing the partnership model presented in this chapter.

The partnership model represents a systematic process for developing, implementing and continuously improving corporate relationships. Without a foundation of effective relationships, efforts to manage the flow of materials and information across the supply chain are likely to be unsuccessful.[4] Partnering between firms is one way to find and maintain competitive advantage for both firms.[5] The partnership model provides a structured and repeatable process to effectively and efficiently build and maintain tailored business relationships that might become an asset for executives looking for competitive advantage.

---

[3] Gardner, John T., Martha C. Cooper and Tom Noordewier, "Understanding Shipper-Carrier and Shipper-Warehouser Relationships: Partnerships Revisited," *Journal of Business Logistics*, Vol. 15, No. 2 (1994), pp. 121-143; and, F. Ian Stuart, "Supplier Partnerships: Influencing Factors and Strategic Benefits," *International Journal of Purchasing and Material Management*, Vol. 29, No. 4 (1993), pp. 22-28.

[4] "Supply Chain Challenges: Building Relationships – A Conversation with Scott Beth, David N. Burt, William Copacino, Chris Gopal, Hau L. Lee, Robert Porter Lynch and Sandra Morris," *Harvard Business Review*, Vol. 81, No. 7 (2003), pp. 64-74.

[5] Mentzer, John T., Soonhong Min and Zach G. Zacharia, "The Nature of Interfirm Partnering in Supply Chain Management," *Journal of Retailing*, Vol. 76, No. 4 (2000), pp. 549-568; and, Jakki Mohr and Robert E. Spekman, "Characteristics of Partnership Success: Partnership Attributes, Communication Behavior, and Conflict Resolution Techniques," *Strategic Management Journal*, Vol. 15, No. 2 (1994), pp. 135-152.

What is a Partnership?

Relationships between organizations can range from arm's length relationships (consisting of either one-time exchanges or multiple transactions) to vertical integration of the two organizations, as shown in Figure 10-1. Most relationships between organizations have been at arm's length. Two organizations conduct business with each other, often over a long period of time and involving multiple exchanges. However, there is no sense of joint commitment or joint operations between management teams in the two organizations. In arm's length relationships, a seller typically offers standard products/services to a wide range of customers who receive standard terms and conditions. When the exchanges end, the relationship ends. While arm's length represents an appropriate option in many situations, there are times when a closer, more integrated relationship, referred to as a partnership, provides significant benefits to both firms.

While the word partnership has been interpreted by some to mean any business-to-business relationship, it is still the most descriptive term for closely integrated, mutually beneficial relationships that enhance supply chain performance. We believe that a partnership is most appropriately defined as follows:[6]

A partnership is a tailored business relationship based on mutual trust, openness, shared risk and shared rewards that results in business performance greater than would be achieved by the two firms working together in the absence of partnership.

> A partnership is a tailored business relationship based on mutual trust, openness, shared risk and shared rewards that results in business performance greater than would be achieved by the two firms working together in the absence of partnership.

A key point of this definition is that the relationship is customized. It is not standard fare, that is, something that would be done for any customer of a particular size. Another key point is that incremental benefits must be gained from the tailoring effort. The tailoring process consumes managerial time and talent, thus it must yield measurable benefits.

A partnership is not the same as a joint venture which normally entails some degree of shared ownership across the two parties. Nor is it the same as vertical integration. Yet a well managed partnership can provide benefits similar to those found in joint ventures or vertical integration without the problems associated with ownership. For instance, a few years ago Pepsi chose to acquire restaurants such as Taco Bell, Pizza Hut and KFC. One of the benefits of these acquisitions was that

Figure 10-1
Types of Relationships

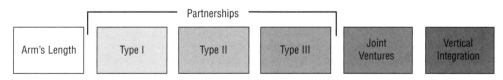

Source: Douglas M. Lambert, Margaret A. Emmelhainz and John T. Gardner, "Developing and Implementing Supply Partnerships," *The International Journal of Logistics Management*, Vol. 7, No. 2 (1996), p. 2.

---

[6] Lambert, Douglas M., Margaret A. Emmelhainz and John T. Gardner, "Developing and Implementing Supply Chain Partnerships," *The International Journal of Logistics Management*, Vol. 7, No. 2 (1996), pp. 1-17; and, Douglas M. Lambert, Margaret A. Emmelhainz and John T. Gardner (1999), "Building Successful Logistics Partnerships," *Journal of Business Logistics*, Vol. 20, No. 1 (1999), pp. 165-181.

PepsiCo could ensure that Coca-Cola would not be sold in these outlets. Coca-Cola achieved a similar result, without the cost of vertical integration, through its partnership with McDonald's. In the late 1990's, PepsiCo got out of the restaurant business saying that it detracted management attention from the core business.

Research also supports the ability of partnerships to achieve cost savings and reduce duplication of efforts by the firms involved.[7] For suppliers, partnerships with industry leaders can enhance operations and prestige,[8] and provide stability in unstable markets.[9] For buyers, partnerships can improve profitability, reduce purchasing costs, and increase technical cooperation.[10]

While most partnerships share some common elements and characteristics, there is no one ideal or "benchmark" relationship which is appropriate in all situations. Because each relationship has its own set of motivating factors driving its development as well as its own unique operating environment, the duration, breadth, strength and closeness of the partnership will vary from case to case and over time. Three types of partnerships exist:

- **Type I** - The organizations involved recognize each other as partners and, on a limited basis, coordinate activities and planning. The partnership usually has a short-term focus and typically involves only one division or a limited number of functional areas within each organization.

- **Type II** - The organizations involved progress beyond coordination of activities to integration of activities. Although not expected to last "forever" the partnership has a long-term horizon. Multiple divisions and functions within the firm are involved in the partnership.

- **Type III** - The organizations share a significant level of operational integration. Each party views the other as an extension of their own firm. Typically no "end date" for the partnership exists.

Normally, a firm will have a wide range of relationships spanning the entire spectrum, the majority of which will not be partnerships at all but arm's length relationships. The largest percentage of partnerships will be Type I with only a limited number of Type III. Type III partnerships should be reserved for two or three percent of suppliers or customers who are critical to an organization's long-term success.

Normally, a firm will have a wide range of relationships spanning the entire spectrum, the majority of which will not be partnerships at all but arm's length relationships.

[7] Herbing, Paul A. and Bradley S. O'Hara, "The Future of Original Equipment Manufacturers: A Matter of Partnerships," *Journal of Business and Industrial Marketing*, Vol. 9, No. 3 (1994), pp. 38-43; Judith S. Whipple, Robert Frankel and David J. Frayer, "Logistical Alliance Formation Motives: Similarities and Differences with the Channel," *Journal of Marketing Theory and Practice*, Vol. 4, No. 2 (1996), pp. 26-36; and, Walter Zinn and A. Parasuraman, "Scope and Intensity of Logistics-Based Strategic Alliances: A Conceptual Classification and Managerial Implications," *Industrial Marketing Management*, Vol. 26, No. 2 (1997), pp. 137-147.

[8] Anderson, James C. and James A. Narus, "Partnering as a Focused Marketing Strategy," *California Management Review*, Vol. 33, No. 3 (1991), pp. 95-113; and, Robert E. Spekman, "Strategic Supplier Selection: Understanding Long-Term Buyer Relationships," *Business Horizons*, Vol. 31, No. 4 (1988), pp. 75-81.

[9] Fram, Eugene H. and Martin L. Presberg, "Customer Partnering: Suppliers' Attitudes and Market Realities," *Journal of Business and Industrial Marketing*, Vol. 8, No. 4 (1993), pp. 43-51.

[10] Ailawadi, Kusum L., Paul W. Farris and Mark E. Parry, "Market Share and ROI: Observing the Effect of Unobserved Variables," *International Journal of Research in Marketing*, Vol. 16, No. 1 (1999), pp. 17-33; and, Sang-Lin Han, David T. Wilson and Shirish P. Dant, "Buyer-Supplier Relationships Today," *Industrial Marketing Management*, Vol. 22, No. 4 (1993), pp. 331-338.

Development of the Model

The partnership model was initially developed using detailed case studies of relationships involving members of The Global Supply Chain Forum who identified 18 relationships which they believed reflected good partnerships that we could learn from (see Table 10-1). These case studies, along with a detailed literature review, and Forum members' input were used as the basis for the development of the partnership model. Over the past few years, the model has been further refined and validated through the facilitation of 20 partnership sessions in a wide variety of contexts. This systematic validation of the model provided support for the value of using the model as well as a number of specific guidelines on implementation issues.

Of the 20 partnership meetings facilitated to validate the model, a major retailer provided an opportunity to use the model with nine product and service suppliers that involved a diverse set of relationships. Both critical component suppliers and support product suppliers were included in the sample. Another nine partnership cases were completed with three companies in the consumer goods

---

Table 10-1
Relationship Cases Used to Develop the Model

Lucent Technologies (formerly known as AT&T Network Systems) and Panalpina for freight forwarding services of telecommunications equipment in the South American Market. Lucent Technologies manufactures and installs telecommunications systems, high-tech fibers, and switching technologies. The systems are shipped in the form of component parts with final assembly and installation in-country. As Lucent entered the Latin America market, it found customs documentation requirements to be particularly burdensome. For instance, the Brazilian government required that the documentation describe every separate part and item. For large systems this was equivalent to taking an automobile apart and shipping it by every nut, bolt, screw, fender, and bumper. Panalpina is a forwarder with offices in facilities in Central and South America and with a well established in-country infrastructure.

A small package express delivery company and a manufacturer for national distribution of healthcare products. This involved an offering of both air and ground transportation on the part of the carrier and a guaranteed volume on the part of the manufacturer.

McDonald's and Martin-Brower for the distribution of products and supplies to franchisees and company stores Martin-Brower is the largest of McDonald's six distributors, handling approximately 40% of McDonald's locations. Martin-Brower

distributes a complete range of products from food supplier to paper items.

McDonald's and OSI for the supply of hamburger patties to McDonald's restaurants. OSI is a manufacturer of beef patties, supplying approximately 25% of McDonald's volume. McDonald's is OSI's only customer.

McDonald's and Coca-Cola for the supply of beverages to McDonald's restaurants. McDonald's is Coke's largest customer and Coke is McDonald's largest supplier. Coca-Cola is the only cola beverage sold in any McDonald's store.

Xerox and Ryder for the delivery, installation, and removal of copiers. In this relationship, Ryder truck drivers deliver, set-up, test, and demonstrate copiers for Xerox. In addition, the drivers also perform initial customer training and remove old equipment.

Xerox and Ryder for inbound transportation services to Xerox's manufacturing locations. Xerox depends upon Ryder Dedicated Logistics to manage the Xerox in-bound network so that JIT requirements are met.

Whirlpool and ERX for the warehousing an distribution of Whirlpool appliances to dealers and customers within 24-48 hours of order placement. Quality Express is a program through which Whirlpool sought to improve its customer service levels by partnering with third party providers. ERX

is a joint venture between MARK VII, a transportation company, and Elston-Richards, a warehousing company, and operates six of eight Quality Exporess programs.

Whirlpool and IP Logistics for the warehousing and distribution of Whirlpool appliances to dealers and customers in one of eight Quality Express program. KP Logistics is a partnership between Kenco, a warehousing company, and Premier Transportation.

Whirlpool and TRMTI (Leaseway) for the warehousing and distribution of appliances to dealers and customers from one of eight Quality Express locations. TRMTI is a division of Leaseway Transportation and had been providing delivery services to builders in Florida for Whirlpool prior to the initiation of Quality Express.

3M and Yellow Freight for less-than-truckload outbound transportation services. This was a relationship which extended from 1981 until 1993 and evolved from a one-year contract to a long-term based arrangement.

Target and 3M for a wide range of consumer products. This arrangement involves seven distinct relationships: one between the two corporations and six others between 3M divisions and Target departments.

Source: Douglas M. Lambert, Margaret A. Emmelhainz and John T. Gardner, "Developing and Implementing Supply Chain Partnerships," *The International Journal of Logistics Management,* Vol. 7, No. 2 (1996), p. 3.

sector and their suppliers. These relationships included suppliers of raw materials and packaging materials as well as a vertically integrated internal relationship between two wholly owned subsidiaries of the same company who also conducted business with companies outside of the relationship. The final two cases involved a major company in the technology sector and two service suppliers.

The methodology used to develop and validate the model addresses a number of frequently cited criticisms of partnership research. For instance, Baba complained that most partnership research was based only on a limited number of interviews, often with just one executive, from only one party to the relationship.[11] Another concern is that much partnership research is based upon mail surveys. While mail surveys enable the gathering of large amounts of data from numerous sources, the extent and richness of the data collected are limited. Also, with a mail survey, there is no assurance that all participants are interpreting the question in the same way or really understand what is meant by partnership.

The methodology used to develop and validate the model addresses a number of frequently cited criticisms of partnership research.

While case studies of partnerships do provide a fuller picture at the micro organizational level, such studies have not followed a unified research framework that would permit replication and generalization of findings. Partnership studies would benefit from research designs aimed at identification and explication of integrative processes that serve to bond partners and strengthen interorganizational relationships. Future research on partnerships must have the partnership dyad as the minimum unit of analysis. Investigations that capture only from one side of a given partnership (even if both partner types are represented in a sample) will fail to reflect accurately the dynamic forces that bond or break partnerships in the long run.[12]

The Partnership Model

The partnership model is comprised of four steps: examination of the drivers of partnership, examination of the facilitators of partnership, calibration of the components of partnership, and the measurement of outcomes.[13] Drivers are the compelling reasons to partner, and must be examined first when approaching a potential partner. Facilitators are characteristics of the two firms that will help or hinder the partnership development process. It is the combination of facilitators and drivers that prescribes the appropriate type of partnership. Components are the managerially controllable elements that can be implemented at various levels depending on the amount of partnership present. How they are actually implemented will determine the type of partnership that exists. Outcomes are the extent to which each firm has achieved its expected performance drivers (see Figure 10-2). Partnerships in practice require a repeatable managerial process that will guide the analysis and implementation of appropriate levels of relationship components. The successes attributed to the use of the model indicate that it is a

---

[11] Baba, Maretta L., "Two Sides to Every Story: An Ethnohistorical Approach to Organizational Partnerships", *City and Society*, Vol. 2, No. 2 (1988), pp. 71-104.

[12] Baba, Maretta L., "Two Sides to Every Story: An Ethnohistorical Approach to Organizational Partnerships", *City and Society*, Vol. 2, No. 2 (1988), p. 75.

[13] Lambert, Douglas M., Margaret A. Emmelhainz and John T. Gardner, "Building Successful Logistics Partnerships," *Journal of Business Logistics*, Vol. 20, No. 1 (1999), pp. 165-181.

Figure 10-2
Partnership Model

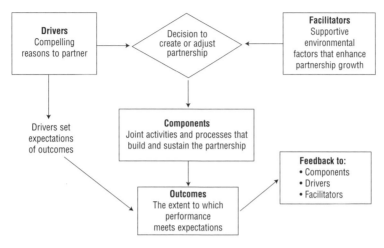

Source: Douglas M. Lambert, Margaret A. Emmelhainz, and John T. Gardner, "Developing and Implementing Supply Chain Partnerships," *The International Journal of Logistics Management*, Vol. 7, No. 2 (1996), p. 4.

valuable tool for implementing supply chain partnerships. Managers consistently report that they would not have considered as many issues and would not have done so as holistically without the structure provided by the model. Some of the outcomes have surprised the users. A retailer used the model with a supplier who subsequently acquired a west coast manufacturing capability to provide full national coverage. The investment had been resisted before the partnership meeting. In another example, a consumer products manufacturer used the model in order to increase the flow of innovation opportunities from key suppliers. During one partnership meeting, a supplier committed to assigning a dedicated salesperson as well as dedicating an employee in their research and development area to this manufacturer. This commitment was made because the partnership meeting identified the concerns of the manufacturer regarding how the confidentiality of joint innovations between the companies would be handled.

Both qualitative and quantitative measures provided by managers support the value of using the model to tailor relationships within the supply chain.

Both qualitative and quantitative measures provided by managers support the value of using the model to tailor relationships within the supply chain. Management of a consumer products manufacturer identified that one of the outcomes of using the model was the implementation of a vendor managed supply system that produced $4.3 million in annual savings. Another case involving this manufacturer resulted in $2.8 million in annual savings by identifying an opportunity to work with the supplier to restructure its supply network. One company attributed the acceleration of a plant opening (a reduction of 2 months) to using the model.

The next section of the chapter provides guidance on how to use the partnership model. First, a description of the preparation that must take place prior to using the model is outlined. Next, the partnership facilitation process is reviewed with a specific focus on providing practical suggestions on how to maximize its effectiveness as a managerial tool. Finally, a set of broader issues concerning the use of the model is detailed.

Preparation for Meeting

All parties involved in the process, meeting process facilitators (MPFs) and participants, have activities that should be completed prior to the meeting. These activities include participant selection decisions, meeting scheduling, meeting planning issues and groundwork issues.

The management team that has made the decision to use the model must determine which business relationship(s) are candidates. Managers may go through a learning curve, therefore, it is beneficial to begin with an important relationship but not a critical relationship in order to gain experience. Once a comfort level with the model has been developed, more critical relationships can be addressed. Additionally, management should consider the word-of-mouth issues associated with the decision to use the model with specific companies. In particular, what might be the reaction within a supplier or customer organization when it is discovered that a competitor has gone through the process and they have not? During several of our facilitations, managers from the company invited to participate in the meeting asked who else had gone through the process.

The meetings are greatly enhanced by the presence of individuals from multiple levels within the organizations and with diverse functional expertise. The make-up of the group sends a message to those in the other firm about the importance of the relationship to the party proposing the meeting. It is important to involve the highest-level executives possible and still have the meeting. The more levels of management above the people in the room, the more likely a change in one of these more senior managers will negatively impact the commitments made in the meeting.

The meetings are greatly enhanced by the presence of individuals from multiple levels within the organizations and with diverse functional expertise.

The need to have the involvement of multiple levels of employees with diverse functional expertise makes scheduling difficult. As was stated by one participant, "this is the first time all of these people have been together in the same room." The best way to handle this challenge is to have a high-level executive both state that the meeting is a priority and also attend the meeting. During our use of the model, the presidents of several of the firms attended the entire meeting.

Some additional insights into the preparation for the meetings can be summed up as follows:

- Publish a detailed agenda in order to establish expectations and maintain focus.
- Schedule sessions of one and a half days (back-to-back partnership meetings are not recommended).
- Schedule a dinner at the end of the first day to enable networking and clarification of the discussions that took place during the day.
- Review the model in advance (this is a must do for all participants).
- Make sure that MPFs are conversant in the business situation.
- Provide a neutral location, spacious rooms, and proper supplies for recording and communicating the process.
- Provide to participants packets that include an agenda, a list of participants, and copies of materials.

While the preparation details appear to be intuitive, some meetings were hampered by a lack of attention to these issues.

The Partnership Meeting

Once the preparatory work is done the partnership meeting is held. This meeting is a complex, multi-session process in which expectations are set, the environment is examined, and action plans are developed and assigned. Specific details related to the partnership meeting are described in the following sections. We describe the sessions as outlined in Table 10-2. The primary sessions include: 1) introduction and expectation setting session; 2) drivers session; 3) facilitators session; 4) targeting session; 5) components session; and 6) the wrap-up session. We include a general overview of the session and where appropriate discussion assessment issues. Information on conducting each of the sessions is provided.

Introduction and Expectation Setting Session. The partnership meeting should begin with an introduction that reinforces the motivations for undertaking the process, a review of the model, and a discussion about expectations. For example, the vice president of one company detailed the corporate goals of increased

Table 10-2
Partnership Facilitation – Key Points and Challenges

Process Stage	Key Points	Challenges
Preparation for Meeting	- review model prior to the meeting - invite appropriate participants to include multiple levels and functions	- scheduling difficulties
Introduction and Expectation Setting Session	- communicate that the business is not at risk - establish expectations of the process	- ensuring candid discussion
Drivers Session	- communicate the need to be selfish when establishing drivers - ensure confidentiality of session - be prepared to present ideas to the other party	- establishing solid driver metrics - explaining the customer service driver to the supplier - learning how to score the drivers
Facilitators Session	- establish environment for the joint session - learning how to jointly score the facilitators	- ensuring candid discussion - establishing the need to provide examples of past behavior
Targeting Session	- explaining the need to use lowest driver score	- communicating to the parties that the goal is the appropriate level of partnership, not to have the highest level
Managerial Components Session	- connecting to drivers and prescribed level of partnership - formulating action plans that address managerial components and drivers	- connecting action items to drivers - prioritizing action items - incorporating driver metrics
Wrap-up Session	- establishing appropriate follow-up schedule - establishing appropriate assessment	- maintaining momentum - ensuring the allocation of managerial resources in order to execute action plans

Source: Douglas M. Lambert, A. Michael Knemeyer and John T. Gardner, "Supply Chain Partnerships: Model Validation and Implementation," *Journal of Business Logistics*, forthcoming.

innovation and profit margin growth as the underlying reason for using the model to build more structure into their relationships with key suppliers. In another firm, the vice president stated that the motivation for using the model was to achieve a structured and consistent approach to supply chain relationship management. Whatever the reason, it is critical for those in attendance to understand that the business is not at risk.

It is common for participants from one of the companies to want more partnership because they feel that somehow it relates to the security of the business. It is important for the MPF to establish from the very beginning of the session that the goal is to tailor the partnership to the most efficient and effective type. It should be made clear that the goal is NOT to have a Type III partnership but to determine the most appropriate type of partnership. The goal should be to obtain the desired business results for the least amount of effort. Incremental benefits must accrue to both firms, if management is going to invest incremental effort. This point should be reinforced throughout the meeting. The managerial time wasted on an unneeded Type III partnership would have large opportunity costs.

> *It should be made clear that the goal is NOT to have a Type III partnership but to determine the most appropriate type of partnership. The goal should be to obtain the desired business results for the least amount of effort.*

Some additional issues concerning the critical role of the MPF are:

- Two MPFs from outside the relationship are needed for the session that develops the drivers for each company.
- The MPF also serves as the lead trainer and pace setter for the process.
- The individual must be skilled in building consensus, probing for more information, assuring closure, and reinforcing agreements on action plans.

These recommendations were drawn from multiple cases. For instance, during a meeting at their customer's location, one supplier stated that the driver session felt like it was taking place back at their own headquarters. This comfort level would be difficult to achieve without an unbiased MPF.

Drivers Session. Both parties must believe that they will receive significant benefits in one or more areas and that these benefits would not be possible without a partnership. The potential benefits which drive the desire to partner include: asset/cost efficiencies, customer service improvements, marketing advantages, and profit stability/growth. In addition, it is important to clarify how best to assess these drivers and how to conduct a drivers session.

> *Both parties must believe that they will receive significant benefits in one or more areas and that these benefits would not be possible without a partnership.*

- **Asset/Cost Efficiencies.** A potential for cost reduction provides a strong reason to partner. Closer integration of activities might lead to reductions in transportation costs, handling costs, packaging costs, information costs, or product costs and may increase managerial efficiencies. A partnership may also enhances the development and use of specialized equipment and processes between the parties, without fear of technology transfer to a competitor.[14] McDonald's found that by establishing partnerships with regional distributors who serve as the single distributor for all products to all stores within a region, delivery and ordering costs were reduced.
- **Customer Service.** Integrating activities in the supply chain through partnerships can often lead to service improvement for customers in the form of reduced inventory, shorter cycle times, and more timely and

---

[14] Williamson, Oliver E., *Markets and Hierarchies: Analysis and Antitrust Implications,* New York: The Free Press, 1975.

accurate information.[15] After discovering that they were significantly slower in deliveries to dealers and had more damage than competitors, Whirlpool developed a Type III partnership with ERX, a logistics service provider. According to a Whirlpool executive, "Our original goal was to be 95% on-time, within the first year. By the fourth month we were at 99%".

- **Marketing Advantage.** A third reason for entering into a partnership is to gain a marketing advantage. A stronger integration between two organizations can: (1) enhance an organization's marketing mix; (2) ease entry into new markets; and, (3) provide better access to technology and innovation.[16] Through its partnership with Ryder for delivery and installation of copiers, Xerox was able to reduce its costs and thus become more price competitive. Target chose to partner with 3M in order to gain access to special packaging, and creative promotional and product strategies.
- **Profit Stability/Growth.** A potential for profit improvement is a strong driver for most partnerships. Strengthening of a relationship often leads to long-term volume commitments, reduced variability in sales, joint use of assets, and other improvements which enhance profitability.[17]

While the presence of strong drivers is necessary for successful partnerships, the drivers by themselves do not ensure success. The benefits derived from the drivers must be sustainable over the long term. If, for instance, the marketing advantage or cost efficiencies resulting from the relationship can be easily matched by a competitor, the probability of long-term partnership success is reduced.

Assessing Drivers. In evaluating a relationship, how does a manager know if there are enough drivers to pursue a partnership? First, drivers must exist for each party. It is unlikely that the drivers will be the same for both parties, but they need to be strong for both. For instance, in the Whirlpool/ERX partnership, improved service was the driver for Whirlpool, while stable, guaranteed volume was the driver for ERX. Second, the drivers must be strong enough to provide each party with a realistic expectation of significant benefits through a strengthening of the relationship.

...drivers must exist for each party. It is unlikely that the drivers will be the same for both parties, but they need to be strong for both.

Each party should independently assess the strength of their specific drivers by using the assessment guide shown in Table 10-3. The guide lists the four drivers and provides examples of each. These examples are not meant to be all inclusive, but rather should be used only as a starting point. Both parties to the potential relationship must develop and agree upon specific descriptors of each driver that are appropriate for the relationship. Further, parameters for measuring each descriptor must be developed. For instance, under the driver Asset/Cost Efficiencies, the parties must decide whether a product cost reduction target should be established. It is important that the descriptors of each driver be specified and agreed upon because the success of the partnership will be measured based upon

---

[15] Weitz, Barton and Sandy Jap, "Relationship Marketing and Distribution Channels", *Journal of the Academy of Marketing Science,* Vol. 23, No. 4 (1995), pp. 305 – 320.

[16] Oliver, Christine, "Determinants of Inter-organizational Relationships: Integration and Future Directions", *Academy of Management Review,* Vol. 15, No. 2 (1990), pp. 241 – 265.

[17] Noordeweir, Thomas G., George John and John R. Nevin, "Performance Outcomes of Purchasing Arrangements in Industrial Buyer-Vendor Relationships", *Journal of Marketing,* Vol. 54, No. 4 (1990), pp. 80 – 93.

Table 10-3
Assessment of Drivers

Drivers are strategic factors which result in a competitive advantage and which help to determine the appropriate level of a business relationship. For each driver, circle the boxed number which reflects the probability of your organization **realistically** achieving a benefit **through forming a tighter relationship**.

		Probability			
ASSET/COST EFFICIENCY	No Chance 0%	25%	50%	75%	Certain 100%
1. *What is the probability that this relationship will substantially reduce channel costs or Improve asset utilization?*	1	2	3	4	5

-product costs savings
-distribution costs savings, handling costs savings
-packing costs savings, information handling costs savings
-managerial efficiencies
-assets to the relationship

If you rated efficiencies in the shaded area and if the advantage is either a sustainable competitive advantage or it allows your firm to match benchmark standards in your industry, circle the I to the right.　　　　　　　　　　　　　1

		Probability			
CUSTOMER SERVICE	No Chance 0%	25%	50%	75%	Certain 100%
2. *What is the probability that this relationship will substantially improve the customer service level as measured by the customer?*	1	2	3	4	5

-improved on-time delivery
-better tracking of movement
-paperless order processing
-accurate order deliveries
-improved cycle times
-improved fill rates
-customer survey results
-process improvements

If you rated customer service in the shaded area and if the advantage is either a sustainable competitive advantage or if it allows your firm to match benchmark standards in your industry, circle the I to the right.　　　　　　　　　1

		Probability			
MARKETING ADVANTAGE	No Chance 0%	25%	50%	75%	Certain 100%
3. *What is the probability that this relationship will lead to substantial marketing advantages?*	1	2	3	4	5

-new market entry
-promotion joint advertising, sales promotion)
-price (reduced price advantage)
-product jointly developed product Innovation, branding opportunities)
-place (expanded geographic coverage, market saturation)
-access to technology
-innovation potential

It you rated marketing advantage in the shaded area and it the advantage is either a sustainable competitive advantage or if it allows your firm to match benchmark standards in your industry, circle the I to the right.　　　　　　　　1

		Probability			
PROFIT STABILITY/GROWTH	No Chance 0%	25%	50%	75%	Certain 100%
4. *What is the probability that this relationship will result in profit growth or reduced variability in profit?*	1	2	3	4	5

-growth
-cyclical leveling
-seasonal leveling
-market share stability
-sales volume
-assurance of supply

It you rated profit stability/growth in the shaded area and if the advantage is either a sustainable competitive advantage or if it allows your firm to match benchmark standards in your industry, circle the 1 to the right.　　　　　　　　1

Add all the boxed numbers which you have circled and place the total in the box to the right. This represents the strength of your motivation to partner.

Source: Douglas M. Lambert, Margaret A. Emmelhainz and John T. Gardner, "Developing and Implementing Supply Chain Partnerships," *The International Journal of Logistics Management*, Vol. 7, No. 2 (1996), p. 6.

whether the desired improvements are actually achieved.

The guide provides a rating scheme with a maximum score of 24. A very low score (below 8) indicates that the potential pay-off from a partnership is so low that it should not be pursued. Therefore, it is not necessary to proceed with the model and evaluate the facilitators. A score of 8 or above indicates that facilitators should be examined. A high score (16 or above) indicates a potential for significant benefits and suggests that a partnership should be pursued.

Conducting a Drivers Session. It is necessary to ensure that the two parties objectively analyze their potential drivers of partnership. Representatives of the two firms should evaluate drivers separately and the evaluation must be from a selfish perspective. In addition, there are several other issues that must be addressed during the session.

A fundamental issue is the potential for double counting. Since profits are a function of costs, service and marketing, there is a possibility for double counting. If a supplier hopes to market better as a result of increased partnership, they will also expect higher profit. A key for success is to warn the participants not to double count. They should use the first three drivers whenever they are appropriate. Only those potential drivers of profit that do not overlap with the others or do not focus on any one of the others should be included in profit stability and growth. If a customer service improvement by the seller yields lower inventories for the buyer, this is asset/cost efficiency for the buyer. If it yields better customer service to the buyer's customers, then it should be counted as a customer service improvement for the buyer. If a joint effort can level volumes, then it should be recorded in profit stability and growth.

Another difficulty with identifying and scoring drivers comes from the need to consider only the incremental gains possible through partnership. Thus, if a cost savings could be gained through hard bargaining or competitive bidding, it should not be scored high as a driver. If a savings due to deploying new technology could only be contemplated in the context of a close, long-term cooperative relationship, then it should be counted. Making this distinction is often difficult.

It can be challenging to get suppliers to think in terms of their own self-interest particularly if the buyer initiated the partnership meeting. Since they respond to the customer in a customer-oriented way in most discussions, taking a selfish perspective is sometimes difficult.

Evaluation of the customer service often poses a problem for sellers. They want to score as a driver, customer service improvements to the potential partner. While these are advantages to the potential partner, they are not compelling reasons for the seller to want a closer relationship. In order for the evaluation to be selfish on the part of the seller, only customer service improvements that can be offered to other customers as a result of more closeness in this relationship should be counted. If a firm, through partnership, can develop a customer service delivery approach that can later be rolled out for non-partner accounts, then the seller can score customer service as a compelling reason to partner.

When evaluating a driver each side should define specific bullets that apply to their business situation. It is important to put measurable goals on each specific bullet identified by the participants. An example for cost efficiency could be to reduce controllable costs in the component parts by five percent per year. A

Representatives of the two firms should evaluate drivers separately and the evaluation must be from a selfish perspective.

marketing advantage that would be harder to quantify in dollars would be to come up with at least five new product ideas over a two-year period, one of which would reach commercialization. After the group comes up with drivers specific to their situation, the MPF should challenge them to come up with measurable goals.

For each partnership driver, the managers of the buying firm and the managers of the selling firm must independently decide on a probability. For the first driver, the question is "What is the probability that this relationship will substantially reduce channel costs or improve asset utilization?" The scoring is on a five-point basis from 1 to 5 ranging from zero percent chance to 100 percent chance. Thus, in the scoring process the managers from each firm will determine four driver scores based on the probability of making substantial gains for their firm. There is no expectation that the drivers will be in the same categories for each firm, nor will the total scores be the same. Each side must assess their own self-interest independently and honestly, which is why the business cannot be at risk.

There is no expectation that the drivers will be in the same categories for each firm, nor will the total scores be the same. Each side must assess their own self-interest independently and honestly, which is why the business cannot be at risk.

Drivers are assessed on "the probability that this relationship will substantially…" with the key word being substantially. If the driver bullets within one of the four drivers are collectively weak on substantiality, then a probability of getting a substantial advantage should be low before factoring uncertainty into the judgment. When one buyer organization assessed the potential for cost avoidance through partnership, they found a large number of potential savings. However, the total savings would only amount to a small part of one percent of the overall costs for the firm. Therefore, the rating had to be a low score even though managers thought achieving the savings was relatively certain.

It is important to have a blank driver form for the recording of driver elements specific to the relationship rather than use the generalized bullet points in the original model. The group should develop an exhaustive list of descriptors for each specific driver and then through discussion reduce it to a parsimonious list that can be summarized in a few bullet points. Each category should be evaluated and scored. Evaluating each and weighting each, then coming up with a probability for each may add a false sense of accuracy, slow the process, and/or defy consensus. The participants should seek consensus for the final number for each of the four drivers. It is not reasonable to average the numbers, since one person's reason to choose a low or high probability may not have been factored into others' thinking. Talking about differences and coming to consensus is very useful in encouraging communication between the participants and facilitating implementation later. Issues come out in the defense of specific ratings that otherwise would not emerge. Also, there needs to be buy-in from the participants if the drivers are to be achieved.

Drivers for the supplier and the buyer will rarely match up in strength by category. It is important to emphasize this to the seller, as they often feel that their score on a particular driver should match their counterpart's score. In fact, often sellers have low customer service scores while buyers often have high customer service scores. It is not important that the scores match, just that both sides have compelling reasons to commit more resources to the relationship than is typical of an arm's-length relationship.

Once each side has scored their drivers, the next step is to come together and present these drivers to the other side. It is important for the other side to explain why the drivers were selected and how they were scored. This represents an expectations-setting session that is critical for partnership success. One of the reasons that partnerships fail is the existence of unrealistic expectations by one of both of the parties involved in the relationship.[18] What each bullet point means as well as the score for the overall driver and the thinking behind that score needs to be understood by both sides of the relationship. If the representatives of the other firm indicate that they cannot or will not help achieve a particular driver, the driver should be reevaluated. If no one in the session objects to the other side's drivers, then management is obligated to help the other firm achieve its drivers as the partnership is implemented.

There is a direct connection between drivers and outcomes. If the drivers are quantified well in the driver assessment process, then the evaluation of the partnership over time is made much easier. An example for asset/cost efficiency would be the reduction of logistics costs by 7% per year over the next three years. By knowing the exact expectation there is more realistic buy-in and better tracking of progress when outcomes are measured over time.

Drivers provide the motivation to partner. But even with a strong desire for building a partnership, the probability of success is reduced if both corporate environments are not supportive of a close relationship.

Facilitators Session. Drivers provide the motivation to partner. But even with a strong desire for building a partnership, the probability of success is reduced if both corporate environments are not supportive of a close relationship. On the other hand, a supportive environment which enhances integration of the two parties will improve the success of the partnership.

Facilitators are elements of a corporate environment which allow a partnership to grow and strengthen. They serve as a foundation for a good relationship. In the short run, facilitators cannot be developed. They either exist or they do not. And the degree to which they exist often determines whether a partnership succeeds or fails. Facilitators include: corporate compatibility, similar managerial philosophy and techniques, mutuality, and symmetry.

- **Corporate Compatibility.** For an integrated relationship to succeed, partners must share compatible values. The cultures and business objectives of the two firms must mesh. They do not have to be identical, but they cannot clash. For instance, the value placed on strategic planning and the approaches used for planning should be similar. The more similar the culture and objectives, the more comfortable the partners are likely to feel, and the higher the chance of partnership success.[19]

- **Managerial Philosophy and Techniques.** Another important facilitator is the compatibility of management philosophy and techniques between the two firms. While corporate culture changes very slowly and business objectives are set at the top, operational level managers implement the objectives through their managerial philosophy and techniques. Such things as organizational structure, attitude toward employee empowerment, the relative importance of teamwork and the level of commitment to continuous improvement are examples of management philosophies.[20] The strong

---

[18] Foster, Thomas A., "Lessons Learned," *Logistics*, No. 4 (1999), pp. 67-70.

[19] Deshpande, Rohit, and Fedrick E. Webster, "Organizational Culture and Marketing: Defining a Research Agenda", *Journal of Marketing*, Vol. 53, No. 1 (1989), pp. 3 -15.

[20] Mohr, Jakki and Robert Spekman, "Characteristic of Partnership Success: Partnership Attributes, Communication Behavior, and Conflict Resolution Techniques", *Strategic Management Journal*, Vol. 15, No. 2 (1994), pp. 135 – 152.

similarities in basic values as well as operating styles between McDonald's and Coca-Cola provides a strong foundation for an highly integrated Type III partnership.

- **Mutuality.** The ability of a management team to put themselves in their partner's shoes is critical in partnering. This ability is usually expressed as a willingness to develop joint goals, share sensitive information, and take a long-term perspective.[21] Mutuality is exemplified by Whirlpool's Quality Express relationships. According to one of Whirlpool's partners, "…in a partnership you are taking on your partner's goals and aspirations… You have to be willing to give up your own identity. You loose your identity, but you grow with your partner." From the Whirlpool side, an executive expressed mutuality this way. "A partnership has to benefit both parties. It cannot be a one way relationship because if you are going to weaken the other side, eventually you are going to weaken the whole operation".

- **Symmetry.** The probability for success is enhanced when the partners are "demographically" similar. Symmetry in terms of importance of each firm to the other's success, relative size, market share, financial strength, productivity, brand image, company reputation, and level of technological sophistication will make a stronger relationship. When firms are relatively symmetrical, there is no junior partner and therefore none of the insecurity, defensiveness and fear which is often found in an unequal relationship.[22] The partnership between McDonald's and Coca-Cola is enhanced by the fact that both have strong brand images and each is the number one firm in its industry. Further, McDonald's is Coca-Cola's largest customer and Coca-Cola is McDonald's largest supplier, adding more symmetry to the relationship.

"A partnership has to benefit both parties. It cannot be a one way relationship because if you are going to weaken the other side, eventually you are going to weaken the whole operation".

Additional Facilitators. The four facilitators already mentioned are universal in that they should exist in any relationship. Their presence strengthens the probability of success and their absence increases the chance of failure. In addition, situation-specific facilitators may be present. While the presence of these facilitators is likely to increase the probability of success, their absence does not spell failure. The additional facilitators include exclusivity, shared competitors, physical proximity, a prior history of working with the partner, and a shared high value end user.

- **Exclusivity.** When managers of both firms are willing to entertain the possibility of exclusivity, then the opportunities for and the likely advantages of the partnership are broadened. For example, Whirlpool views the Quality Express relationship with ERX as a significant competitive advantage. While ERX management may consider providing a similar service to manufacturers of complimentary non-competitive products, such as kitchen cabinets or televisions, this service would not be offered to direct competitors of Whirlpool. In the case of a branded product where exclusivity would not be possible, exclusivity can be addressed by

---

[21] Cooper, Martha C., and John T. Gardner, "Good Business Relationships: More than Just Partnerships or Strategic Alliances", *International Journal of Physical Distribution and Logistics Management*, Vol. 23, No. 6 (1993), pp. 14-36.

[22] Langley, John C. and Mary C. Holcomb, "Creating Logistics Customer Value", *Journal of Business Logistics*, Vol. 13, No. 2 (1992), pp. 1-27.

establishing a separate division that deals solely with the large partner or by providing unique packaging.

- **Shared Competitors.** In the relatively rare case when both parties face a common competitor, the partnership is likely to have a stronger foundations. An excellent example of this is the McDonald's and Coca-Cola relationship in which they both faced Pepsi as a competitor. "Now that Pepsi is in the hamburger business… it has given us a synergy that has added to the partnership," stated a McDonald's executive.
- **Close Proximity.** If key players from both firms are located near each other, this can enhance the relationship. The relationship between Target and 3M reflects the influence of proximity. According to a 3M representative, "[the relationship] developed over time since both companies are based in the Twin cities."
- **Prior History.** Firms with a prior history of positive interaction will have an advantage when building partnerships. Having worked closely and successfully with a partner in the past strengthens the chance of future successful interactions.[23]
- **Shared End User.** In the case where both partners are serving the same end user, and that end user is of particularly high value, the partnership is likely to be strengthened. For example, both McDonald's and Coke place emphasis on the young consumer market and this strengthens their relationship.

Facilitators apply to the combined environment of the two potential partners. Therefore, unlike drivers which are assessed by managers in each firm independently, facilitators should be assessed jointly.

Assessing Facilitators. Facilitators apply to the combined environment of the two potential partners. Therefore, unlike drivers which are assessed by managers in each firm independently, facilitators should be assessed jointly. The discussion of corporate values, philosophies, and objectives often leads to an improved relationship even if no further steps toward building a partnership are taken. The strength of facilitators can be assessed using a 25 point rating guide shown in Table 10-4. The higher the facilitators, the better the chance of partnership success. A very low score (below 8) would suggest that even with strong drivers, a partnership is likely to fail because of a hostile environment. Conversely, very high facilitators (16 or above) could lead to partnership success even in the face of low drivers (8-11 points).

Conducting a Facilitators Session. The facilitators should not be examined at the outset of a relationship. After a period of working together, the two firms will have a much easier time assessing each facilitator. In a new relationship, a logistics service provider and a large telecommunications manufacturer went through the process when the relationship was just beginning. The managers felt it was not possible to complete the facilitators because they lacked experience working together and decided to wait six months before finishing the process. The experience gained over these months sharpened the managers' views about how well the two firms would naturally mesh.

It is critical that the person leading the session emphasize the disfunctionality of painting an overly positive picture of the environment. The result will be to

---

[23] Graham, T. Scott, Patricia J. Daugherty and William N. Dudley, "The Long-term Strategic Impact of Purchasing Partnerships", *International Journal of Purchasing and Material Management*, Vol. 30, No. 4 (1994), pp. 13-18.

Table 10-4
Assessment of Facilitators

Facilitators are factors which provide a supportive environment for the growth and maintenance of a partnership. For each facilitator, indicate the probability of it being a factor in this relationship, by circling one of the boxed numbers.

	Probability				
CORPORATE COMPATIBILITY	**No Chance** 0%	25%	50%	75%	**Certain** 100%
1. *What is the probability that the two organizations will mesh smoothly in terms of.,*	1	2	3	4	5

(a) CULTURE?
-Both firms place a value on keeping commitments
-Constancy of purpose
-Employees viewed as long term assets
-External stakeholders considered important

(b) BUSINESS?
-Strategic plans and objectives consistent
-Commitment to partnership ideas
-Willingness to change

	Probability				
MANAGEMENT PHILOSOPHY AND TECHNIQUES	**No Chance** 0%	25%	50%	75%	**Certain** 100%
2. *What is the probability that the management philosophy and techniques of the two companies will match smoothly?*	1	2	3	4	5

-Organizational structure
-Commitment to continuous improvement
-Degree of top management support
-Types of motivation used
-Importance of teamwork
-Attitudes toward "personnel churning"
-Degree of employee empowerment

	Probability				
MUTUALITY	**No Chance** 0%	25%	50%	75%	**Certain** 100%
3. *What is the probability both parties have the skills and predisposition needed for mutual relationship building?*	1	2	3	4	5

Management skilled at:
-two-sided thinking and action
-taking the perspective of the other company
-expressing goals and sharing expectations
-taking a longer term view
-mutual respect

Management willing to:
-share financial information
-integrate systems

	Probability				
SYMMETRY	**No Chance** 0%	25%	50%	75%	**Certain** 100%
4. *What Is the probability that the parties are similar on the following important factors that will affect the success of the relationship:*	1	2	3	4	5

-Relative size in terms of sales
-Relative market share in their respective industries
-Financial strength
-Productivity
-Brand imagetreputation
-Technological sophistication

ADDITIONAL FACTORS (BONUS POINTS)

	Yes	No
5. *Do you have shared competitors which will tend to unite your efforts?*	1	0
6. *Are the key players in the two parties in close physical proximity to each other?*	1	0
7. *Is there a willingness to deal exclusively with your partner?*	1	0
8. *Do both parties have prior experience with successful partnerships?*	1	0
9. *Do both parties share a high value end user?*	1	0

Add all the boxed numbers which you have circled on this page aid place the total in the box to the right. This represents the strength/ability to sustain and grow the partnership.

Source: Douglas M. Lambert, Margaret A. Emmelhainz and John T. Gardner, "Developing and Implementing Supply Chain Partnerships," *The International Journal of Logistics Management*, Vol. 7, No. 2 (1996), p. 9.

move the firms into more partnership than the situation demands and consume more managerial resources than necessary. The participants should be challenged to give examples of each claim and to relate each example of how it might result in a partnership being easier to implement. If both sides claim employee empowerment, then a concrete example of empowered decision-making is in order. In one case, both sides were indicating a strong quality focus, but one was a six sigma supporter and the other was focused on relationships not process. Both firms were very strong and successful with their approach, but these differences could make joint work more difficult.

Bonus points are given for environmental factors that cannot be reasonably expected in every relationship but when they are present they strengthen the relationship. Managers regularly want to claim close proximity based on something other than the two headquarters being in the same metropolitan area. A field office for one firm located close to the headquarters of the other or an on-site account manager is not close proximity as defined by the model. It is hard to have informal and social contacts between top management and others up and down both organizations if they are not closely co-located. When claims of prior experience with partnership are made, they should be based on the style of relationship described previously. As was the case with drivers, it is important to gain consensus on the facilitator scores.

Targeting Session. If both parties realistically expect benefits from a partnership and if the corporate environments appear supportive, then a partnership is warranted. However, not all partnerships are the same. Three types of partnering exist, each with different degrees of integration. The appropriateness of any one type of partnership is a function of the combined strength of the drivers and facilitators. A combination of strong drivers and strong facilitators would suggest a Type III partnership while low drivers and low facilitators suggest an arm's length relationship, as shown in Figure 10-3.

The appropriateness of any one type of partnership is a function of the combined strength of the drivers and facilitators.

While it might seem managers should attempt to change all of their corporate relationships into Type III partnerships, this is not the case. In partnering, more is not always better. The objective in establishing a partnership should not be to have a Type III partnership, rather it should be to have the most appropriate type of partnership given the specific drivers and facilitators. In fact, in situations with low drivers and/or facilitators, trying to achieve a Type III partnership is likely to be counterproductive. The necessary foundation is just not there. Having determined

Figure 10-3
Propensity to Partner Matrix

		DRIVER POINTS		
		8-11 Points	12-15 Points	16-24 Points
FACILITATOR POINTS	8-11 Points	Arm's Length	Type I	Type II
	12-15 Points	Type I	Type II	Type III
	16-25 Points	Type II	Type III	Type III

Source: Douglas M. Lambert, Margaret A. Emmelhainz and John T. Gardner, "Developing and Implementing Supply Chain Partnerships," *The International Journal of Logistics Management*, Vol. 7, No. 2 (1996), p. 10.

that a partnership is warranted and should be pursued, the next step is to actually put the partnership into place. This is done through the components (see Figure 10-2).

Conducting a Targeting Session. The model uses a three-by-three matrix to prescribe partnership type and therefore is subject to the difficulties present with any grid approach. The MPF needs to be sensitive to the fact that a single point change on either drivers or facilitators can move a relationship from a Type II partnership to a Type III or to a Type I. The prescriptions near the intersections of the boxes need to be evaluated with care. If a Type III partnership is indicated, but no joint investment is demanded to achieve the drivers, a low target for the financial component is fine. It is possible to place a relationship squarely between two types of partnership, as well. The goal is to tailor the relationship to fit the drivers and the environment not to match the grid.

Since the drivers are being assessed independently, it is possible for the firms to have driver scores that fall into two different categories (low, medium, or high). When one firm has a driver score in a higher category than the other, the low driver score is used. Like any relationship, the party that wants it the least determines the outcome. The relationship is only as strong as the weakest commitment. There will be only one facilitator score since facilitators are evaluated jointly.

An issue is how to handle a mismatch in driver scores. Initially, there was considerable concern about the potential for disparity in driver scores. After experiencing two cases of large disparity in scores, it appears that this situation need not damage an otherwise good business relationship. It is important for the MPF to note the disparity as it emerges and encourage the representatives of the lower-scoring organization to emphasize how their drivers were scored. The MPF should reinforce the idea that the reason for using the lowest driver score is because the firm with the least amount to gain will determine the level of focus on the relationship.

By the end of the targeting session, both parties should have a clearer understanding of the joint expectations of their relationship. This is critical for partnership success as well as useful if a partnership is not indicated. In the latter case, both parties benefit from a better understanding of why an arm's length relationship is the best fit.

By the end of the targeting session, both parties should have a clearer understanding of the joint expectations of their relationship.

In summary, the assessment of the drivers and facilitators is used to determine the potential for a partnership. That is, should a partnership be implemented and if so what type of partnership is appropriate? However, it is the management components and how they are implemented which determine the type of relationship that is actually in place.

Components Session. Components are the activities and processes that management establishes and controls throughout the life of the partnership. Components make the relationship operational and help managers create the benefits of partnering. Every partnership has the same basic components, but the way in which the components are implemented and managed varies. Components include: planning, joint operating controls, communications, risk/reward sharing, trust and commitment, contract style, scope, and financial investment.[24]

---

[24] Macnell, Ian R., *The New Social Contract, an Inquiry into Modern Contractual Relations*, New Heaven, CT: Yale University Press, 1980; and, Robert Dwyer, Paul H. Schurr and Sejo Oh, "Developing Buyer-Seller Relationships", *Journal of Marketing*, Vol. 51, No. 2 (1987), pp. 11-27.

- **Planning.** Joint planning, a key component of effective partnerships, can range from the sharing of existing plans to the joint development of strategic objectives. Effective joint planning adds both flexibility and strength to a relationship. In the McDonald's and Coca-Cola relationship, joint planning is done at multiple levels, on both a periodic and continual basis.[25]
- **Joint Operating Controls.** In a partnership, either party should be able to change the operations of the other for the good of the partnership. The ability to make changes can range from being encouraged to suggest changes to being empowered to operationalize a change without needing prior approval or notification from the partner. Within the Whirlpool Quality Express partnership, ERX can change the delivery schedule to a customer, without first obtaining approval, or even notifying Whirlpool.[26]
- **Communications.** Effective communication, on both a day-to-day and a non-routine basis, is a key component of successful partnerships. Integrated E-mail systems, regularly scheduled meetings and phone calls, and the willingness to share both good and bad news, as well as communication systems such EDI, all contribute to the success of a partnership. The more breadth and depth that exists in communication patterns, the stronger the partnership is likely to be. Communication links should be across all levels of the organizations including strategic, tactical, operational, interpersonal, and cultural.[27]
- **Risk/Reward Sharing.** At the core of a partnership is the concept of "shared destiny". Mechanisms need to be in place to ensure that not only are the benefits and rewards of the partnership shared, but that the costs and risks are also shared. A strong commitment to shared risk is evident when either party is willing to take a short-term "hit" in order to help out the partner and to strengthen the partnership over the long-term. In one of our cases, a firm deliberately delayed a planned price increase because its partner was not meeting its financial goals due to competitive pressures. In another case, productivity gains above a stated level are shared 50/50.[28]
- **Trust and Commitment.** No partnership can exist without trust and commitment. Loyalty to each other, loyalty to the partnership, and a long-term focus are all elements of trust and commitment. True partners do not have to constantly worry about being replaced. While most executives involved in partnerships found it difficult to precisely define trust, they all intuitively knew when it existed.
- **Contract Style.** The type of contract which governs a partnership speaks volumes about the relationship. The strongest partnerships generally have

---

[25] La Londe, Bernard J. and Martha C. Cooper, *Partnerships in Providing Customer Service: A Third Party Perspective*, Oak Brook, IL: Council of Logistics Management, 1989.

[26] Gardner, John T., Martha C. Cooper and Thomas G. Noodewier, "Understanding Shipper-Carrier and Shipper-Warehouser Relationships: Partnerships Revised", *Journal of Business Logistics*, Vol. 15, No. 2 (1994), pp. 121-143.

[27] Ellram, Lisa M., "A Managerial Guideline for the Development and Implementation of Purchasing Partnerships", *Journal of Purchasing and Materials Management*, Vol. 27, No. 3 (1991), pp. 2-8.

[28] Cooper, Martha C. and Lisa M. Ellram, "Characteristics of Supply Chian Management and the Implications for Purchasing and Logistics Strategy", *The International Journal of Logistics Management*, Vol. 4, No. 2 (1993), pp. 13-24.

the shortest and least specific agreements or not written agreement at all. A one to two-page document, outlining the basic philosophy and vision for the partnership, is all that is needed when the parties are truly integrated. The partnership contract for the Quality Express program is only about three pages long, and most managers operating under the contract had not seen it and were not aware that it existed. The "contract" between McDonald's and Coca-Cola is not in writing. It is an agreement based on trust and sealed with a handshake.[29]

- **Scope.** A partnership is made stronger by including more of the economic activities of each firm within the relationship. The number and complexity of the value-added steps covered and the amount of business involved are key elements of a partnership. In the partnership between Xerox and Ryder, Ryder performed light assembly and testing of equipment and Ryder truck drivers delivered the new machines, set them up, demonstrated them for customers, and removed the old equipment.[30]

- **Financial Investment.** A partnership can be strengthened by the sharing of financial resources across the relationship. Shared assets, joint investment in technology, exchange of key personnel, and joint research and development reflect a high degree of financial interdependence. Such interdependence leads to a stronger partnership.[31]

Each of the eight components will be evident in every partnership, regardless of type. However, the amount of each component, ranging from low to high, and the way in which the component is managed will vary depending upon the type of the partnership. For instance, while every partnership will have some degree of joint planning, that planning can range from infrequent, ad-hoc sharing of individual plans (low) to systematic, multi-level, joint strategic planning (high). Table 10-5 shows the various levels of implementation of the components.

Assessing the Components. After determining appropriate type of partnership and the associated level of component implementation, the parties must agree on how each component is specifically going to be put into place and managed. For instance, if it is determined that a Type III partnership is appropriate, this means that the majority, but not necessarily all, of the components should be implemented at a high level. Therefore some decisions must be made on which of the components will be implemented at a high level, and which may be more appropriately implemented at a medium level, as well as a timetable for implementation and the resources needed.

At Texas Instruments, this model was used with a major supplier. After deciding that a Type II partnership was appropriate, the parties agreed to specifics on how communications were to take place, what type of joint planning was to be done, the operations which would be jointly managed and other aspects of the components. Each partner then determined what resources were necessary in

After determining appropriate type of partnership and the associated level of component implementation, the parties must agree on how each component is specifically going to be put into place and managed.

---

[29] Gundlatch, Gregory T. and Patrick C. Murphy, "Ethical and Legal Foundations of Relational Marketing Exchanges", *Journal of Marketing*, Vol. 57, No. 4 (1993), pp. 36-46.

[30] Harrigan, Kathryn Rudie, "Matching Vertical Integration Strategies to Competitive Conditions", *Strategic Management Journal*, Vol. 7. No. 4 (1996), pp. 535-555.

[31] Heide, Jan B. and George John, "The Role of Dependence Balancing in Safeguarding Transaction-Specific Assets in Conventional Channels", *Journal of Marketing*, Vol. 52, No. 1 (1988), pp. 20-35.

Table 10-5
Partnership Component Levels

Partnership Component		Low	Medium	High
PLANNING	• Style	• On ad-hoc basis	• Regularly scheduled	• Systematic: Both scheduled and ad hoc
	• Level	• Focus on projects or tasks	• Focus is on process	• Focus is on relationship
	• Content	• Sharing of existing plans	• Performed jointly, eliminating conflicts in strategies	• Performed jointly and at multiple levels, including top management; objective is to mesh strategies; each party participates in other's business planning.
JOINT OPERATING CONTROLS	• Measurement	• Performance measures are developed independently and results are shared	• Measures are jointly developed and shared; focused on individual firm's performance.	• Measures are jointly developed and shared; focused on relationship and joint performance
	• Ability to make changes	• Parties may suggest changes to other's system	• Parties may make changes to other's system after getting approval	• Parties may make changes to other's system without getting approval
COMMUNICATIONS	NON-ROUTINE	• Very limited, usually just critical issues at the task or project level	• Conducted more regularly, done at multiple levels; generally open and honest	• Planned as a pad of the relationship; occurs at all levels; sharing of both praise and criticism; parties "speak the same language"
	DAY-TO-DAY • Organization	• Conducted on ad-hoc basis, between individuals	• Limited number of scheduled communications; some routinization	• Systematized method of communication; may be manual or electronic; communication systems are linked
	• Balance	• Primarily one-way	• Two-way but unbalanced	• Balanced two-way communications flow
	• Electronic	• Use of individual system	• Joint modification of individual systems	• Joint development of customized electronic communications
RISK/REWARD SHARING	• Loss tolerance	• Very low tolerance for loss	• Some tolerance for short-term loss	• High tolerance for short-term loss
	• Gain Commitment	• Limited willingness to help the other gain	• Willingness to help the other gain	• Desire to help other party gain
	• Commitment to fairness	• Fairness is evaluated by transaction	• Fairness is tracked year to year	• Fairness is measured over life of relationship
TRUST AND COMMITMENT	• Trust	• Trust is limited to belief that each partner will perform honestly and ethically	• Partner is given more trust than others, viewed as "most favored" supplier	• There is implicit, total trust; trust does not have to be earned
	• Commitment to each other's success	• Commitment of each party is to specific transaction or project; trust must be constantly "re-earned"	• Commitment is to a longer term relationship	• Commitment is to partner's long term success; commitment prevails across functions and levels in both organizations
CONTRACT STYLE	• Timeframe	• Covers a short time frame	• Covers a longer time frame	• Contracts are very general in nature and are evergreen, or alternatively the entire relationship is on a handshake basis
	• Coverage	• Contracts are specific in nature	• Contracts are more general in nature	• Contract does not specify duties or responsibilities; rather, it only outlines the basic philosophy guiding the relationship
SCOPE	• Share	• Activity of partnership represents a very small share of business for each partner	• Activity represents a modes share of business for at least one partner	• Activity covered by relationship represents significant business to both parties
	• Value-added	• Relationship covers only one or a few value-added steps (functions)	• Multiple functions, units are involved in the relationship	• Multiple functions and units are involved; partnership extends to all levels in both organizations
	• Critical activities	• Only activities which are relatively unimportant for partner's success	• Activities that are important for each partner's success are included	• Activities that are critical for each partner's success are included
INVESTMENT	• Financial	• There is low or no investment between the two parties	• May jointly own low value assets	• High value assets may be jointly owned
	• Technology	• No joint development of products/technology	• There is some joint design effort and there may be some joint R&D planning	• There is significant joint development; regular and significant joint R&D activity
	• People	• Limited personnel exchange	• Extensive exchange of personnel	• Participation on other party's board

Source: Douglas M. Lambert, Margaret A. Emmelhainz and John T. Gardner, "Developing and Implementing Supply Chain Partnerships," *The International Journal of Logistics Management*, Vol. 7, No. 2 (1996), p. 12.

terms of dollars, time and personnel; and commitments were obtained from top management for those resources. As a result, both parties understood and accepted the expectations and requirements of the partnership.

Conducting a Components Session. This session is critical since it involves developing the action plan. The first three components, planning, joint operating controls, and communications, are the keys to a successful relationship. Setting these three at the appropriate position typically takes the most time. To help the process along each participant should have the table of management components available as well as a note page to record current and desired state as well as action items, timelines and responsible parties.

The first step is to assess the current relationship component by component. In fact, the level of the analysis should be bullet by bullet within the components, as each component can be implemented at different levels. Thus, a relationship can entail joint planning on a regularly scheduled basis but focusing on tasks. A typical review of the current state of management components found many of them with bullet points in different columns. The current implementation of the management components reveals the amount of partnership that has been implemented in the relationship. This review provides initial guidance on managerial components that need more or less focus depending on the desired level of partnership.

The eight components should be reviewed again to determine the target level of implementation based on the targeted partnership type. The participants will be determining action items such as forming a task force to set up communications links that support the attainment of the targeted partnership. In one relationship, management chose to form a steering committee charged with developing a vision for the relationship. This committee was responsible for ensuring that progress was made towards reaching the desired levels of implementation of the management components.

If specific actions are properly identified, then responsibility can be placed on individuals and due dates established. It is not enough to say that metrics for a particular hard-to-measure driver should be jointly developed. The parties need to determine who should be involved, who leads, when the work will be completed, and to whom they will report. If this level of detail is achieved in the managerial components session, the outcomes assessment to be done later will be that much easier and the probability of the relationship staying on track is higher. The action items from the managerial components session need to become part of the ongoing operations planning process, such as a quarterly business review.

If specific actions are properly identified, then responsibility can be placed on individuals and due dates established.

The final, but very important, step in the components session is to review the drivers to ensure that each has been addressed. Drivers from each side should be available to all participants. If a driver for the seller (as is often the case) is to gain access to other business units within the parent company, then the trust and commitment components need to have specific action items. An example item would be to communicate examples of the level of commitment and trust in the relationship within their respective company newsletters. This was an action item in one relationship which was only added after a review of the drivers indicated that the marketing driver of the seller was not fully covered in the components after the first pass at setting action plans.

For each specific managerial component, we have additional suggestions. Based on our experiences, we recommend the following:

- **Planning.** Participants often have difficulty with the distinction between process and relationship as the focus of planning. An example of a process focus is the development of a method for making changes to the partner's delivery parameters. A relationship focus institutionalizes the partnership by putting the maintenance of the relationship within senior managers' job description for each firm.

- **Joint Operating Controls.** Participants should be clear that this component refers to the operations at the interface between the firms. It is unlikely that management would allow a key value-adding step to be modified by a partner independently. It is important to give realistic examples. The distinction between suggesting changes and making changes after approval is subtle.

- **Communications.** The electronic component remains an important consideration, however it is becoming less of a question about whether electronic communication is used or not. The new differentiator is the types of electronic communication taking place between the organizations and the degree of tailoring of these tools to the specific relationship.

- **Risk and Reward Sharing.** When addressing this item the managers should be challenged to provide examples of what sharing will take place and how it will take place. Will there be a gain-sharing program developed? How would management in each firm react to some fairly realistic hypothetical scenarios regarding the sharing of the potential costs and benefits of jointly developed initiatives?

- **Trust and Commitment.** This should be distinguished from the mutuality construct in the facilitator portion of the model. Where mutuality is a propensity, here it is specific to the two firms. Trust is managerially built as a spiral of commitment, performance, and communications throughout the organizations. These three are repeated as the spiral raises the level of trust. Each of these three is under managerial control and should be considered.

- **Contract Style.** If no supplier or no customer operates on a contract, then the absence of a contract should not be interpreted as a Type III partnership. Conversely, if the legal department makes everyone write a detailed contract, but the parties do not use it to manage the relationship, then the existence of the contract is not the issue either. The key is the amount of tailoring of the business relationship.

- **Scope.** Including more value-added steps in the relationship typically makes the bonds tighter. The key issue to be considered is what would happen if this partner disappeared. How would the loss of the partner affect the business unit or the corporation?

- **Investment.** As mentioned above, financial commitment only makes sense if there is a need to make an investment in order to achieve relationship drivers.

Components need to be examined three times, each with a different goal: 1) to determine the current state; 2) to determine desired state; and, 3) to make sure nothing was omitted.

Components need to be examined three times, each with a different goal: 1) to determine the current state; 2) to determine desired state; and, 3) to make sure nothing was omitted. The determination of the current state is best achieved through a group discussion of Table 10-5 as it relates to the relationship. Table 10-5 also provides a good overview of the amount of effort it will take to get to the desired state. After developing action plans, a quick final review of the components will be beneficial.

Wrap-up Session. A key aspect of the final wrap-up session is to reinforce to the participants that the outcomes of the process should result directly from the drivers, which is why it is so important to articulate with detail each organization's drivers. If both parties are achieving their drivers, the partnership will be viewed as a success. Therefore, during the components session it is important to bring back the drivers and establish specific action plans for achieving the drivers. The most common approach is to establish a set of action items with assignment of responsibility and due dates. This is needed in order to maintain the momentum gained in the meeting.

One meeting failed to develop these action plans before ending the process. Their plan was to follow-up the partnership meeting with a videoconference focused on developing the action plan and assigning time frames and responsibilities for achieving the drivers. The follow-up videoconference failed to demonstrate the same level of focus and energy that existed during the partnership meeting. According to one of the managers, "we had to schedule an additional team building meeting in order to regain the momentum that was lost by waiting to establish an action plan." Thus, action plans, time frames and responsibilities should be included in the process whenever possible.

Assessing Outcomes. A partnership, if appropriately established and effectively managed, should improve performance for both parties. Profit enhancement, process improvements, and increased competitive advantage are all likely outcomes of effective partnerships. Specific outcomes will vary depending upon the drivers which initially motivated the development of the partnership. It should be noted, however, that a partnership is not required to achieve satisfactory outcomes from a relationship. Typically, organizations will have multiple arm's length relationships which meet the needs of and provide benefits to both parties. One of our case study relationships, between an express delivery company and a national manufacturer, was viewed by both parties at the beginning of the research as a partnership, since both parties were receiving their desired outcomes: a service improvement and cost reduction for the manufacturer and a revenue increase for the delivery company. At the completion of the research, it was clear to management in the manufacturing firm the researchers that this relationship was not a partnership. The components of a partnership were not present. The desired benefits resulted from the fact that the parties were appropriately using an effective arm's length relationship.

A partnership, if appropriately established and effectively managed, should improve performance for both parties.

Applications of the Model

The model was designed primarily as a tool to help develop new partnerships. However, it can be used to diagnose an existing relationship, strengthen a key relationship and to create a common vision of partnership within the organization.

Establishing a New Partnership

When used to establish a new partnership, the party desiring a partnership should first use the model internally to assess the drivers and the appropriateness of partnering. The potential partner should then do the same. If both parties decide that a partnership has potential, they must jointly evaluate the facilitators and agreement must be reached on the type of partnership and the implementation of the components.

AlliedSignal, a long-term customer of Sea-Land Services, asked the carrier's management to consider a partnership. AlliedSignal's goal was to combine all the services of CSX, Sea-Land's parent company, into a single relationship. This included barge, intermodal, rail and trucking, as well as the existing container business. Sea-Land representatives suggested the use of the model as a guideline for understanding and implementing a partnership.

Two very positive results emerged from this experience. First, the model clearly indicated to the parties the difference between a partnership and a long-term contract with volume and price guarantees (which is often mistakenly thought of as a partnership). According to one manager, "…the mode identified eight or nine behaviors which we needed to change, as well as eight or nine behaviors we thought they could change."

Second, in a multi-division firm it is difficult to put a single-face forward. The model helped CSX coordinate the response of different business units to a partnership opportunity. In the words of a Sea-Land manager, "If we are looking at a corporate solution for the customer, one CSX unit might have to do something that in the short run will be suboptimal, but in the long run will be positive for CSX Corporation as a whole as a result of positive gains made by other CSX units. Or we may have to gamble and set rates and service commitments, which we know the competitor will match; and we will have to rely on the customer's integrity to deliver on their promise." Sea-Land was willing to make these commitments as long as a partnership was in place and other CSX divisions were on board.

Diagnosing an Existing Relationship

In addition to being used as a tool for assessing a new relationship, the model can be used to diagnose existing relationships.

In addition to being used as a tool for assessing a new relationship, the model can be used to diagnose existing relationships. It works as an excellent check to ensure that a relationship is the appropriate type. By jointly working through the model, partners can determine if the relationship needs to be strengthened, needs to be loosened or should be left as is.

For example, Goodyear and Yellow Freight had a strong relationship for a number of years and they closely coordinated efforts and participated in numerous joint activities for distribution of tires. Although no problems existed in the relationship, management in Goodyear's Logistics and Product Supply Group decided to evaluate the partnership using the model.

Teams from both Goodyear and Yellow evaluated the drivers and facilitators using the assessment forms. Multiple personnel, at various levels, in both firms assessed the relationship. The scores were analyzed to identify gaps or inconsistencies between levels within each corporation, as well as between the two corporations.

The assessment of the drivers and facilitators confirmed that a strong (Type II) partnership was appropriate. The components were them reviewed in a systematic way by joint teams. Management from both firms believe that working through the model has strengthened the partnership and has identified areas for improvement.

Strengthening a Key Relationship

Texas Instruments used the model to strengthen its relationship with Photronics, a key supplier of photomask. Texas Instruments purchased 99 percent of its domestic market photomask requirements from Photronics, which represented about 36 percent of Phonotronics' sales. Photronics had five facilities in the U.S., including one in Texas dedicated to Texas Instruments.

Realizing the importance of the relationship, the two firms used the model to determine how the partnership might more effectively be managed. Initially, considerable time was spent in joint meetings agreeing upon the meanings of each element of the drivers, facilitators, and components. Then each party independently assessed the drivers. This was done by multiple people at various levels in both firms (10 people from Photronics and 25 people from Texas Instruments.) After assessing both drivers and facilitators, the firms agreed that the most appropriate type of relationship was a Type II. In a meeting attended by vice-presidents from Texas Instruments, the president, the chairman and vice-presidents from Photronics, and numerous operational personnel from both firms, agreement was reached on the specific implementation of the components. The team prioritized the components and developed a detailed implementation plan outlining what each party would do to ensure successful implementation. Over a four month period, the teams held approximately five to six hours of meetings per week, involving eight to 10 people from each firm.

Both firms are now more satisfied with the direction of the partnership and its current working arrangement. They shared and meshed five year plans and each has made a commitment to the other. Even though their existing contract expired, they chose to move forward with no contract.

Creating a Common Partnership Vision

The model is also useful in harmonizing the partnership process throughout an organization. It provides a way to systematize the approach to partnering. Texas Instruments has used the model as a partnership marketing tool within the firm. The common language of drivers, facilitators, and components helps executives see the importance and potential of partnerships.

The model further serves as a screening tool in deciding where to allocate scarce resources. A firm can have a Type III partnership with only a limited number of partners. This limitation makes it critical that the correct relationship style is used in each business-to-business link. The model suggests which relationships offer the best potential pay-back and should be given the most attention and resources.

Institutionalizing the Partnership Process

Partnering is critical to long-term competitive success, and the partnership model can help managers develop and implement a cohesive, focused partnership strategy. Based upon the experiences of the case study firms, institutionalizing the partnership approach so that it will survive the departure/transfer of a key executive requires a recognition of the importance of: a champion, preselling, education, organization, empowering employees and reporting.

Partnering is critical to long-term competitive success, and the partnership model can help managers develop and implement a cohesive, focused partnership strategy.

As with any major organizational change, systematizing the approach to partnership management requires a champion or change agent who will promote the partnership concept throughout the organization. Texas Instruments' success with the partnership model was due, in large part, to the aggressive leadership of a change agent.

The model has been most successful in those firms where a change agent first sold top management on the concept of partnering and then introduced the details at an operational level. Short presentations, customized to each individual firm, and emphasizing the systematic approach to partnering were used as a "hook" to gain the interest of managers, customers and/or suppliers, as well as to gain a commitment to further education.

When the effort was made to educate managers about the details of the model, its use was a success. On the other hand, in those cases, where the process was only briefly explained, frustration and failure resulted, at least initially. It is imperative that all parties on both sides of the partnership have a common understanding of language and terms. Everyone should be using the same meaning for a Type III partnership, for instance.

Building and developing partnerships takes time and resources. A "partnership organization" within the firm enhances the probability of continued availability of those resources. The most common "structure" seen within the case study firm was one of teams. In the Goodyear/Yellow Freight partnership, there are seven teams at various locations, with members from both parties participating on each team. These teams greatly facilitate the communications and planning necessary for an on-going commitment to partnering.

A partnership can enhance an organization's ability to empower its own employees as well as those of its partner.

A partnership can enhance an organization's ability to empower its own employees as well as those of its partner. In the partnership between Whirlpool and ERX, ERX drivers were empowered to evaluate shipping damage and negotiate settlement, thus solving a potentially damaging customer service issue immediately. This eliminated the need for a damage adjuster and enhanced customer goodwill. Both parties felt comfortable with this arrangement due to the partnership components which were in place, joint planning and training took place, close communications were established, and a high level of trust existed.

Similarly, Xerox empowered Ryder Systems delivery personnel to unpack, set-up and test copiers, thus eliminating the need for multiple visits from Xerox personnel including technical representatives, sales people, and technician who removed the old equipment. In doing so, Xerox was placing its quality reputation on the line and in the hands of Ryder personnel. Trust, planning, operating controls, and risk sharing all had to be in place for this system to work.

In order to keep the partnering process on track, there needs to be regular reporting and communication about the partnership and its progress both within each firm and across the organizations. In case study firms, this reporting was done at joint team meetings, through internal newsletters, and in written managerial reports. The initiation of a new partnership between CSX and AlliedSignal was widely announced in corporate newsletters. This kept all potential contacts across the two organizations aware of the partnering initiative.

Conclusions

Partnerships are an important aspect of successful supply chain management. A well-designed facilitation process for establishing the appropriate level of partnership with other members of the supply chain network has substantial benefits. These benefits are especially relevant when addressing an organization's critical supply chain linkages. In today's competitive environment with leaner organizations it is necessary to form closer relationships with key suppliers, customers and third-party providers in order to maintain a leadership position and to grow. But the same forces that provide the benefits of partnering make it impossible to develop these relationships with everyone. Trying to develop a partnership where one is not warranted will waste valuable resources while providing minimal return. Not having a partnership when one is appropriate squanders an opportunity for competitive advantage.

The partnership model described in this chapter is a systematic method for ensuring that partnerships are developed and managed in the most beneficial way for both firms. Users have found that the most helpful aspect of the model is not the specific scores obtained, but rather that the process leads to a disclosure of all important issues. However, the partnership model alone is not sufficient to guarantee effective relationship management. Business will continue "as usual" unless managers are provided with incentives and are rewarded for building and maintaining effective partnerships. Top management must not only embrace partnership ideals, they must recognize and reward cooperative behavior.

The partnership model described in this chapter offers a systematic method for ensuring that partnerships are developed and managed in the most beneficial way for both firms.

Supply Chain Management Performance Measurement

Douglas M. Lambert and Terrance L. Pohlen

Overview

Most discussions and articles about supply chain metrics are, in actuality, about internal logistics performance measures.[1] The lack of a widely accepted definition for supply chain management and the complexity associated with overlapping supply chains make the development of supply chain metrics difficult. Despite these problems, managers continue to pursue supply chain metrics as a means to increase their "line of sight" over areas they do not directly control, but have a direct impact on their company's performance. We provide a framework for developing supply chain metrics that translates performance into shareholder value. The framework focuses on managing the interfacing customer relationship management and supplier relationship management processes at each link in the supply chain. The translation of process improvements into supplier and customer profitability provides a method for developing metrics that enable management to identify opportunities for improved profitability and align objectives across firms in the supply chain.

Introduction

It is generally believed that a well-crafted system of supply chain metrics can increase the chances for success by aligning processes across multiple firms, targeting the most profitable market segments, and obtaining a competitive advantage through differentiated services and lower costs. The lack of proper metrics for a supply chain will result in failure to meet consumer/end-user expectations, suboptimization of departmental or company performance, missed opportunities to outperform the competition, and conflict within the supply chain. However, there is no evidence that meaningful performance measures that span the entire supply chain actually exist. Many factors contribute to this situation including: the lack of a supply chain orientation, the complexity of capturing metrics across multiple organizations, the unwillingness to share information among organizations, and the inability to capture performance by customer,

...there is no evidence that meaningful performance measures that span the entire supply chain actually exist.

---

[1] This chapter is adapted from Douglas M. Lambert and Terrance L. Pohlen, "Supply Chain Metrics," *The International Journal of Logistics Management*, Vol. 12, No. 1 (2001), pp. 1-19.

product or supply chain. A major contributor to the lack of meaningful supply chain management performance measures is the absence of an approach for developing and designing such measures.

In most companies, the metrics that management refers to as supply chain metrics are primarily internally focused logistics measures such as lead time, fill rate, or on-time performance. In many instances, these measures are financial (inventory turns and overall profitability), but they do not provide insight regarding how well key business processes have been performed or how effectively the supply chain has met customer needs. In a growing number of firms, management is beginning to measure performance outside the firm, but these efforts have been limited to evaluating the performance of Tier 1 suppliers, customers, or third-party providers. These metrics do not capture how the overall supply chain has performed and fail to identify where opportunities exist to increase competitiveness, customer value, and shareholder value for each firm in the supply chain.

In this chapter, we present a framework for developing metrics that measure the performance of the supply chain management processes, identify how each firm affects supply chain performance, and can be translated into shareholder value. First, we describe the problems with current metrics and the need for comprehensive supply chain management performance measures. Second, we explain the need for supply chain metrics. Third, we describe the relationship between supply chain metrics and strategy. Fourth, we present a framework for developing supply chain metrics. Finally, we provide conclusions.

Problems with Existing Metrics

The performance measures used in most companies have several problems that prevent them from effectively measuring supply chain performance. Many measures identified as supply chain metrics are actually measures of internal logistics operations as opposed to measures of supply chain management. The majority are single firm logistics measures such as fill rate, lead time, on-time performance, damage and responsiveness[2] and are not the multi-firm measures that are necessary to measure the performance of the supply chain.[3] Similar measures were provided in seminar programs held at multiple locations in the United States and abroad, when we asked executives to identify examples of supply chain metrics. Typically, the executives identified inventory turns as one of the measures

Many measures identified as supply chain metrics are actually measures of internal logistics operations as opposed to measures of supply chain management.

[2] Gilmour, Peter, "A Strategic Audit Framework to Improve Supply Chain Performance," *Journal of Business and Industrial Marketing,* Vol. 14, No. 5/6 (1999), pp. 355-363.

[3] Beamon, Benita M., "Measuring Supply Chain Performance," *International Journal of Operations and Production Management,* Vol. 19, No. 3 (1989), pp. 275-292; and, James S. Keebler, Karl B. Manrodt, David A. Durtsche, and D. Michael Ledyard, *Keeping Score,* Oak Brook, IL: Council of Logistics Management, 1999.

[4] Lapide, Larry, "What About Measuring Supply Chain Performance?" *Achieving Supply Chain Excellence Through Technology,* David L. Anderson editor, San Francisco, CA: Montgomery Research, 1999, pp. 287-297; *Energizing the Supply Chain: Trends and Issues in Supply Chain Management,* New York, NY: Deloitte Consulting, 1999, p. 15; *Supply Chain Operations Reference Model Overview of SCOR Version 3.1,* Pittsburgh, PA: Supply Chain Council, 2000, p. 9; "High Performance Value Chains: A Report of the 2000 Value Chain Survey," New York, NY: Cap Gemini Ernst & Young and *Industry Week,* 2000, p. 7; Debra Seaman Langdon, "Measure the Whole," *iSource Business,* March 2001, pp. 33-36; and, David L. Anderson, Franke E. Britt, and Donavon J. Favre, "The Seven Principles of Supply Chain Management," *Supply Chain Management Review,* Vol. 1, No. 1 (1997), pp. 31-41.

of supply chain performance, a view shared by several authors.[4] However, as a supply chain metric, inventory turns is not an effective measure and provides a useful example of why new metrics are needed for managing the supply chain.

An inventory turns measurement fails to capture key differences in product cost, form, and risk within the supply chain. Figure 11-1, which illustrates inventory positions and flows across four tiers of a supply chain, helps make this point. As inventory moves closer to the point of consumption, it increases in value. That is, the out-of-pocket cash investment in the inventory increases. The cash value of inventory increases from $5 at the suppliers, to $25 at the manufacturers, to $62 at the wholesalers, to $72 at the retailers.

Consequently, if the opportunity cost of money and the inventory turns are similar, inventory carrying costs are much higher at the retail level, and an inventory turn improvement by the retailer has a much greater effect on overall supply chain performance than a turn improvement by the supplier, or manufacturer, and a greater impact than a turn improvement by the wholesaler. Referring to Table 11-1, if the supplier, manufacturer, wholesaler and retailer are all achieving six turns and have a similar inventory carrying cost of 36 percent, an improvement to seven turns would be worth $0.04, $0.21, $0.53, and $0.62 per unit sold for each of the parties, respectively. This example illustrates that the common practice of pushing inventory forward in the supply chain might reduce overall supply chain performance. Current inventory turns at each level within the supply chain also must be considered. Figure 11-2 shows how the inventory carrying cost per unit changes with the number of inventory turns. While Figure 11-2 reflects the manufacturer data from Table 11-1, the shape of the curve is

...an inventory turn improvement by the retailer has a much greater effect on overall supply chain performance than a turn improvement by the supplier...

Figure 11-1
Inventory Flows Within the Supply Chain

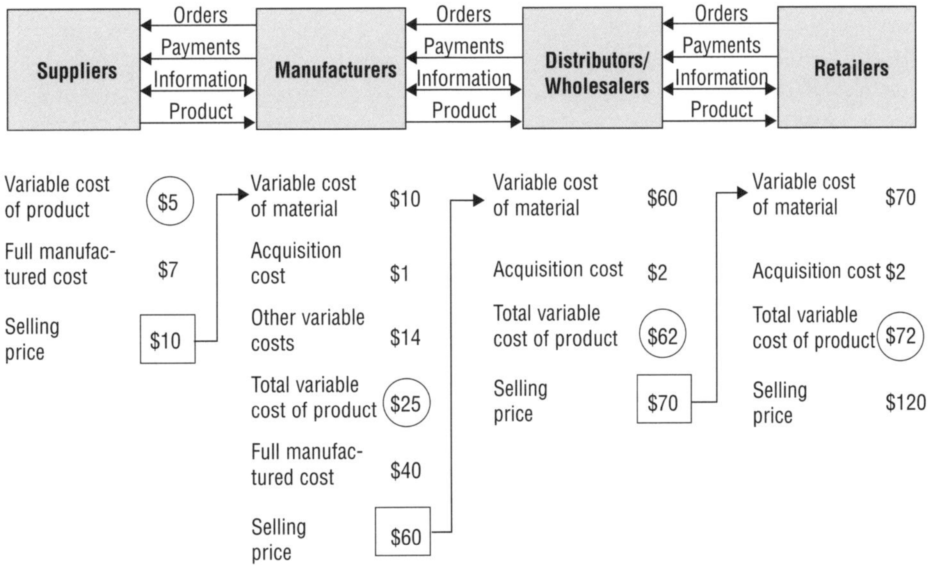

Source: Adapted from Douglas M. Lambert and Mark L. Bennion, "New Channel Strategies for the 1980s," in *Marketing Channels: Domestics and International Perspectives,* ed. Michael G. Harvey and Robert F. Lusch, Norman: Center for Economic Management Research, School of Business Administration, University of Oklahoma, 1982, p. 127.

Table 11-1
How Supply Chain Position Affects Inventory Carrying Cost

		Supplier	Manufacturer	Distributor/ Wholesaler	Retailer
Cash value of inventory:*		$5	$25	$62	$72
Inventory carrying cost %:		36%	36%	36%	36%
ICC/unit with:	1 turn	$1.80	$9.00	$22.32	$25.92
	2 turns	$0.90	$4.50	$11.16	$12.96
	3 turns	$0.60	$3.00	$7.44	$8.64
	4 turns	$0.45	$2.25	$5.58	$6.48
	5 turns	$0.36	$1.80	$4.46	$5.18
	6 turns	$0.30	$1.50	$3.72	$4.32
	7 turns	$0.26	$1.29	$3.19	$3.70
	8 turns	$0.23	$1.13	$2.79	$3.24
	9 turns	$0.20	$1.00	$2.48	$2.88
	10 turns	$0.18	$0.90	$2.23	$2.59
	11 turns	$0.16	$0.82	$2.03	$2.36
	12 turns	$0.15	$0.75	$1.86	$2.16

*Based on data provided in Figure 11-1

Figure 11-2
Annual Inventory Carrying Costs Compared to Inventory Turns

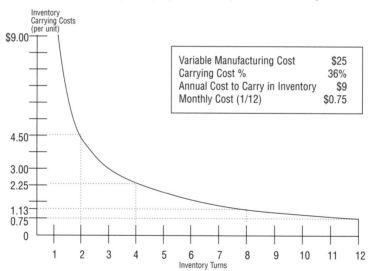

Variable Manufacturing Cost	$25
Carrying Cost %	36%
Annual Cost to Carry in Inventory	$9
Monthly Cost (1/12)	$0.75

Source: Adapted from Jay U. Sterling and Douglas M. Lambert as referenced in Douglas M. Lambert and James R. Stock, *Strategic Logistics Management*, Burr Ridge, IL: Irwin McGraw-Hill, 1993, p. 390.

identical for the supplier, distributor/wholesaler and retailer. Now, let's reconsider how existing inventory turns at various tiers in the supply chain will affect the general rule that inventory, or inventory ownership, should be moved backward in the supply chain. If the manufacturer is only achieving five turns and wholesaler has eleven turns, a one turn improvement equates to $0.30 per unit sold for the manufacturer and $0.17 per unit sold for the wholesaler. In this case, the general rule is broken.

In addition, an inventory turn rate does not recognize the different forms or the risk of holding inventory. Raw materials held by the supplier might be used for multiple products or customers which makes it difficult to determine how downstream changes would affect the amount of inventory held by the supplier. The inventory turns metric does not consider risk. The further downstream the inventory, the greater the risk that it does not exactly meet consumers' requirements. Pushing the inventory backwards and postponing its final form permits the supply chain to avoid higher obsolescence costs and the cost of repositioning inventory when it has been deployed to the wrong location.

A single inventory turn metric for the supply chain cannot capture the differences that an improvement in turns will have at each level or for the total supply chain. Performance, as measured by total inventory carrying costs, would be a better measure since it considers both the cash value of the inventory at various positions in the supply chain as well as varying opportunity costs for inventory investments for various supply chain members.[5] Total inventory carrying cost is improved by pushing inventory backwards in the supply chain toward the point of origin. The further back, the lower the overall inventory carrying costs for the entire supply chain. In summary, inventory turns and other commonly used logistics measures are inadequate for evaluating and aligning performance across multiple companies in the supply chain.

...inventory turns and other commonly used logistics measures are inadequate for evaluating and aligning performance across multiple companies in the supply chain.

Another problem with metrics stems from the lack of a widely accepted definition for supply chain management. Many logistics practitioners, academics, and consultants view supply chain management as an extension of logistics outside the firm to include customers and suppliers.[6] However, the Council of Logistics Management revised its definition of logistics in 2003 to reflect that logistics is only a part of supply chain management:

> Logistics is that part of Supply Chain Management that plans, implements and controls the efficient, effective forward and reverse flow and storage of goods, services, and related information between the point-of-origin and the point-of-consumption in order to meet customers' requirements.[7]

Supply chain management has a much broader scope and considers functions other than logistics:

> Supply chain management is the integration of key business processes from end user through original suppliers that provides products, services, and information that add value for customers and other stakeholders.[8]

---

[5] Stock, James R. and Douglas M. Lambert, *Strategic Logistics Management,* 4th Ed., Burr Ridge, IL: McGraw-Hill Irwin, 2001, pp. 187-221.

[6] Coyle, John J., Edward J. Bardi and Robert A. Novack, *Transportation,* 5th Ed., Cincinnati: South-Western College Publishing, 2000; William C. Copacino, *Supply Chain Management The Basics and Beyond,* Boca Raton, FL: St. Lucie Press, p. 7; Robert B. Handfield and Ernest L. Nichols, Jr., *Introduction to Supply Chain Management,* Upper Saddle, NJ: Prentice Hall Inc., 1999, p. 7; and, David Simchi-Levi, Philip Kaminsky, and Edith Simchi-Levi, *Designing and Managing the Supply Chain,* Boston, MA: Irwin McGraw-Hill, 2000, p. 1.

[7] Oak Brook, IL: Council of Logistics Management, 2003. See: www.clm1.org

[8] Lambert, Douglas M. and Martha C. Cooper, "Issues in Supply Chain Management," *Industrial Marketing Management,* Vol. 29, No. 1 (2000), pp. 65-83.

Figure 11-3
Supply Chain Management:
Integrating and Managing Business Processes Across the Supply Chain

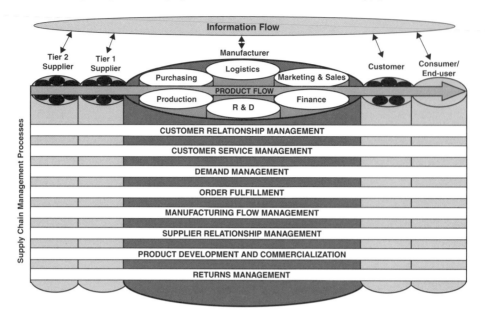

Source: Adapted from Douglas M. Lambert, Martha C. Cooper, and Janus D. Pagh, "Supply Chain Management: Implementation Issues and Research Opportunities," *The International Journal of Logistics Management,* Vol. 9, No. 2 (1998), p. 2.

Figure 11-3 shows the eight processes that must be implemented in the supply chain. The use of supply chain management as another name for logistics has led to observations that most companies have been using logistics metrics instead of measures that capture supply chain performance.[9]

More research is needed to develop supply chain metrics and to overcome the implementation barriers.[10] Most of the literature has focused on analyzing and categorizing performance measurement systems but little research has been devoted to supply chain performance measures.[11] The supply chain must be viewed as one entity and any measurement system should span the entire supply chain.[12] Managers need to see the areas where supply chain performance can be improved, so they can focus their attention, and obtain higher levels of performance.[13]

[9] Lee, Hau L. and Corey Billington, "Managing Supply Chain Inventory: Pitfalls and Opportunities," *Sloan Management Review,* Vol. 33, No. 3 (1992), pp. 65-73; Larry Lapide, "What About Measuring Supply Chain Performance?" *Achieving Supply Chain Excellence Through Technology,* San Francisco, CA: Montgomery Research, 1999, pp. 287-297; Peter Gilmour, "A Strategic Audit Framework to Improve Supply Chain Performance," *Journal of Business and Industrial Marketing,* Vol. 14, No. 5/6 (1999), pp. 355-363; and, James S. Keebler, Karl B. Manrodt, David A. Durtsche and D. Michael Ledyard, *Keeping Score,* Oak Brook, IL: Council of Logistics Management, 1999.

[10] Cooper, Martha C., Douglas M. Lambert and Janus D. Pagh, "Supply Chain Management: More Than a New Name for Logistics," *The International Journal of Logistics Management,* Vol. 8, No. 1 (1997), pp. 1-14.

[11] Beamon, Benita M., "Measuring Supply Chain Performance," *International Journal of Operations and Production Management,* Vol. 19, No. 3 (1989), pp. 275-292.

[12] Holmberg, Stefan, "A Systems Perspective on Supply Chain Measurements," *International Journal of Physical Distribution and Logistics Management,* Vol. 30, No. 10 (2000), pp. 847-868.

Why Supply Chain Metrics?

Several factors are contributing to management's need for new types of measures for managing the supply chain including:

- The lack of measures that capture performance across the entire supply chain.
- The requirement to go beyond internal metrics and take a supply chain perspective.
- The need to determine the interrelationship between corporate and supply chain performance.
- The complexity of supply chain management.
- The requirement to align activities and share joint performance measurement information to implement strategy that achieves supply chain objectives.
- The desire to expand the "line of sight" within the supply chain.
- The requirement to allocate benefits and burdens resulting from functional shifts within the supply chain.
- The need to differentiate the supply chain to obtain a competitive advantage.
- The goal of encouraging cooperative behavior across corporate functions and across firms in the supply chain.

Measures spanning the entire supply chain do not exist,[14] and logistics or other functional measures do not adequately reflect the scope of supply chain management.[15] Managers can only determine whether they have met their corporate goals after the fact, by diagnosing poor financial results or when they lose a key customer.[16] The measures used have little to do with supply chain strategy and objectives and might actually conflict resulting in inefficiencies for the overall supply chain.[17] Metrics integrating performance across multiple companies are emerging,[18] but they are not comprehensive financial measures.

The adoption of a supply chain approach holds numerous consequences for the measurement and control of individual business activities[19] and the performance measures used. The shift from a functional to a process focus requires the development of new types of measures, financial as well as operational.[20]

---

[13] van Hoek, Remko I., "Measuring the Unmeasureable—Measuring and Improving Performance in the Supply Chain," *Supply Chain Management,* Vol. 3, No. 4 (1998), pp. 187-192.

[14] Mentze, John T., editor, *Supply Chain Management,* edited by John T. Mentzer, Thousand Oaks, CA: Sage Publishing, 2001, p. 435.

[15] Caplice, Chris and Yossi Sheffi, "A Review and Evaluation of Logistics Performance Measurement Systems," *The International Journal of Logistics Management,* Vol. 6, No. 1 (1995), pp. 61-74.

[16] Lapide, Larry, "What About Measuring Supply Chain Performance?" *Achieving Supply Chain Excellence Through Technology,* David L. Anderson editor, San Francisco, CA: Montgomery Research, 1999, pp. 287-297.

[17] Lee, Hau L. and Corey Billington, "Managing Supply Chain Inventory: Pitfalls and Opportunities," *Sloan Management Review,* Vol. 33, No. 3 (1992), pp. 65-73.

[18] "Supply Chain Solutions: Linking the Chains," Kevin Francella and Katherine Doherty editors, Supplement to *Food Logistics,* March 1998.

[19] van Hoek, Remko I., "Measuring the Unmeasureable—Measuring and Improving Performance in the Supply Chain," *Supply Chain Management,* Vol. 3, No. 4 (1998), pp. 187-192.

[20] Kallio, Jukka, Timo Saarinen, Markku Tinnila and Ari P. J. Vepsalainen, "Measuring Delivery Process Performance," *The International Journal of Logistics Management,* Vol. 11, No. 1 (2000), pp. 75-87.

Supply chains, rather than the functional operations within a single company, become the new focus.[21] Supply chain members become accountable for the joint performance of these key business processes, and they require an integrated information system to enable multiple members of the supply chain to gain access to performance measures.[22] Management needs to understand the activities and costs of upstream and downstream supply chain members.[23]

In order for management to understand the interrelationship between corporate and supply chain performance, more holistic measures are required. These measures must integrate corporate financial and non-financial performance.[24] The translation of these measures into long-term shareholder value is critical for resolving conflicting objectives and supporting cost trade-offs across the supply chain especially in areas where cost or asset increases are required by some member(s). Existing measurement systems provide little assistance or insight regarding the question "What's in it for me?"[25] Future supply chain management innovations will come under increasing scrutiny to determine if and when they yield a positive impact on corporate performance.

Future supply chain management innovations will come under increasing scrutiny to determine if and when they yield a positive impact on corporate performance.

The complexity of the supply chain requires a different approach for designing metrics and measuring performance. In the case of a manufacturer, a supply chain can be represented as an uprooted tree, where the roots are the suppliers and the branches are the customers (see Figure 11-4). Managers require an understanding of what each branch or root adds to the value of the supply chain. The complexity of most supply chains makes it difficult to understand how activities at multiple tiers are related and influence each other. Performance measures must reflect this complexity and consider cross-company operations from original suppliers to the end customer.[26]

Relationship Between Supply Chain Metrics and Strategy

Implementing a supply chain strategy requires metrics that align performance with the objectives of other members of the supply chain.[27] Managers need to work collaboratively to generate the greatest mutual gains and savings.[28] Aligned metrics can assist in shifting managers' focus to attaining the operational goals of the enterprise-wide supply chain.[29] The alignment of metrics enables managers to identify

Implementing a supply chain strategy requires metrics that align performance with the objectives of other members of the supply chain.

---

[21] Keebler, James S., Karl B. Manrodt, David A. Durtsche and D. Michael Ledyard, *Keeping Score,* Oak Brook, IL: Council of Logistics Management, 1999.

[22] Lee, Hau L. "Creating Value Through Supply Chain Integration," *Supply Chain Management Review,* Vol. 4, No. 4 (2000), pp. 30-40.

[23] "Supply Chain Solutions: Linking the Chains," Kevin Francella and Katherine Doherty editors, Supplement to *Food Logistics,* March 1998.

[24] *Performance Measurement: Applying Value Chain Analysis to the Grocery Industry,* Joint Industry Project on Efficient Consumer Response, 1994.

[25] van Hoek, Remko I., "Measuring the Unmeasureable—Measuring and Improving Performance in the Supply Chain," *Supply Chain Management,* Vol. 3, No. 4 (1998), pp. 187-192.

[26] "Supply Chain Solutions: Linking the Chains," Kevin Francella and Katherine Doherty editors, Supplement to *Food Logistics,* March 1998.

[27] "Supply Chain Solutions: Linking the Chains," Kevin Francella and Katherine Doherty editors, Supplement to *Food Logistics,* March 1998.

[28] Keebler, James S., Karl B. Manrodt, David A. Durtsche and D. Michael Ledyard, *Keeping Score,* Oak Brook, IL: Council of Logistics Management, 1999.

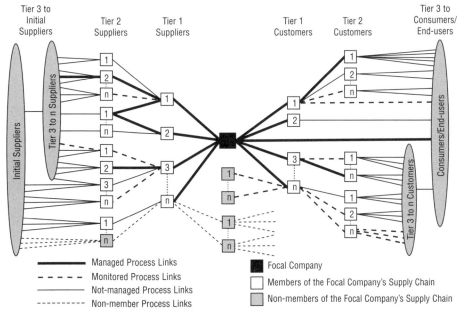

Figure 11-4
Types of Inter-company Business Process Links

Tier 3 to Initial Suppliers

Tier 2 Suppliers

Tier 1 Suppliers

Tier 1 Customers

Tier 2 Customers

Tier 3 to Consumers/End-users

Initial Suppliers

Tier 3 to n Suppliers

Consumers/End-users

Tier 3 to n Customers

——— Managed Process Links
- - - - Monitored Process Links
——— Not-managed Process Links
-------- Non-member Process Links

■ Focal Company
□ Members of the Focal Company's Supply Chain
▨ Non-members of the Focal Company's Supply Chain

Source: Adapted from Douglas M. Lambert, Martha C. Cooper and Janus D. Pagh, "Supply Chain Management: Implementation Issues and Research Opportunities," *The International Journal of Logistics Management,* Vol. 9, No. 2 (1998), p. 7.

and institutionalize the organizational, operational, and behavioral changes[30] needed to manage relationships in the supply chain. Aligned metrics can direct management attention and effort to the areas requiring improvement leading to higher levels of performance for the supply chain.[31] By establishing metrics for the supply chain, managers will be more likely to reach overall corporate goals and business strategies.[32] Integrating business processes across the supply chain is difficult because of the many constituencies, each with their own metrics and individual objectives.[33] Their objectives might have little in common resulting in potential conflict and inefficiencies for the supply chain.[34] Conflicting objectives preclude managers from effectively managing trade-offs across functions[35] as well as across companies.

[29] Walker, William T., "Use Global Performance Measures to Align the Enterprise Trading Partners," *Achieving Supply Chain Excellence Through Technology,* David L. Anderson, editor, San Francisco, CA: Montgomery Research, 1999.

[30] "Strategic Channel Management," *A Mercer Commentary,* Mercer Management Consulting, Undated.

[31] van Hoek, Remko I., "Measuring the Unmeasureable—Measuring and Improving Performance in the Supply Chain," *Supply Chain Management,* Vol. 3, No. 4 (1998), pp. 187-192.

[32] van Hoek, Remko I., "Measuring the Unmeasureable—Measuring and Improving Performance in the Supply Chain," *Supply Chain Management,* Vol. 3, No. 4 (1998), pp. 187-192.

[33] Sherman, Richard J., *Supply Chain Management for the Millennium,* Oak Brook, IL: Warehousing Education and Research Council, 1998.

[34] Lee, Hau L. and Corey Billington, "Managing Supply Chain Inventory: Pitfalls and Opportunities," *Sloan Management Review,* Vol. 33, No. 3 (1992), pp. 65-73.

[35] Lee, Hau L. and Corey Billington, "Managing Supply Chain Inventory: Pitfalls and Opportunities," *Sloan Management Review,* Vol. 33, No. 3 (1992), pp. 65-73.

Managers need to extend their "line of sight" across the supply chain by measuring the performance of activities and companies they do not directly control.[36] Management of a single company rarely controls the supply chain from point of origin to point of consumption and cannot see areas for improvement across the entire supply chain.[37] Increased visibility and shared metrics assist management with the integration, synchronization, and optimization of these inter-enterprise processes. The visibility makes the supply chain more transparent and can lead the way for performance improvements. Managers can determine how well the supply chain performed against the expectations of their customers[38] and use the information to determine where performance improvements need to occur. The identification of deficiencies outside a company's span of control can lead to programs aimed at improving performance or taking some level of control of upstream or downstream supply chain activities. Managers rarely have face-to-face contact with the end users, and supply chain metrics enable all the linked members to better respond to changes in consumer demand.[39]

Functional shifts and cost trade-offs made across multiple firms require metrics capable of measuring the resulting benefits and burdens. Individual companies might have to sacrifice internal efficiencies or perform additional functions to reduce or optimize total supply chain costs.[40] Consequently, some firms will benefit from the realignment of activities of functions while others will incur additional burdens or costs. Management needs the capability to measure where any benefits or burdens have occurred and a mechanism for negotiating an equitable redistribution of the benefits among firms.[41]

The commoditization of products and the number of competitive product offerings are forcing management to differentiate the firm's offerings through increased performance. As a result, managers must examine the supply chain to determine additional revenue opportunities and where they can obtain the greatest leverage to differentiate the brand and/or to eliminate costs.[42] Integrated metrics allow management to assess the overall competitiveness of the supply chain and to determine which internal improvement efforts produce the greatest impact on overall competitiveness.[43]

Integrated metrics allow management to assess the overall competitiveness of the supply chain and to determine which internal improvement efforts produce the greatest impact on overall competitiveness.

---

[36] Lapide, Larry, "What About Measuring Supply Chain Performance?" *Achieving Supply Chain Excellence Through Technology,* David L. Anderson, editor, San Francisco, CA: Montgomery Research, 1999, pp. 287-297; and, Andrew K. Reese, "Metrics Mentality," *iSource Business,* June 2001, pp. 67-70.

[37] van Hoek, Remko I., "Measuring the Unmeasureable—Measuring and Improving Performance in the Supply Chain," *Supply Chain Management,* Vol. 3, No. 4 (1998), pp. 187-192

[38] Reese, Andrew K., "Metrics Mentality," *iSource Business,* June 2001, pp. 67-70.

[39] Lummus, Rhonda R. and Robert J. Vokurka, "Managing the Demand Chain Through Managing the Information Flow: Capturing 'Moments of Information,'" *Production and Inventory Management Journal,* Vol. 40, No. 1 (1999), pp. 16-20.

[40] van Hoek, Remko I., "Measuring the Unmeasureable—Measuring and Improving Performance in the Supply Chain," *Supply Chain Management,* Vol. 3, No. 4 (1998), pp. 187-192.

[41] La Londe, Bernard J. and Terrance L. Pohlen, "Issues in Supply Chain Costing," *The International Journal of Logistics Management,* Vol. 7, No. 1 (1994), pp. 1-12.

[42] Keebler, James S., Karl B. Manrodt, David A. Durtsche and D. Michael Ledyard, *Keeping Score,* Oak Brook, IL: Council of Logistics Management, 1999.

[43] van Hoek, Remko I., "Measuring the Unmeasureable—Measuring and Improving Performance in the Supply Chain," *Supply Chain Management,* Vol. 3, No. 4 (1998), pp. 187-192.

Rewards and incentives are usually based on performance measurements that are focused internally rather than on the consumer or the supply chain.[44] The metrics used influence the behavior of individuals and determine supply chain performance.[45] The metrics provide the means for management to determine whether the performance of the firm's supply chain members has improved or degraded and what factors have contributed to the situation. Behavior of managers in individual firms can be influenced by measurements such as increases in value or competitiveness, or through the use of rewards and sanctions.[46]

The focus on internal logistics metrics results in performance measures and activities not being aligned with supply chain strategy. The operational objectives of the companies frequently conflict with one another leading to inefficiencies in the supply chain.[47] Many of the measurements used within firms are developed in isolation and incentives are linked to an individual's functional performance rather than strategy. The missing connection between strategy and measurements promotes an internal focus that becomes an obstacle to developing supply chain metrics[48] and contributes to many of the strategic level measures appearing unrelated or not actionable at lower levels in the corporate hierarchy.

Many of the measurements used within firms are developed in isolation and incentives are linked to an individual's functional performance rather than strategy.

Framework for Developing Supply Chain Management Metrics

Complexity makes the development of supply chain management metrics very difficult (see Figure 11-5). For example, consumer goods manufacturers such as Colgate-Palmolive, Procter & Gamble and Unilever sell to the same customers and purchase from the same suppliers. Competing supply chains appear more like interconnected or overlapping networks than a mutually exclusive "supply chain versus supply chain" form of competition. The overlap results in many instances of shared inventories, shared services, and shared assets between supply chains.[49] Managers cannot easily determine how business practices within specific companies drive total supply chain performance. As was pointed out earlier, you cannot simply add up inventory turns for participating firms and arrive at a total for the supply chain.

Despite the complexity and overlap existing in most supply chains, managers can develop metrics to align the performance of key business processes across

[44] Neely, Andy, Mike Gregory and Ken Platts, "Performance Measurement System Design," *International Journal of Operations and Production Management,* Vol. 15, No. 4 (1995), pp. 80-116.

[45] Lapide, Larry, "What About Measuring Supply Chain Performance?" *Achieving Supply Chain Excellence Through Technology,* David L. Anderson, editor, San Francisco, CA: Montgomery Research, 1999, pp. 287-297.

[46] Neely, Andy, Mike Gregory and Ken Platts, "Performance Measurement System Design," *International Journal of Operations and Production Management,* Vol. 15, No. 4 (1995), pp. 80-116.

[47] Holmberg, Stefan, "A Systems Perspective on Supply Chain Measurements," *International Journal of Physical Distribution and Logistics Management,* Vol. 30, No. 10 (2000), pp. 847-868.

[48] Mentzer, John T., editor, *Supply Chain Management,* Thousand Oaks, CA: Sage Publishing, 2001; Stefan Holmberg, "A Systems Perspective on Supply Chain Measurements," *International Journal of Physical Distribution and Logistics Management,* Vol. 30, No. 10 (2000), pp. 847-868; and, M. E. Kuwaiti and John M. Kay, "The Role of Performance Measurement in Business Process Reengineering," *International Journal of Operations, and Production Management,* Vol. 20. No. 12 (2000), pp. 1411-1426.

[49] Rice, James B. Jr. and Richard M. Hoppe, "Supply Chain vs. Supply Chain: The Hype & The Reality," *Supply Chain Management Review,* Vol. 5, No. 5 (2001), pp. 46-54.

Figure 11-5
Supply Chain Complexity

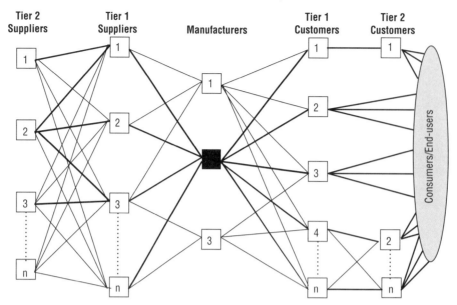

multiple companies. We propose a framework that aligns performance at each link (supplier-customer pair) within the supply chain. The framework begins with the linkages at the focal company and moves outward a link at a time. The link-by-link approach provides a means for aligning performance from point-of-origin to point-of-consumption with the overall objective of maximizing shareholder value for the total supply chain as well as for each company. The framework consists of seven steps:

We propose a framework that aligns performance at each link (supplier-customer pair) within the supply chain.

- Map the supply chain from point-of-origin to point-of-consumption to identify where key linkages exist.
- Use the customer relationship management and supplier relationship management processes to analyze each link (customer-supplier pair) and determine where additional value can be created for the supply chain.
- Develop customer and supplier profit and loss (P&L) statements to assess the effect of the relationship on profitability and shareholder value of the two firms.
- Realign supply chain management processes and activities to achieve performance objectives.
- Establish non-financial performance measures that align individual behavior with supply chain management process objectives and financial goals.
- Compare shareholder value and market capitalization across firms with supply chain objectives and revise process and performance measures as necessary.
- Replicate steps at each link in the supply chain.

Map the Supply Chain

The framework begins with the mapping of the supply chain from point-of-origin to point-of-consumption. In the map, the various paths that materials, information and financial flows may take from source to the final consumer are identified (see Figure 11-4). Managers can use the map to identify the different companies and linkages comprising the supply chain. The key supply chain linkages are those that are most critical to success. The initial focus should be on managing those supplied/customer dyads with the greatest potential for increasing profitability and developing a sustainable competitive advantage. Customer relationship management (CRM) and supplier relationship management (SRM) are the two processes that capture the overall performance of a supplier-customer relationship and can be used to link up the entire supply chain.

Customer relationship management (CRM) and supplier relationship management (SRM) are the two processes that capture the overall performance of a supplier-customer relationship and can be used to link up the entire supply chain.

Analyze Each Link

The supplier applies the CRM process to define how it will manage relationships with customers. Key customers are identified and the supplier's CRM teams work with these accounts to tailor product and service agreements that meet their requirements and specify the level of performance. The CRM process creates value by working with the customer to improve performance. For example, the CRM team may negotiate with the customer's team to implement supplier managed inventory (SMI). Successful SMI implementation might lead to increased revenues as the customer allocates a larger proportion of the business to that supplier. If the relationship reduces costs and can yield a price reduction for the consumer, revenues should increase as total sales for the supply chain increase. Revenues should increase as a result of better in-stock availability at the end of the supply chain. The cost of goods sold (COGS) should decrease through better scheduling of material requirements and more efficient utilization of plant capacity and labor. When SMI is implemented, the supplier experiences a one-time decrease in sales and the customer uses up existing inventory. The supplier's expenses will increase as the company assumes ownership of, and responsibility for, the customer's inventory; however, other expenses should decrease due to reduced order processing and forecasting costs. Inventory carrying costs should decrease as point-of-sale data are used to schedule shipments instead of forecasting requirements and maintaining safety stock. Better capacity utilization and collaborative planning and forecasting of requirements should reduce the need for customer specific assets. If these cost reductions in total do not more than offset the increased costs, then some other method of sharing benefits must occur. For example, the customer could write the supplier a check. The process improvements obtained through CRM can be translated into increased shareholder value through the use of an economic value-added (EVA) model as illustrated in Figure 11-6.

On the opposite side of the dyad, the customer uses the SRM process to manage supplier relationships. The customer selects and develops relationships with suppliers based on their contribution and criticality. The SRM process is the mirror image of the CRM process. As with the CRM process, it is possible to identify how SRM affects EVA (see Figure 11-7). Referring to the previous example, the SRM process captures the value created through SMI implementation. The relationship might produce increased revenues through cost reductions, lower

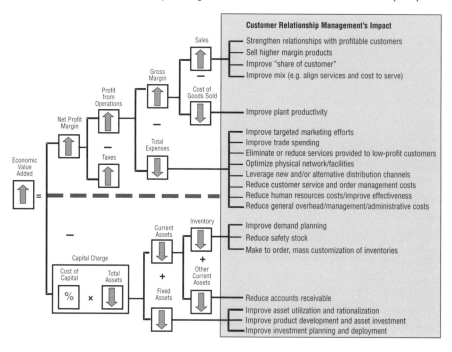

Figure 11-6
How Customer Relationship Management Affects Economic Value Added (EVA)

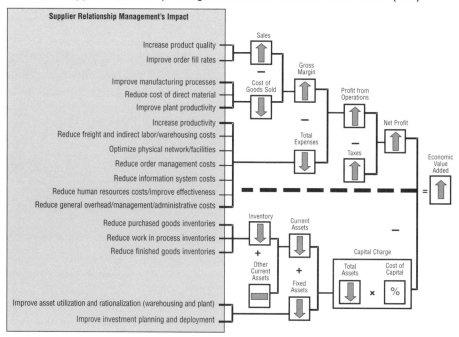

Figure 11-7
How Supplier Relationship Management Affects Economic Value Added (EVA)

consumer prices, and improved quality obtained by working with a select group of suppliers. The COGS might be reduced through the leveraging of larger buys with a smaller number of suppliers. Expenses decrease as the supplier assumes responsibility for order placement and inventory management. Pushing the ownership of inventory backwards to the supplier reduces inventory carrying costs for the customer and for the total supply chain since the supplier owns the inventory at a lower cash value (see Figure 11-1). Together, the CRM and SRM processes capture the total value, adjusted for the cost of money, created by the supplier-customer relationship. Exhibits similar to Figures 11-6 and 11-7 have been developed for the other six supply chain management processes and were included in prior chapters of this book.

Develop Profit and Loss Statements

The development of customer and supplier P&L statements provides a complete picture of how the relationship affects profitability for both firms (see Table 11-2). Initiatives undertaken by the two firms are reflected in these P&Ls, as are improvements in performance of the other six processes (see Figure 11-3). While performance metrics must be developed for all eight processes in order to motivate the desired behavior, the financial performance of all eight processes is captured in the customer P&Ls. When the customer P&Ls are aggregated for all customers and corporate joint costs deducted, the results represent overall firm performance.

When the customer P&Ls are aggregated for all customers and corporate joint costs deducted, the results represent overall firm performance.

Table 11-2 illustrates combined customer-supplier profitability analysis for a manufacturer selling to a wholesaler or retailer. In the case of the supplier (manufacturer), variable manufacturing costs are deducted from net sales to calculate a manufacturing contribution. Next, variable marketing and logistics

Table 11-2
Combined Customer-Supplier Profitability Analysis:
A Contribution Approach with Charge for Assets Employed

Supplier	Customer A	Customer	Supplier A
Net Sales		Sales	
Cost of Goods Sold (Variable Mfg. Cost)		Cost of Goods Sold	
Manufacturing Contribution	____	Gross Margin	____
		Plus: Discounts and Allowances	
Variable Marketing & Logistics Costs:		Market Development Funds	
Sales Commissions		Slotting Allowances	
Transportation		Co-Op Advertising	____
Warehousing (Handling in and out)		Net Margin	____
Special Packaging		Variable Marketing & Logistics Costs:	
Order Processing		Transportation	
Charge for Investment in Accts. Rec.	____	Receiving	
Contribution Margin	____	Order Processing	____
		Contribution Margin	____
Assignable Nonvariable Costs:		Assignable Nonvariable Costs:	
Salaries		Salaries	
Segment Related Advertising		Advertising	
Slotting Allowances		Inventory Carrying Costs Less:	
Inventory Carrying Costs		Charge for Accounts Payable	
Segment Controllable Margin	____	Segment Controllable Margin	____
Charge for Dedicated Assets Used	____	Charge for Dedicated Assets Used	____
Net Segment Margin	____	Net Segment Margin	____

costs are deducted to calculate a contribution margin. Assignable nonvariable costs, such as slotting allowances and inventory carrying costs, are subtracted to obtain a segment controllable margin. The net margin is obtained after deducting a charge for dedicated assets. In the case of the customer (wholesaler or retailer), product costs are deducted from sales to obtain a gross margin to which discounts and allowances are added to obtain the net margin. The remaining steps are similar to those taken by the supplier to obtain the net segment margin. These statements contain opportunity costs for investments in receivables and inventory and a charge for dedicated assets. Consequently, they are much closer to cash flow statements than a traditional P&L. They contain revenues minus the costs (avoidable costs) that disappear if the revenue disappears. If the supplier is selling an undifferentiated commodity to a customer that is another manufacturer, then the customer's report on the supplier is a total cost analysis unless revenue can be attributed to a source of supply (e.g., better quality or fewer returns). The customer compares the total cost for the current period to similar periods in the past or to comparable suppliers to determine the change in performance.

Realign Supply Chain Management Processes

The P&Ls provide the best measure of supply chain management performance and can be used to align performance across processes and firms. In our SMI example, implementation may cause the supplier to incur additional costs in some areas while obtaining cost reductions in others. The supplier's P&L reflects the resulting total cost as well as changes in assets (because of charges for assets employed), revenue, and profitability. Similarly, the customer's P&L reflects any changes due to SMI implementation. A combined profitability analysis captures the total effort and enables management to better understand how aligning their actions with supply chain objectives drives profitability in their firms. They can use this information as a basis for negotiating how to equitably split any benefits or burdens resulting from supply chain process improvements. In order to evaluate proposed programs, proforma P&Ls can be developed.

The P&Ls provide the best measure of supply chain management performance and can be used to align performance across processes and firms.

If the profitability reports are developed correctly, they will capture the impact of improved performance in all of the eight supply chain management processes (see Figure 11-8). The figure shows that the manufacturer (M) is generating profitabily reports for each customer and report C_1 represents retailer (R). While each process, such as order fulfillment, will have its inidividual metrics the overall performance is captured in the customer profit and loss statement. Figure 11-9 illustrates how management in the two organizations might identify process improvement opportunities by activities performed in each process.

Functional measures, such as inventory turns, cannot capture the full extent of management cost trade-offs and can be easily "gamed." Inventory carrying cost is a better measure, but it does not capture the costs incurred to achieve the reduction in inventory. Increases in production setup costs, transportation costs, ordering costs and lost sales costs might more than offset any gains made in inventory carrying costs. Typically, inventory reductions have a greater impact on total supply chain performance if they occur at the retail level. Generally speaking, making to order, pushing inventory backwards or pushing inventory ownership backwards in the supply chain improves overall performance.

Figure 11-8
Customer and Supplier Profitability Reports Should Capture the Impact of Improved Performance in Each Process

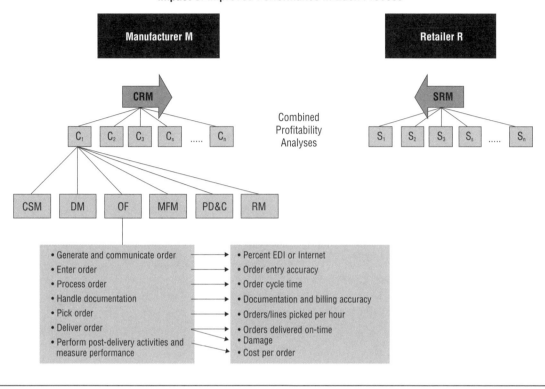

Figure 11-9
Identifying Process Improvement Opportunities

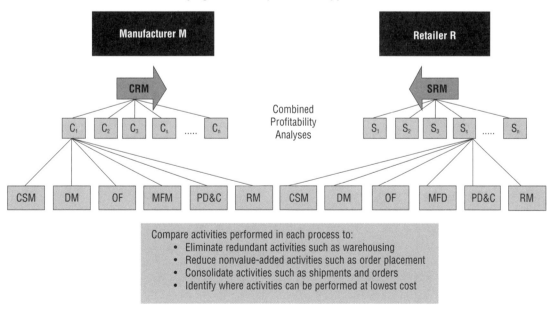

A combined customer-supplier profitability analysis will capture how the repositioning of inventory improves total supply chain performance, whereas inventory turns does not reflect any of the cost trade-offs within a firm or in the supplier-customer link.

Align Non-Financial Measures with P&Ls

P&Ls and EVA measures alone are not sufficient to effect improvements in supply chain performance or to align behavior. Supply chain and corporate metrics must be cascaded down to develop performance measures at the lowest level in the organization. For example, managers begin with the objectives identified in Figure 11-10 for developing performance measures for the order fulfillment process (see Order Fulfillment's Impact in Figure 11-10). These represent high level drivers of financial performance. It is necessary to develop more specific measures of performance (see Order Fulfillment's Performance Metrics in Figure 11-10).

A warehouseman or order fulfillment specialist supporting this process may not be able to relate how more efficient order picking and picking accuracy impact profitability or shareholder value, but they can focus on reducing order pick time and errors. Reducing order pick time while increasing productivity reduces the cost per order. Reducing order pick errors results in faster payment of customer invoices and reduces the cost of returned goods. By outperforming the competition, a faster order cycle time might lead to increased sales. Individual performance measures must be tied to the specific objectives required to improve profitability and shareholder value at each link in the supply chain. The relationship between improved non-financial

A combined customer-supplier profitability analysis will capture how the repositioning of inventory improves total supply chain performance, whereas inventory turns does not reflect any of the cost trade-offs within a firm or in the supplier-customer link.

Figure 11-10
How Order Fulfillment Affects Economic Value Added (EVA®)

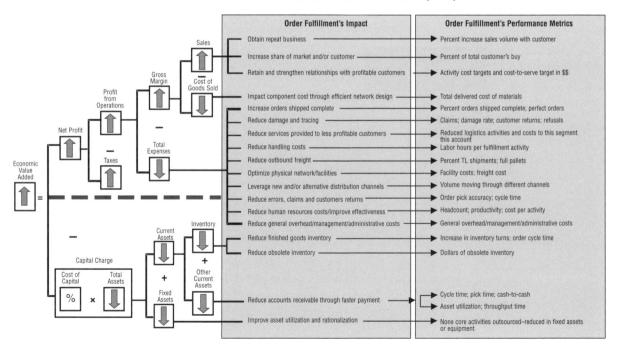

performance and shareholder value can be accomplished by converting activities into costs through such means as activity-based costing, identifying any revenue or asset implications, and inserting this information into an EVA or profit analyses.

Compare Across Firms and Replicate

The final steps in the framework compare the resulting shareholder value and market capitalization across firms (see Figure 11-11) and replicate these steps at every link in the supply chain. Overall performance might be measured by the increase in profit or market capitalization for each firm in the supply chain. The wholesaler/distributor's P&L for C as a supplier and the manufacturer's cost saving for D as a supplier are not included in the market capitalization metric to avoid double counting as an increase in profit or expense reduction from a supplier is captured in the customer P&Ls. In the case of the retailer/end user, it would be unusual to have customer P&Ls so overall profitability is determined by summing supplier P&Ls and deducting corporate joint costs. While management's goal is to increase shareholder value, economic conditions or other events can lead to depressed price-earnings (P/E) multiples in the short run. In these situations, it may be better to simply sum the changes in net profits. In Figure 11-11, all firms show an increase in profits because management uses the financial data to negotiate an equitable sharing of the costs and benefits.

Managers should assess whether the process changes and metrics employed have produced the targeted levels of profitability and shareholder value. They may need to refine the processes or make additional trade-offs to achieve the targets. In many instances, managers may find second or third tier customers and suppliers

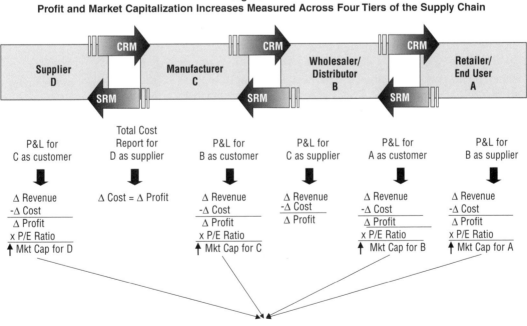

Figure 11-11
Profit and Market Capitalization Increases Measured Across Four Tiers of the Supply Chain

Supply Chain Performance = Increase in Market Cap for A, B, C, and D

provide additional opportunities to reduce cost, increase quality, and accelerate product development. Some intermediaries that do not add value might be eliminated from the supply chain or others added if it can increase the profitability of certain segments; for example, a distributor may be used to service a large number of small accounts or to achieve distribution in a remote geographic region.

The customer-supplier profitability analysis should be applied at each link in the supply chain. By analyzing the processes at each link and understanding the value the link creates, managers can align the supply chain processes in order to provide the best value for consumers/end-users and the highest profitability and shareholder value for each company. This framework increases management's understanding of how their firm contributes to the overall competitiveness and value created by the supply chain and provides the opportunity for a dynamic realignment of the supply chain. Management maximizes performance at each linkage and over time, the firms obtain the best performance. Eventually the processes become more efficient and effective and the supply chain naturally migrates to the point that maximizes profitability for each party and the whole. The process is on-going and requires continual adjustment. Managers can take proactive action within their firm as well as negotiate with other firms to further increase overall supply chain performance. Management must understand how value is created by each process at each link in the supply chain, take collaborative action to increase value, and replicate these steps across the entire supply chain. Ultimately, it is the value provided to retail customers or industrial end-users (product and service quality relative to price) that determines the competitiveness of the supply chain and the profitability of its members.

By analyzing the processes at each link and understanding the value the link creates, managers can align the supply chain processes in order to provide the best value for consumers/end users and the highest profitability and shareholder value for each company.

Conclusions

Most of the performance measures called supply chain metrics are nothing more than logistics measures that have an internal focus and do not capture how the firm drives value or profitability in the supply chain. These measures may actually prove to be dysfunctional by attempting to optimize the firm's performance at the expense of the other firms in the supply chain, an approach that eventually decreases the value of the entire supply chain. The use of customer and supplier contribution reports avoids this situation. The customer-supplier P&Ls capture cost trade-offs as well as revenue implications, and any action taken by one firm is reflected in both firms' P&Ls. The combined P&Ls provide the necessary foundation for improving performance in the supply chain. Although one firm may incur additional costs, the combined analysis reflects whether the costs associated with a process improvement increased profitability through a larger share of the customer's business or increased supply chain competitiveness. By maximizing profitability at each link, supply chain performance migrates toward management's objectives and maximizes performance for the whole.

By maximizing profitability at each link, supply chain performance migrates toward management's objectives and maximizes performance for the whole.

12 Implementing Supply Chain Management

Douglas M. Lambert, Sebastián J. García-Dastugue,
A. Michael Knemeyer and Keely L. Croxton

Overview

The preceding chapters have detailed The Global Supply Chain Forum (GSCF) process-based framework of supply chain management, described a partnership model that can be used to tailor key supply chain relationships, and presented a method for developing a performance measurement system to identify opportunities for improved profitability and align objectives across firms in the supply chain. In this chapter, we provide additional insights on how to implement supply chain management. An alternative process-based supply chain management framework (Supply-Chain Operations Reference - SCOR) is compared and contrasted with the GSCF framework. Our goal is to provide management with an understanding of the strengths and weaknesses of both frameworks in order to determine which can bring the most value to their organization. Also, managerial guidelines for implementing the GSCF framework are detailed. These include the characteristics of an assessment tool to assist with the implementation of the GSCF processes and a model for facilitating the required organizational transformation.

Introduction

Given that a supply chain is the network of companies, or independent business units, from original supplier to end-users, management of this network is a broad and challenging task. As detailed in the previous chapters of this book, managers who desire to implement a relationship-oriented supply chain management framework will be challenged to focus their efforts on implementing cross-functional business processes. These processes provide the structure to manage the relationships with key members of the supply chain.

...managers who desire to implement a relationship-oriented supply chain management framework will be challenged to focus their efforts on implementing cross-functional business processes.

The focus of this chapter is to highlight considerations for managers who want to implement the GSCF framework. The chapter initially compares the GSCF framework to another supply chain management framework, SCOR, which also prescribes the implementation of business processes. While many authors have talked about the importance of implementing processes, these two frameworks represent the only alternatives available with a sufficient level of detail to assist management in implementation. While both frameworks are process-based, they take distinctly different approaches to supply chain management. Therefore, comparing them will provide useful insight to management interested in implementation of one or both of the frameworks. The chapter also presents guidelines for managers who adopt the GSCF framework. The guidelines deal with assessment and change management activities that support management's implementation efforts.

The chapter is organized as follows. First, the GSCF and SCOR frameworks are described. Second, the frameworks are compared and the strengths and weaknesses are identified. Third, guidelines for implementing the GSCF framework are suggested. Finally, conclusions are presented.

Process-Based Frameworks for Supply Chain Management

While there has been much discussion about the need to implement cross-functional business processes in the supply chain, there are only two frameworks that identify what processes are involved and provide enough detail for implementation. The SCOR and GSCF frameworks prescribe the implementation of business processes, but the goals of each are different. We briefly describe each framework and provide an evaluation of the strengths and weaknesses of each.

The SCOR and GSCF frameworks prescribe the implementation of business processes, but the goals of each are different.

The GSCF Framework

As described throughout this book, the GSCF defines supply chain management as *"the integration of key business processes from end user through original suppliers that provides products, services, and information that add value for customers and other stakeholders."* Implementation is carried out through three elements: the supply chain network structure, the business processes, and the management components. The following eight supply chain management processes are included in the GSCF framework.

- Customer Relationship Management - provides the structure for how relationships with customers are developed and maintained.
- Customer Service Management - provides the firm's face to the customer and provides a single source of customer information.
- Demand Management - provides the structure for balancing the customers' requirements with supply chain capabilities, including reducing demand variability and increasing supply chain flexibility.
- Order Fulfillment - includes all activities necessary to define customer requirements, design the logistics network, and fill customer orders.
- Manufacturing Flow Management - includes all activities necessary to obtain, implement and manage manufacturing flexibility and move products through the plants in the supply chain.
- Supplier Relationship Management - provides the structure for how relationships with suppliers are developed and maintained.
- Product Development and Commercialization - provides the structure for developing and bringing to market new products jointly with customers and suppliers.
- Returns Management - includes all activities related to returns, reverse logistics, gatekeeping, and avoidance.

Customer relationship management and supplier relationship management form the critical links of the supply chain and the other six processes are coordinated through them.

The GSCF framework is shown in Figure 12-1. Customer relationship management and supplier relationship management form the critical links of the supply chain and the other six processes are coordinated through them. Each of the eight processes is cross-functional and cross-firm, and can be broken down into a sequence of strategic sub-processes, and a sequence of operational sub-processes. Each sub-process is described by a set of activities. Cross-functional teams are used to define the structure for managing the process at the strategic level and to implement it at the operational level.

The Supply-Chain Operations Reference (SCOR) Framework

A second process-based framework, SCOR, was developed in 1996 by the Supply-Chain Council (SCC), a nonprofit organization founded by Pittiglio, Rabin, Todd & McGrath (PRTM), a consulting company, and AMR Research.[1] Initially, SCOR included four business processes: plan, source, make, and deliver, which are to be implemented within the firm and eventually connected across firms in the supply chain. Return, the fifth process, was added in 2001.[2] The SCOR framework has three components: business process reengineering, benchmarking and best practices analysis. SCOR prescribes the use of business process reengineering techniques to capture the current state of a process and then determine the "to-be" state.

Figure 12-1
Supply Chain Management:
Integrating and Managing Business Processes Across the Supply Chain

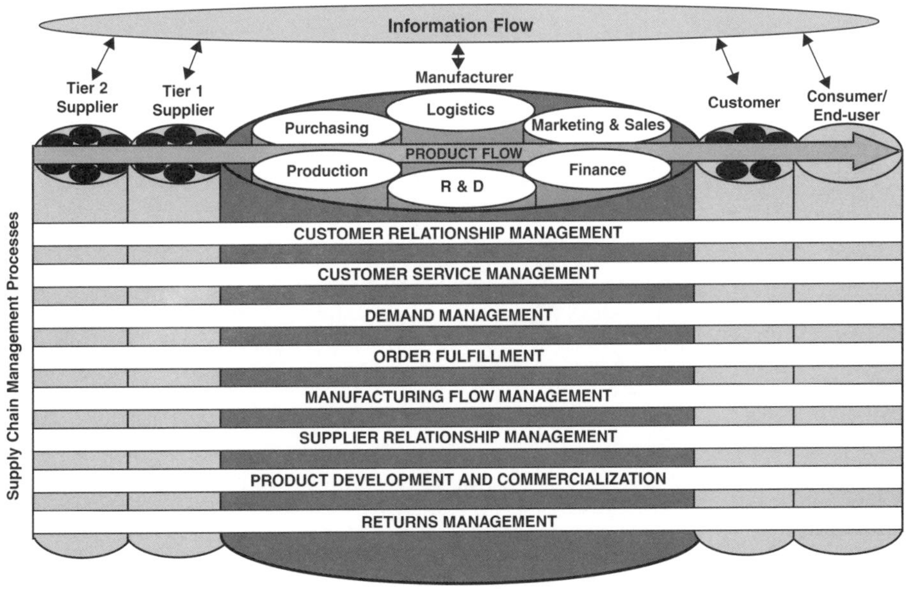

Source: Adapted from Douglas M. Lambert, Martha C. Cooper, and Janus D. Pagh, "Supply Chain Management: Implementation Issues and Research Opportunities," *The International Journal of Logistics Management,* Vol. 9, No. 2 (1998), p. 2.

[1] Supply-Chain Council, "Supply-Chain Operations Reference-model. Overview of SCOR Version 1.0," 1996.

[2] Supply-Chain Council, "Supply-Chain Operations Reference-model. Overview of SCOR Version 5.0," 2001.

Benchmarking is used to determine target values for operational performance metrics. Best practice analysis identifies management practices and software solutions used successfully by similar companies that are considered top performers.[3]

SCOR is organized around five processes (see Figure 12-2), which are:

- Plan - balances aggregate demand and supply to develop a course of action which best meets sourcing, production, and delivery requirements.
- Source - includes activities related to procuring goods and services to meet planned and actual demand.
- Make - includes activities related to transforming products into a finished state to meet planned or actual demand.
- Deliver - provides finished goods and services to meet planned or actual demand, typically including order management, transportation management, and distribution management.
- Return - deals with returning or receiving returned products for any reason and extends into post-delivery customer support.

Each of these processes is implemented in four levels of detail. Level One defines the number of supply chains as well as what metrics will be used. Level Two defines the planning and execution processes in material flow. Level Three defines the inputs, outputs and flow of each transactional element. At Level Four, the implementation details of the processes are defined.

Strengths and Weaknesses of the Two Frameworks

Each framework has its strengths and weaknesses which must be recognized for managers to understand the value that each can bring to their organizations, and the potential issues that must be addressed in implementing each.[4]

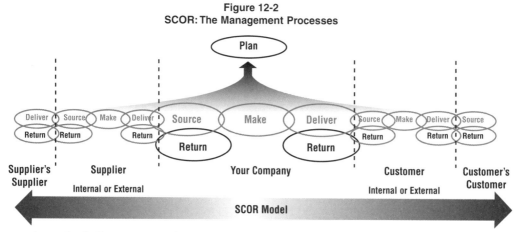

Figure 12-2
SCOR: The Management Processes

Source: Supply-Chain Operations Reference Model, Overview of SCOR Version 6.0, ©Copyright 2003, Supply-Chain Council.

---

[3] The presentation of the SCOR framework is based on Supply-Chain Council, "Supply-Chain Operations Reference-model. Overview of SCOR Version 6.0," 2003; and, Peter Bolstorff and Robert Rosenbaum, *Supply Chain Excellence: a Handbook for Dramatic Improvement Using the SCOR Model*, New York: AMACOM, 2003.

[4] This section is based on material included in Douglas M. Lambert, Sebastián García-Dastugue and Keely L. Croxton, "An Evaluation of Process-Oriented Supply Chain Management Frameworks," *Journal of Business Logistics*, forthcoming.

Focus

The focus of the two frameworks can be summarized as follows: SCOR focuses on transactional efficiency, while GSCF focuses on relationship management.

The focus of the two frameworks can be summarized as follows: SCOR focuses on transactional efficiency, while GSCF focuses on relationship management. While managers need to aim for transactional efficiency, cost minimization across the supply chain cannot be achieved without managing key relationships. Failure to recognize the value of a relationship orientation will limit supply chain efficiency.

Several of the companies that have helped to develop the GSCF framework are also using SCOR.[5] Some managers find that SCOR is a useful tool for identifying areas of improvement to achieve quick pay-back opportunities that satisfy top-management's desire for cost reductions and asset efficiency. Identifying quick-hits is possible because the SCOR framework involves functions that are more easily integrated, and because the focus is on cost reduction and improved asset utilization. In many companies, opportunities still exist for transactional process improvements that might be found during the implementation of SCOR.

The GSCF framework is more strategic and focuses on increasing long-term shareholder value through closer cross-functional relationships with key members of the supply chain. The business settings that will tend to favor the implementation of the GSCF framework are those in which the capability to identify, build and maintain business relationships is considered to be a competitive advantage. In many businesses, management has begun to recognize the importance of intangibles in the marketing of products and that to succeed, interactivity, connectivity and ongoing relationships are needed.[6]

An executive summarized his experience working with both frameworks as follows:

> The difference between the SCOR and GSCF approaches lies in the fact that SCOR addresses symptoms through tactics. The GSCF framework provides a strategic approach to address supply chain management processes incorporating the knowledge, expertise and objectives of all functions (Ernie Elliot, Rear Admiral Retired, Supply Corps, USN; VP Supply Chain, xpedx, an International Paper Company).

Strategic Alignment

Each of the GSCF processes is aligned with the corporate strategy and the appropriate functional strategies either directly or indirectly through the customer relationship and supplier relationship management processes. For example, the manufacturing flow management process starts by reviewing the corporate, manufacturing, sourcing, marketing and logistics strategies. This link between the processes, and the corporate and functional strategies is needed in order to assure alignment and make functional activities responsive to the market.[7]

SCOR processes are developed based on the operations strategy.[8] While the

---

[5] The lists of members for both groups are available through the web. The list of members for GSCF: http://fisher.osu.edu/scm/members/index.html and for SCC: http://www.supply-chain.org/html/mlist_nolink.asp

[6] Vargo, Stephen L. and Robert F. Lusch, "Evolving to a New Dominant Logic for Marketing," *Journal of Marketing*, Vol. 68, No. 1 (2004), pp. 1-17.

[7] Day, George S., *Market Driven Strategy*, New York: Free Press, 1999.

[8] Bolstorff, Peter and Robert Rosenbaum, *Supply Chain Excellence: a Handbook for Dramatic Improvement Using the SCOR Model*, New York: AMACOM, 2003.

operations strategy should be developed based on the corporate strategy and be aligned with the other functional strategies,[9] SCOR does not explicitly consider these other strategies. A disconnect between functional strategies and corporate strategies might jeopardize the organization-wide alignment of resources. Management pursuing the implementation of SCOR and interested in having the model provide the broadest impact should focus on positioning SCOR within the overall corporate strategy. This will help to align resources and goals, and prioritize implementation initiatives that result from the use of the framework.

Breadth of Activities

The GSCF framework is very broad in its scope, including activities such as product development, demand generation, relationship management and returns avoidance. Some respond to the model with comments like, "It includes everything." This breadth is intentional. Since the focus of the framework is to provide a structure to maintain stable relationships in the supply chain, the framework provides direction on all the activities that need to be managed in order to identify, develop and maintain key relationships with both customers and suppliers.[10] This breadth is why participation of all the functional areas is so critical in the GSCF framework. The activities included in the eight processes will touch all aspects of managing the business.

In contrast, the scope of the SCOR framework is limited. As stated in the SCOR literature, "SCOR does not attempt to describe every business process or activity, including: sales and marketing (demand generation), research and technology development, product development, and some elements of post-delivery customer support."[11] The activities that are included are those related to the forward and backward movement of the products, and the planning required to efficiently manage these flows.

In some respects, the breadth of the GSCF framework might be both its biggest strength and its biggest weakness. It is a strength because it increases the opportunity for supply chain management to provide value. For instance, if managers implement the returns process as it is suggested in SCOR, they are focused on reverse logistics and might miss avoidance opportunities, such as improving the product or the processes so that fewer returns are incurred. The GSCF framework includes avoidance as a key part of implementing the returns process, so the potential for providing bottom-line value through the process is increased. As another example, the demand management process of the GSCF framework has a broader scope than the plan process of SCOR. The plan process views demand as an input while in demand management the team works to actively manage demand finding ways to reduce variability.

However, the breadth of the GSCF framework provides some implementation challenges. For some people, the concept of supply chain management has grown

"SCOR does not attempt to describe every business process or activity, including: sales and marketing (demand generation), research and technology development, product development, and some elements of post-delivery customer support."

---

[9] Berry, William L., Terry J. Hill and Jay E. Klompmaker, "Customer-driven manufacturing," *International Journal of Operations & Production Management*, Vol. 15, No. 3 (1995), pp. 4-15.

[10] Lambert, Douglas M., Martha C. Cooper and Janus D. Pagh, "Supply Chain Management: Implementation Issues and Research Opportunities," *The International Journal of Logistics Management*, Vol. 9, No. 2 (1998), pp. 1-19.

[11] Supply-Chain Council, "Supply-Chain Operations Reference-model. Overview of SCOR Version 6.0," 2003.

out of the logistics, production or purchasing function, and it is difficult to shift to this very broad view. The breadth also makes it challenging to start small because all functions are involved and interfaces exist among the eight supply chain management processes. To achieve the full benefits, management should commit to implementing all eight processes. However, if this is not possible, implementing one process at a time can result in enhanced performance. It might also be difficult to manage the interfaces between firms in the supply chain while there is substantial change going on within the focal firm. While the full value of these processes cannot be achieved without including customers and suppliers in the implementation, it is possible to improve the performance of the firm by implementing some of the activities and internal interfaces before implementing the full framework.

Cross-Functional Involvement

SCOR and GSCF are similar in that they both advocate cross-functional involvement and recognize that business processes will not replace corporate functions. However, the number of corporate functions included in each framework is different and the type of cross-functional involvement differs as well.

Because the GSCF framework touches all aspects of the business, it is critical that each process team includes representation from all incumbent functions including, but not limited to, marketing, production, finance, purchasing and logistics.

Because the GSCF framework touches all aspects of the business, it is critical that each process team includes representation from all incumbent functions including, but not limited to, marketing, production, finance, purchasing and logistics. The team members provide their functional expertise and assure that the decisions are the right ones for the whole firm. Figure 12-3 shows examples of how each functional area provides input to each business process. Working in cross-functional teams can be difficult to accomplish.[12] With long histories of a "functional silo" orientation, it is often difficult for management to put together cooperative cross-functional teams that can bring together the necessary functional expertise to successfully develop and implement innovative solutions for the supply chain. Top management has to commit to the vision and reward team activities in order to successfully achieve the cross-functional involvement necessary for the GSCF framework.

In the case of SCOR, the cross-functional involvement is pursued primarily within three functions: logistics, production and purchasing. Figure 12-4 shows what input each function provides into the SCOR processes.[13] Focusing on just three functions might make SCOR easier to implement since in many firms the activities of these three functions are more likely to be somewhat integrated within the corporate structure. The tradeoff is that management is attempting to manage the supply chain without critical input from marketing, finance and research and development. This limited functional involvement can yield sub-par performance and can even result in failed initiatives.

For example, a manufacturer of consumer durable goods implemented a rapid delivery system that provided retailers with deliveries in 24 to 48 hours anywhere in

---

[12] Webber, Sheila S., "Leadership and Trust Facilitating Cross-functional Team Success," *Journal of Management Development*, Vol. 21, No. 3 (2002), pp. 201-214.

[13] Evaluation based on Supply-Chain Council, "Supply-Chain Operations Reference-model. Overview of SCOR Version 6.0," 2003; and, Peter Bolstorff and Robert Rosenbaum, *Supply Chain Excellence: a Handbook for Dramatic Improvement Using the SCOR Model*, New York: AMACOM, 2003.

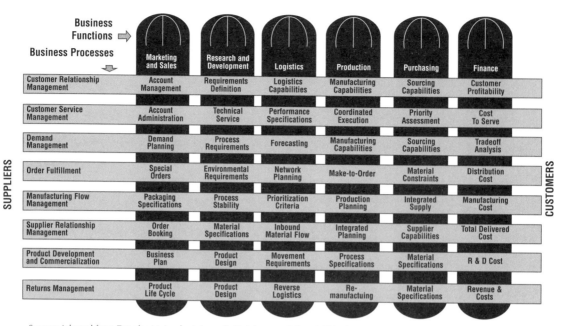

Figure 12-3
Functional Involvement in the GSCF Processes

Business Processes	Marketing and Sales	Research and Development	Logistics	Production	Purchasing	Finance
Customer Relationship Management	Account Management	Requirements Definition	Logistics Capabilities	Manufacturing Capabilities	Sourcing Capabilities	Customer Profitability
Customer Service Management	Account Administration	Technical Service	Performance Specifications	Coordinated Execution	Priority Assessment	Cost To Serve
Demand Management	Demand Planning	Process Requirements	Forecasting	Manufacturing Capabilities	Sourcing Capabilities	Tradeoff Analysis
Order Fulfillment	Special Orders	Environmental Requirements	Network Planning	Make-to-Order	Material Constraints	Distribution Cost
Manufacturing Flow Management	Packaging Specifications	Process Stability	Prioritization Criteria	Production Planning	Integrated Supply	Manufacturing Cost
Supplier Relationship Management	Order Booking	Material Specifications	Inbound Material Flow	Integrated Planning	Supplier Capabilities	Total Delivered Cost
Product Development and Commercialization	Business Plan	Product Design	Movement Requirements	Process Specifications	Material Specifications	R & D Cost
Returns Management	Product Life Cycle	Product Design	Reverse Logistics	Re-manufacturing	Material Specifications	Revenue & Costs

Source: Adapted from Douglas M. Lambert, Larry C. Guinipero and Gary J. Ridenhower, "Supply Chain Management: A Key to Achieving Business Excellence in the 21st Century," unpublished manuscript.

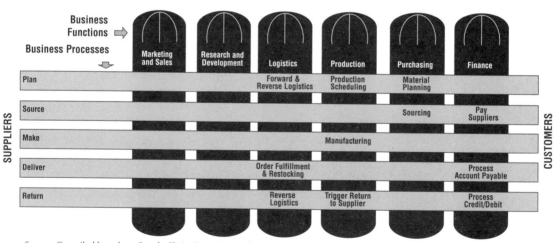

Figure 12-4
Functional Involvement in the SCOR Processes

Business Processes	Marketing and Sales	Research and Development	Logistics	Production	Purchasing	Finance
Plan			Forward & Reverse Logistics	Production Scheduling	Material Planning	
Source					Sourcing	Pay Suppliers
Make				Manufacturing		
Deliver			Order Fulfillment & Restocking			Process Account Payable
Return			Reverse Logistics	Trigger Return to Supplier		Process Credit/Debit

Source: Compiled based on: Supply-Chain Operations Reference Model. Overview of SCOR Version 6.0 ©Copyright 2003 Supply-Chain Council; and, Bolstorff, Peter and Robert Rosenbaum, *Supply Chain Excellence: a Handbook for Dramatic Improvement Using the SCOR Model*, New York: AMACOM, 2003.

the United States. The rapid delivery system was designed to enable the retailers to improve service while holding less inventory. Six years later, the company had not seen the inventory reductions and reduced the service promise to 48 to 72 hours. The rapid delivery system never achieved its full potential because the marketing organization still provided the customers with incentives to buy in large volumes.[14] This example should make it clear that failure to manage all the touches might diminish the impact of supply chain initiatives. Failure to include all functions has a cost. Those left out have the potential to maliciously or inadvertently undermine the initiatives. Using the GSCF framework increases the likelihood of success because all functions are involved in the planning and implementation of the initiative.

Failure to include all functions has a cost. Those left out have the potential to maliciously or inadvertently undermine the initiatives.

Process and Performance Benchmarking

In conversations with users of SCOR, a perceived strength is the set of benchmarking tools. The concept of benchmarking has received considerable attention in both the management and research communities.[15] Most consider two types of benchmarking: performance and process benchmarking.[16] Performance benchmarking is about learning how competitors or firms in comparable industries are performing on key operational metrics such as inventory turns or fill rates, while process benchmarking, or what SCOR calls best-practice analysis, is concerned with learning about and duplicating best practices.

To offer assistance with performance benchmarking, the SCC, the organization that leads the development of SCOR, provides a source of data and information compiled from its members. Some managers have found the SCC data to be useful in their benchmarking efforts. However, there are issues related to the accuracy and use of these data.[17] Specifically, SCC collects these data by survey and while they provide very detailed instructions on how the numbers are to be developed, there should be concerns about the effort that managers expend on reworking their organization's data to fit the SCC's specifications.

Some managers have found the SCC data to be useful in their benchmarking efforts.

SCOR users also find value in the SCC's best-practice analysis. In line with the focus of SCOR, this list of best practices includes tools primarily aimed at improving transactional efficiency in the supply chain, such as activity-based costing, advanced-shipping notification, Kanban and supplier certification programs. Information on how to implement these practices can be obtained through the SCC. In this way, the SCC might provide value to those implementing the GSCF framework, as the teams evaluate these best practices in the context of the eight supply chain management processes. For example, CPFR might be a practice implemented in the context of the demand management process. However, some managers find the process benchmarking might omit creativity.

A drawback to benchmarking best practices is a lack of creativity and the possibility of missing an opportunity to completely change the

[14] Lambert, Douglas M. and Renan Burduroglu, "Measuring and Selling the Value of Logistics," *The International Journal of Logistics Management*, Vol. 11, No. 1 (2000), pp. 1-17.

[15] Dattakumar, R. and R. Jagadeesh, "A review of literature on benchmarking," *Benchmarking: An International Journal*, Vol. 10, No. 3 (2003), pp. 176-209.

[16] Bhutta, Khurrum S. and Faizul Huq, "Benchmarking - Best Practices: an Integrated Approach," *Benchmarking: an International Journal*, Vol. 6, No. 3 (1999), pp. 176-209.

[17] Hammer, Michael and James Champy, *Reengineering the Corporation: a Manifesto for Business Revolution*, New York, NY: Harper Business, 1993; David Longbottom, "Benchmarking in the UK: an Empirical Study of Practitioners and Academics," *Benchmarking: an International Journal*, Vol. 7, No. 2 (2000), pp. 98-117; Andrew Cox and Ian Thompson, "On the Appropriateness of Benchmarking," *Journal of General Management*, Vol. 23, No. 3 (1998), pp. 1-19; and, Andrew Campbell, "Tailored, Not Benchmarked," *Harvard Business Review*, Vol. 77, No. 2 (1999), pp. 41-47.

process. The real strength of the GSCF framework is to start with the objectives and develop strategies and tactics to achieve them in a rapidly changing business environment. The GSCF framework has the potential to create greater value through leading change and/or being the first mover. (Ernie Elliot, Rear Admiral Retired, Supply Corps, USN; VP Supply Chain, xpedx, an International Paper Company).

"The GSCF framework has the potential to create greater value through leading change and/or being the first mover."

To perform process benchmarking using the GSCF framework, management can rely on the descriptions of the eight supply chain management processes. The GSCF processes represent the combined knowledge of the executives that participated in The Forum's meetings over the past 10 years. In other words, the subprocesses and activities are the best practices to successfully manage a business and develop sustained competitive advantages.

Since the implementation of an improvement initiative is costly, management should not pursue one just because a competitor, known or unknown, is doing it. Management should identify to what extent each process needs to be formalized. Assessment tools for the supply chain management processes are under development.[18] The assessment tools are designed to enable management to evaluate their firms' current business practices in terms of these processes and identify improvement opportunities.

Value Creation

Managers have four ways to create value: increase revenue, reduce operating cost, reduce working capital, and increase asset efficiency. The two frameworks use different approaches to measuring how the efforts of supply chain management can be used to create value.

In the GSCF framework, operational measures are tied to the firm's EVA and to profitability reports for customers and suppliers. Therefore, central to the successful implementation of GSCF is the identification of the revenue implications associated with all activities performed within the firm and by the firm's supply chain members. This will enable the development of profitability reports which provide information about the value that each key supplier provides to the customer as well as the value that the customer provides to each of the key suppliers. GSCF is intended not only to measure cost reduction and increased asset utilization but also to identify the revenue implications from more closely managing relationships with key suppliers and customers. For example, including customers in the product development and commercialization process should shorten time to market and yield products that better meet customer requirements, generating more profit for the firm.

Because the objective of SCOR is operational efficiency, the drivers of value creation are focused on cost reductions and improvements in asset utilization. This makes measurement easier because it tends to be less subjective to determine how much will be saved by a particular program than to estimate how a segment of customers will respond to a service improvement, a new marketing effort, or a new product. Also, cost reductions will yield large savings when inefficiencies are present. However, when efficiency levels are high, incremental improvements tend to be smaller. Thus, managers of firms with lower levels of efficiency might find

Because the objective of SCOR is operational efficiency, the drivers of value creation are focused on cost reductions and improvements in asset utilization.

---

[18] For more information, see www.scm-institute.org

bigger and more immediate benefits from the implementation of SCOR, while those that have achieved high levels of internal efficiency will find more value focusing on managing relationships outside the firm, as prescribed in the GSCF framework. The GSCF framework has the advantage of considering revenue generation as well as cost reduction. For long-term financial success, it is necessary to focus on revenue enhancement.

The GSCF framework has the advantage of considering revenue generation as well as cost reduction.

While the GSCF and SCOR frameworks both focus on the implementation of cross-functional processes in the supply chain, the GSCF framework is more inclusive since all business functions are involved and a broader set of activities is included. In the next section, we will provide quidelines for implementing the GSCF framework.

Guidelines for Implementing the GSCF Framework

All organizations exist in one or more supply chains, but few managers truly understand the underlying business relationships that take place with their key customers and suppliers.[19] Thus, most mangers typically have a fragmented approach to supply chain management. As managers develop the capabilities for implementing the GSCF framework, they must start with a clear understanding of the current state of their organization with respect to the supply chain management processes and then decide how best to lead their organization with implementation of the framework. Managers will require skills and/or tools that support both assessment of the processes and change management.

Assessment of the Supply Chain Management Processes

Self-assessment has been popularized by various high profile quality awards such as the Deming Prize and Malcolm Baldrige National Quality Award.[20] Self-assessment is a comprehensive, systematic and regular review of an organization's activities and results compared to a model of business excellence.[21] When implementing the GSCF framework, self-assessment allows management to identify the firm's capabilities and areas for improvement.

Why should managers assess their firm's supply chain management activities prior to implementing the GSCF framework? Self-assessments are valuable when managers sense a performance problem, but lack an understanding of its severity or its source.[22] The self-assessment of a firm's supply chain management processes should serve as an information system for managers as they begin the implementation of the GSCF framework. In addition, the self-assessment should provide the following benefits:[23]

---

[19] Handfield, Robert B. and Ernest L. Nichols, Jr., *Supply Chain Redesign: Converting Your Supply Chain into an Integrated Value System*, Upper Saddle River, NJ: Financial Times Prentice Hall, 2002.

[20] Lascelle, D. and R. Peacock, *Self Assessment for Business Excellence*, London, UK: McGraw Hill, 1996.

[21] European Foundation for Quality Management, 1994.

[22] Ford, Matthew W. and James R. Evans, "Models for Organizational Self-Assessment," *Business Horizons*, Vol. 45, No. 6 (2002), pp. 25-33.

[23] Tennant, Charles and Paul Roberts, "The Creation and Application of a Self-Assessment Process for New Product Introduction," *International Journal of Project Management*, Vol. 21, No. 1 (2003), pp. 77-87; and, Francisco B. Benavent, "TQM Self-Assessment Evolves and Promotes Strategic Learning at Ericsson Espana S.A.," *Journal of Organizational Excellence*, Vol. 22, No. 2 (2003), pp. 65-75.

- Measure and target improvements related to GSCF framework implementation.
- Highlight and share best practices with respect to the management of successful relationships and the supply chain management processes.
- Provide strategic direction for implementing the GSCF framework.
- Make inter-divisional comparisons for each business process.
- Facilitate the integration of supply chain management principles into other business practices.
- Foster learning of the GSCF framework in the organization.

Figure 12-5 provides an overview of the activities involved with a self-assessment of a firm's supply chain management processes.[24] The cyclic nature of the self-assessment enables management to improve the organization's position on a continuous basis.[25] Thus, an initial assessment should be performed prior to beginning implementation of the GSCF framework. In addition, there should be periodic assessments during implementation to provide management with an update of the progress implementing the framework.

Necessary criteria for a successful self-assessment of the firm's status with

Figure 12-5
Self-Assessment Process for the GSCF Framework

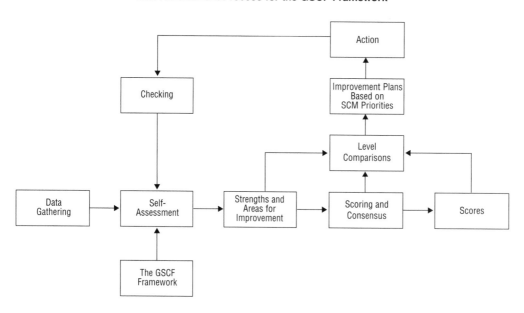

Source: Adapted from F., Balbastre and M. Moreno-Luzon, "Self-assessment Application and Learning in Organizations: A Special Reference to the Ontological Dimension," *Total Quality Management*, Vol. 14, No. 3 (2003), pp. 367-388.

---

[24] Adapted from F., Balbastre and M. Moreno-Luzon, "Self-assessment Application and Learning in Organizations: A Special Reference to the Ontological Dimension," *Total Quality Management*, Vol. 14, No. 3 (2003), pp. 367-388.

[25] Balbastre, F. and M. Moreno-Luzon, "Self-assessment Application and Learning in Organizations: A Special Reference to the Ontological Dimension," *Total Quality Management*, Vol. 14, No. 3 (2003), pp. 367-388.

respect to implementing the GSCF framework should include:[26]

- Gaining commitment and support from all levels of organization.
- Evaluating actions taken from previous self-assessments.
- Increasing awareness of the use of the GSCF framework.
- Incorporating self-assessment into the implementation of the GSCF framework implementation.
- Ensuring that self-assessment is not "added on" to employees existing workload.

Self-assessment will be an important tool for managers to use during implementation of the GSCF framework.

Self-assessment will be an important tool for managers to use during implementation of the GSCF framework. Management could use the GSCF self-assessment tool or consider other options. Managers wishing to use other methods of self-assessment should consider the following questions:[27]

- Is the model from a conceptual domain similar to the area requiring assessment?
- Does the model relate to experience and real-life events?
- Does the model allow managers to understand process strengths and weaknesses, and guide them toward areas that need corrective action or improvement?
- Does the model's affiliation lend legitimacy to the model, which will enhance the self-assessment initiative?
- Does the model improve the probability of accurate conclusions and effective actions stemming from the self-assessment?

Change Management

Implementing the GSCF framework will require managers to be skilled in the art of change management. Several established change models are available to guide and instruct managers as they implement a change.[28] Probably the most well known is Kotter's strategic eight-step model for transforming organizations. This section provides a brief description of the model and provides guidance to managers as they lead an organizational change process focused on implementing the GSCF framework.

Kotter's model is based on a study of over 100 organizations varying in size and industry type. The model is strategically focused and is designed to help managers avoid mistakes when implementing change. The two key lessons from the model are that the change process goes through a series of phases, each lasting a considerable amount of time, and that critical mistakes in any of the phases can have a devastating impact on the momentum of the change process. The eight-steps of Kotter's model for transforming an organization are as follows:[29]

---

[26] Ritchie, L. and B. G. Dale, "Self-assessment using the Business Excellence Model: A Study of Practice and Process," *International Journal of Production Economics*, Vol. 66, No. 3 (2000), pp. 241-255.

[27] Adapted from Ford, Matthew W. and James R. Evans, "Models for Organizational Self-Assessment," *Business Horizons*, Vol. 45, No. 6 (2002), pp. 25-33.

[28] See for example: Jick, T., *Implementing Change*, Note 9-191-114, Boston, MA:Harvard Business School Press, 1991; and, John P. Kotter, "Leading Change: Why Transformation Efforts Fail," *Harvard Business Review*, Vol. 74, No. 2 (1995), pp. 59-65.

[29] Mento, Anthony J., Raymond M. Jones, and Walter Dirndorfer, "A Change Management Process: Grounded in both Theory and Practice," *Journal of Change Management*, Vol. 3, No. 1 (2002), pp. 45-59.

- Establishing a sense of urgency.
- Forming a powerful guiding coalition.
- Creating a vision.
- Communicating the vision.
- Empowering others to act on the vision.
- Planning for and creating short-term wins.
- Consolidating improvements and producing still more change.
- Institutionalizing new approaches.

The establishment of a sense of urgency is essential because getting a change program started requires the aggressive cooperation of many individuals within the firm.[30] This is especially true when implementing the GSCF framework. Each of the eight supply chain management processes requires the support of several functions within a firm, as well as customers and suppliers. According to Kotter, the urgency rate within the organization is right when about 75% of a company's management is honestly convinced that business-as-usual is totally unacceptable.[31] Thus, when implementing one of the GSCF processes, management must build a compelling case for why change is needed. In addition, management must build this compelling case for the key supply chain members beyond the walls of the firm. This is best achieved by demonstrating how financial performance or competitive positioning is being affected negatively by the current system. The previous chapters provide examples of how each process can be tied back to financial measures such as EVA. In order to build a case, management must identify the financial consequences of not changing.

Forming a powerful guiding coalition involves not only active support from the CEO level, but also a cross-functional leadership team. While a small group or team can begin the implementation of the GSCF framework, they will not get very far without the active involvement of upper management from the functions. Someone needs to assist the formation of a guiding coalition, help them develop a shared assessment of their organization's problems and opportunities, and create a minimum level of trust and communication. Moen Inc. began implementation of the GSCF order fulfillment process with their team launch program. This structured program provided an opportunity for a diverse group of cross-functional representatives to build some momentum for the task of changing the firm's order fulfillment process to one that is in line with the GSCF framework. The off-site meeting launching the program allowed these managers who typically worked within their own function to develop a level of trust and commitment with people from other functions.

Forming a powerful guiding coalition involves not only active support from the CEO level, but also a cross-functional leadership team.

The creation of a vision clarifies the direction in which an organization needs to move.[32] The various chapters within this book can serve as an effective starting point for creating a vision within your organization. For example, management at Moen Inc. handed out copies of the order fulfillment process chapter to each member of the cross-functional team charged with developing the new process. The team members used significant time within the launch meeting to discuss the

---

[30] Kotter, John P., "Leading Change: Why Transformation Efforts Fail," *Harvard Business Review*, Vol. 74, No. 2 (1995), pp. 59-65.

[31] Ibid.

[32] Ibid.

chapter and clarify the team's vision of where they wanted to move the order fulfillment process. Kotter suggests that a useful rule of thumb is to reach a point where you can communicate the vision to someone in five minutes or less and get a reaction that signifies both understanding and interest.[33] At Moen, having the key team members review the chapter and discuss the process enabled them to develop an increased ability to communicate the vision to others.

Communicating the vision requires that management goes beyond the typical mass e-mail announcing that a cross-functional team is developing a new approach to supply chain management. The successful change efforts leverage all existing communication channels to broadcast the vision. This could include newsletters, meetings, and training activities. One potential approach for communicating the vision throughout the organization is to provide training in the GSCF framework for employees in every business function. Several organizations have made investments in training programs designed specifically to communicate the GSCF process-based vision of supply chain management to employees. In addition, upper management must focus on "walking the talk." Managers who promote the values of the process-based, cross-functional approach of the GSCF framework must not revert to the functional perspective in their daily activities such as rewarding functional performance independently. Nothing undermines change more than behavior by high level individuals that is inconsistent with their words.[34]

Managers who promote the values of the process-based, cross-functional approach of the GSCF framework must not revert to the functional perspective in their daily activities such as rewarding functional performance independently.

Empowering others to act on the vision looks for employees to be emboldened to try new approaches, to develop creative ideas, and to provide leadership. The only constraint is that the actions must fit within the vision established by the GSCF framework. Ultimately, the more people involved, the better the chances of succeeding with the implementation. Sharing the supply chain management vision requires not only communication, but the removal of potential obstacles to that vision. These obstacles can take the form of individuals, organizational structures, performance-appraisal systems, or job categories to name a few. As an example, managment at Colgate-Palmolive wanted to have more involvement of a key supplier in the product development and commercialization process, but the existing organizational structure at the supplier was an obstacle. The supplier's account representative had one of Colgate's major competitors as a customer making it difficult to involve her on a product development and commercialization team. At Colgate's request the supplier assigned a dedicated account representative who provided the level of trust and safeguards required to include the supplier on the team. In addition, the supplier agreed that the R&D people who work on Colgate's new product development would not work on projects with Colgate's direct competitors.

Planning for and creating short-term wins involves managers charged with implementing the GSCF processes to quickly identify areas where the implementation can provide examples of improvement. Implementing the GSCF framework or an individual process within the framework will take time. Thus, implementation efforts might lose momentum if there are no short-term goals to meet and celebrate. Without short-term wins, people might give up or join the ranks

---

[33] Ibid.

[34] Ibid.

of those who have been resisting change.[35] As part of the management team's efforts to implement the order fulfillment process at Moen Inc., the team focused initially on documenting improvements in the existing process that were achieved as part of the implementation. These improvements demonstrated the team was making measurable progress and enabled them to reinforce the value of the implementation. The team leadership also drove the team to increase the expectations for improvements over time in order to expand the firm's perspective beyond process improvement to the implementation of the complete process.

Managers must consolidate improvements and then produce still more change. Instead of declaring victory, leaders of successful change efforts use the credibility afforded by the short-term wins to tackle even bigger problems.[36] Two key aspects of this step for those implementing the GSCF framework are to realize that the changes will not take place overnight and that the hiring, promoting and development of employees must be supportive of the new vision. The natural tendency of change teams is to want to see quick implementation of the new framework. This can lead to failure of the effort because team members become frustrated with the pace of change. Leadership should continuously look to reinvigorate the process with new projects, themes and change agents that are consistent with the overall goal of implementing the GSCF framework.

Focusing on institutionalizing new approaches involves articulating connections between the new supply chain management approach and overall corporate success. In addition, there needs to be a means for ensuring leadership development and succession so that the GSCF framework reaches its full potential. It is important that the GSCF framework is seen throughout the organization as the way things are done. Thus, as progress is made implementing the GSCF framework, it is critical that the connection with improved corporate performance is communicated up and down the organization. As part of this, employee reward systems should include some compensation based on the financial impact of the employee's process activities and not just their functional activities.

It is important that the GSCF framework is seen throughout the organization as the way things are done.

Conclusions

In this chapter, we compared the GSCF framework with the SCOR framework developed by the Supply-Chain Council. Both frameworks acknowledge that the supply chain is a network of companies, or independent business units, from original suppliers to end-users and suggest the implementation of cross-functional business processes. However, the approach to business process implementation prescribed by SCOR and GSCF differ and they represent distinct ways of managing the business; SCOR is focused on achieving transactional efficiency within the realm of purchasing, manufacturing, and distribution; while GSCF focuses on relationship management and integrating all activities within the firm and with key members of the supply chain.

Guidelines for implementing the GSCF framework were presented. The areas of initial assessment and change management were described as being particularly important as companies implement supply chain management.

---

[35] Ibid.

[36] Ibid.

In order to create the most value for the company's shareholders and the whole supply chain including consumers/end-users, management must take action to integrate the supply chain. The time for action is now.

At the Spring 2004 meeting of The Global Supply Chain Forum, a series of break-out sessions were devoted to the topic "the supply chain of the future". At the end of the day, the conclusion of the group was that when an organization's management had successfully implemented all eight of the SCM processes, they would have achieved the supply chain of the future and would be able to respond to whatever challenges the business might face. Where is your company in terms of successful implementation of cross-functional business processes? In order to create the most value for the company's shareholders and the whole supply chain including consumers/end-users, management must take action to integrate the supply chain. The time for action is now.